THE REEZON WHY

A Deeply Personal Story That Showcases the Power of
Resilience and Triumph in the Inner City Streets

SHERRIE MICHELE DAVIS

DEDICATION

This book is dedicated to my big brother Terrance Lamont Copeland who lost his battle with Mental Illness and substance abuse four days before his forty fifth birthday on February 6, 2020.

Brother, I wish I could have helped you heal your past and save you from your addiction. I promise that I will never stop fighting to save others from themselves. You no longer have to suffer in this cold world. Rest up Bro! Kiss Grandma for me. I will continue to keep fighting for the both of us.

CONTENTS

Dedication iii

1. Gemini 1

2. Butterfly 33

3. Runaway... 57

4. Promiscuity 81

5. The Trap 109

6. Rehab 143

7. The Block Is Hot..173

8. Mommy Is A Baby Too 197

9. Major Changes 211

10. All We Got Is Us 233

11. The Last Stroke 247

12. Family Matters 263

13. Let It Burn 293

14. Atl Shawty...317

15. Recount Biz..345

16. Shrink Me Please 363

17. Rewrite Your Life...................................... 375

Acknowledgements 415

About The Author 418

1

GEMINI

Mom's name is Stacey. She was the only girl, the oldest of three brothers who were born in stair steps; meaning one was born a year after the next, and the last two were born less than a year apart. Although she was spoiled, rotten, and had everything she wanted, she was lonely being the oddball and not having anyone to play with. Her father never let her brothers play with her or play in her room; she was his princess! Her female cousins would come over from time to time, but no one liked her because she was a spoiled brat. She was born and raised in Bellevue Square Housing projects, but she thought that she was rich because of the lavished lifestyle they lived. She would tell me about the Cadillac's her parents drove, and the fancy clothes she wore. Her father's mother lived in Charter Oak housing projects and ran a gambling house. Both her parents were hustlers and sold lots of drugs.

Her mother had an identical twin sister who had three girl kids and one boy; the complete opposite of her mom. Another one of her mother's sisters had seven kids, with the three of them being girls. However, mommy wasn't the popular cousin. She was the oldest girl cousin, so her clothes were the ones that were passed down. I'm sure she bragged all the time because she still does so to this day! I can't even imagine her as a kid because I would have beat her up myself.

Mom would go to Charter Oak Village projects to her grandma's house all the time. She said that her father took her away from her mom for some reason, but to this day, she doesn't know why. Her father brought her to live with her grandma, whose name was Tom Cat. Her immediate family called her momma. Momma was a gold tooth wearing, shotgun in every closet having, moonshine sipping gangster from Georgia. Momma had six sisters and a brother. They all were high yellow with long silky hair down their backs and extremely gorgeous women. They used their good looks to their advantage too. Mom told me that her grandma and great aunts were ruthless and had men eating out of the palm of their hands. These are the women that she looked up to, so she put herself on a pedestal compared to her regular lil cousins.

She thought she was better than them since she had a daddy! Not just any daddy, he was the MAN! He used to be in a jazz band singing his heart out to the ladies and was a very smooth talker! All the ladies loved this mild-mannered, soft-spoken, handsome man. He never married grandma, but she was his main woman and his favorite! They all lived in Bellevue Square, where grandma had lived since she was a kid. Grandma grew up in the projects and raised her kids there too. Grandma had so much respect in the hood that they called my granddad Mr. Copeland, which was my grandma's last name. To this day, people still don't know that he has a different last name.

Once mom got old enough to understand life a bit, she realized that no one had 9 to 5 jobs as the other families did. Everyone in her family lived the fast life. From number runners, boosters, gamblers, Madames, pimps to drug dealers. This was the only way of life that she had known her entire life!

By the time mom was 12 years old, she was pregnant with her first baby, and it was a boy. She was ashamed and embarrassed, especially when the boy's family denied paternity when the baby was born. The baby was very light-skinned and much lighter than him or her. This caused more trauma for mom as she was already so young and now made out to be a liar, and some type of hoe. They said that the baby was a white man's baby. However, my big brother grew up to be the spitting image of that man, and that family ended up loving my brother to pieces.

Mom was now 13 with a baby and still living with her parents and brothers. She had lots of support to finish school, though. But she still had a baby, and she needed more money, so she started selling joints to her classmates in school. She was stealing the joints from her mom, who sold weed in the manila envelopes with a red dot on it. I don't know what the red dot was for back then, and it's not like they had high grades in the 70's, but whatever!

It didn't take long before she started selling cocaine. Between her and her parents, they now had a full-blown trap house. Granddad sold heroin, grandma sold weed, and mom sold cocaine! They were hood rich! They had all kinds of Cadillacs and had crazy money! Mom finished high school and met a smooth-talking gangsta named Joe Davis from the other side of town in WestBrook Village projects. They instantly fell in love with each other; both Virgos; both raised in the projects, and both living life in the fast lane. They were like Bonnie and Clyde. Mom was 19, and my dad 21 when they celebrated their birthdays during Virgo season and conceived me, a Gemini. Mom knew that she would marry my dad one day, so she gave me his last name. Sherrie Davis.

I was born on June 6, 1980, and my dad jumped over the fence to escape from the county jail in the meadows just so he could see me. The meadows were over the train tracks on the north end of Hartford. That's where the jail, the police station, and the main post office were located. The meadows were where they took the city offenders who weren't sentenced yet. After sentencing, offenders would go to the state or federal corrections system.

My dad loved the ground that my mom walked on, but he was just a bad boy and didn't know how to be straight and narrow! Grandma drove dad back to the jail, where he climbed the fence to get back in! They tell this story saying how my dad had always been crazy about me. He was raised in WestBrook Village, but he was from Albany Avenue all the way! Just an angry man who grew up without a father figure and made the world pay for it. He could walk into a store and walk out with the cash register without even getting noticed. Although he received his first felony charge at the age of 18 for armed robbery, this was the beginning of his career as a criminal. He was very handsome and charming and a true ladies' man. However, all he wanted to do was make a free buck. He was an opportunist and had women buying him fur coats, gators, leather, and anything worth having just for a piece of his time. When he met my mom, he was different, though. She wasn't having any of that foolishness that he was about. He had to step up his game to get with her. Just like he had women showering him with gifts, my mom had the same effect on men. Together they had true love, no hidden agendas, just real love.

I would always go to visit my daddy in jail, but I was told it was his school that I was visiting. I'm sure my mom's family didn't come up with that lie because none of them went away to school. My dad only had one sister, and she didn't go to college either, so why were they trying to play me? Either way, I knew who my daddy was, and I knew why I couldn't see him when I wanted to, whether it was the truth or not.

Before we left Bellevue Square, we had a big integrated family. I grew up with so many people in the household, and I thought it was normal. It was my grandmother and grandfather, my mom, her 3 brothers, my grandmother's sister's three kids, my brother and I. We only had a 4 bedroom apartment with 11 residents.

My mom's first cousin used to wake up and make me cereal with ice in it. I thought that was normal until I found out that no one else did this. I was always in his room because he had cool graffiti on the wall and wooden canes carved into snakes, fists, and other fun shapes. He had a whole collection of them. He was later found guilty of several different child predatory cases. I often wondered what he did to me. I was so young when we lived together and shouldn't have been anywhere close to someone like that. All of a sudden, he was sent to Georgia to live with his older brother and stepfather. It was a closed mouth situation, and no one even talks about him leaving or why he was sent away to begin with. How could someone do so many things to other kids later in life, but didn't touch me as close as I was to him? I would never know if this predator did any of these things to me because I was too young to remember anything else about him. However, what would happen next caught everyone off guard. One night while everyone was asleep, both of the doors were kicked in! BOOM! Everyone on the floor, hands up, get down, GET DOWN! All I remember was lots of loud screaming, dogs, double-barreled shotguns, and more police than I'd ever seen in my entire life. I was only about 5 years old. When I heard the first bang on the door, I thought it was that crazy lady whom my granddad was sleeping with, who had an axe and kept banging on the door, trying to get in and chop everyone up. She was chopping on both doors. I heard my family saying if she ever gets in, they would shoot her. She was my granddad's mistress. She used to babysit my mom and her brothers, but then she had three secret kids for granddad right under my grandma's nose. I don't know if granddad ever told her that he would leave grandma, but he didn't, and she was never happy about it. I guess she wanted to scare my grandma, but she didn't know there was a whole mob in the house, and she only had an axe. I was the youngest and only 5 years old, and I'd already been through so much trauma!

Needless to say everyone was separated after the police raid. It's like the police took my family away, and to this day, seeing the police gives me anxiety. I went to live with my mom's first cousin, Kelis! She lived on main and pavilion across the street from the projects, so I still attended Sands elementary school, which was the school that I was previously districted in. Not long after we moved in, Kelis was arguing with her boyfriend, Crip. One day they were loud in the room screaming and throwing things. Then we heard a big BANG! Craig slammed Kelis on the floor. We all ran to the room where she was laying on the floor, hurting, screaming, and couldn't get up. The kids were running around the apartment as everyone was yelling and screaming, trying to fight him. My mother's middle brother, Shawn, was also living there with his girlfriend Joan and their two babies. Kelis's older sister Linique was living with us too. We all were trying to fight him before he ran out of the house! It was so loud, and everyone was going bat shit crazy as they were helping Kelis off the floor! I started crying because I thought her legs were broken. They told us, "kids, go into the room." But it was only a two bedroom apartment, and our room was right across the hall from all of the chaos and drama that was going on on the other side of the door, so we still heard everything.

In the room, there was a twin bed, which was Linique's bed. Tommy, Kelis's youngest, and only son slept on the bottom bunk, and Tennille and I slept on the top bunk. Tennille was Kelis's oldest daughter, but she was my sister and we were closer than anyone else! She was as close to a sister that I would get.

I taught both of my little cousins how to ride a bike in the backyard. The backyard was shared with three other buildings and each of the four buildings held twelve families. So we had lots of friends in the backyard. My cousin Val also lived right across the street in the projects, but she would come over to play with me sometimes. I taught her how to ride a bike also. I had a (peaches and cream) bike with the long seat, a front storage basket, and pink and red ribbons on the handles. I loved that bike. It was brand new. The big girls had bikes and didn't want to play with us because we were too young. But when they found out that I was Terrance's little sister, all of a sudden they wanted me to chill with them sometimes. My brother didn't like any of them. He would be mean to them and call them names. One day, I brought my brand new twin cabbage patches upstairs to Channel and Rochelle's house. They were sisters and about 4 or 5 years older than me I! All their friends didn't want me around, but I kept coming back daily. They used to run through the hallways to get me lost in the building so that they could get away from me. Why didn't they want to be my big sisters? They tricked me into leaving my dolls in their house and going to the store with them. When we came back from the store, we didn't go right back upstairs, so I forgot about my dolls because I wanted to stay outside and play. I was riding the big wheel outside around the whole building. When I rode back in the back yard, I heard firecrackers and a man running past me towards the front of the building. He was holding his neck, and his blood was spraying all over the place, on me, and the big wheel as he ran by. There were so many firecrackers that everyone began to scream and run. Someone snatched me off the big wheel and threw me on the porch so I could run into the house. Everyone ran in different directions, screaming! I didn't know what was going on. We just had to get on the floor and lay there until the firecrackers stopped. When it did finally stop, I had to take a bath to get the blood off me. It was a real-life scary movie as I kept seeing a flashback of that man with a familiar face running with blood spilling out of his neck. I had nightmares about him grabbing me and getting me shot too, because he used me as a shield to protect himself. I'll never forget that experience while riding my big wheel. Especially since I remember that man from the projects, my whole family knew him.

Later that night, I tried to get my dolls back from the mean sisters, but somehow nobody knew where my dolls were. These old bitches stole my babies and their birth certificates. I was about 6 years old with missing teeth, and they were preteens stealing certified baby dolls. If you had birth certificates for your cabbage patch, you could adopt that baby, but she was kidnapped before I could adopt her. The big girls had lots of friends. I tried to hang with them, but they only really let me play double dutch and kick ball with them, and because I was good at both, just smaller than them.

When my mom came around, I always wanted to show her that I was a big girl, and she didn't have to leave me behind anymore because I could take care of myself. I wanted her to

know that she didn't need anyone to watch me anymore, which meant I could go out with her when she went out, because she always left me behind. One day, she was on her way across the street to the projects. I had my bike and begged her to go out with her because I didn't know when I'd see her again. She finally said that I could join her; I was so excited because in times past I hardly got to go for a walk with her. Whenever I had a bike, I had to walk it across the street instead of riding it across in order to stay safe, but I wanted to show my mom that I knew how to cross the street by myself, and she doesn't have to keep treating me like a baby, holding my hand. As we headed over to the projects, I rode to the corner and could hear her yell and tell me not to cross that street with that bike. She knew that I was hard-headed, so she had to warn me not to be bad before I did something bad. I got off that bike at the corner, but she was still so far away from the corner where she wanted me to wait for her to hold my hand. I hated it when she did that because I cross this street at least twice every day to go to school, so why do I need her to hold my damn hand now? Maybe it's because I have my bike with me! That's when I dropped my bike at the corner and thought; my mom can walk the bike across the street herself because I'm not waiting! I have to move fast because she is almost at the corner. She could tell that I was about to do something bad because she started yelling louder and screaming, "Don't cross that street!" I looked back at her one last time as I thought of being rebellious and crossing the street anyway! As soon as I put one foot in the street, she screamed my name, and I turned to look at her with a bad kid grin on my face daring her to stop me. She yelled one last time, and I started running across the street, but my body was turned toward her. When I took my second step off the curb, I twisted my ankle and fell in the street. Mom started running towards me, and so did Bean who was the big dude from the projects that knew my whole family. He picked me up off the ground and carried me back home, where I went to the hospital and spoiled my mom's plans that day. She was pissed but still didn't punish me, so I guess it wasn't that bad. I had a cast on my foot for the rest of that summer! I couldn't play double dutch, ride a bike, or do anything else because of that cast. I still tried, though! I pretended that my foot didn't hurt, but it did! That didn't stop me from playing and having fun when nobody was watching me and that was always!

That was the summer of 1987. Shortly after breaking my ankle, my brother and I went to Philly for two weeks with my uncle Troy! He was in the Navy but was living in Philly with his baby mama, Lynn. My uncle loved her so much that he made a rap song about her. She just had a baby boy for my uncle, but also had an older daughter named Cassie, who was my age. I played with Cassie all summer, but I don't think she liked me. I was too wild for her; she wasn't used to that wild shit. My brother and I had fun that summer; our first time living outside of the slums, even if it was for a hot minute. My brother rode his skateboard in the parking lot without any drug dealers, broken glass, bottle tops, or gunshots. It was so quiet there, and nobody was hanging outside. We even went to the movie theater to watch a movie called "money can't buy me, love." This was my first time being in a movie theater. I thought only rich people did that. The summer didn't last long enough as my brother, my cast and I were on the train riding back home. What's funny is; if I just turned 7, that means my brother just turned 12. Here, we are traveling on the Amtrak train from CT to PA and back like it's no big deal. I can see if it was an airplane, but Amtrack had about thirty different stops on each trip. Here we are though, heading back to Hartford.

Kelis has a new boyfriend name Rick who sometimes takes us fishing with the Thorntons. The Thorntons were another popular family in Bellevue Square which my family grew up with. Ms.Thorntons was my grandmother's best friend, so they raised their kids together, and we grandkids, grew up as cousins. Ms. Thornton had lots of grandkids, so the cousins that were still living in the Square were Deep as hell! All of my real cousins had already moved out of the projects.

In fact, I was the last of my generation to be born there. We all went fishing one day, and we the kids were told to stay up on the log, but of course, my hard-headed ass fell in the water and had to sit on the wet clothes because I wasn't ruining anybody's fishing trip. They brought home some catfish. They had to clean it, scale it, and gut it like they do the other fish they catch. But this fish was different for some reason. Once they cut the catfish, the head flew one way, and the body flew another way. Both pieces of the severed fish would still flap like the fish was still alive. The mouth would move up and down, but without a body attached to it. The tail would flap as if it's still swimming in the water. I had nightmares about the alien fish, and didn't want to eat catfish anymore after that. Ever! Kelis moved to her new sister-in-law's house on Nelson street between Barbour and Clark street. Of course, I lived there too. Now, enrolled in Clark Street school, which was right across the street.

Mom moved us to Charter Oak with my mom's grandmother, 'momma.' Momma had poker parties all the time; there were so many people in the house almost every day. During the early part of the day, I would sneak and play with the poker chips when nobody was looking. I don't know where my mom was, but I slept with momma and all of her titties. She was like sleeping with a big pillow. It was soft everywhere, and I would push up close to her in the bed because she was warm. My cousin Tabitha slept on the other side of her big bed with her. Tabitha was momma's youngest granddaughter, my mom's first cousin, but she was close to my brother's age and about 8 years older than me. I would follow her around with her big friends, but most of the time, she would run away from me. I would be on the other side of the projects trying to find her and her friends, but she knew shortcuts for getaways, so I often had to go back home before I got lost. I always asked her for everything she had, and she was tired of sharing with me and getting in trouble for leaving me outside alone. One day, she had a lot of chocolate candy, and I asked her for some like I always did. This time I didn't have to beg her and cry to my great grandmother about her not sharing with me. She was nice this time and gave me the whole candy bar. I ate it so fast because I thought she was tricking me and would take it back from me. She and her friends were laughing as they watched me eating the candy. I thought they dropped it on the ground being mean to me, but I didn't care because it was good, and I already ate candy off the ground before. Within minutes, I felt doo-doo sliding down my legs! I started crying because I couldn't stop pooping on myself. I ran behind the car to hide. Tabitha and her friends were laughing as they went to tell on me about crapping on myself outside!! Momma was yelling for me to get in the house, but I kept hiding because I was too embarrassed. Tabitha got in trouble for giving me some of mama's laxatives. I didn't know what laxatives were, but I knew that they make you poop on yourself outside, in front of everyone!! Why would anyone want to do that? The big kids never wanted me to play with them, but the little kids were so boring and didn't know how to be a big kid. They were babies and didn't know how to have fun like my big brother and cousin. Sometimes my brother or cousin would let me play high low with them in the parking lot. High low was a game that you either had to jump over the rope or under like limbo. One day we were playing, and the rope was low enough for me to jump over, so I got a running and about to jump, but once I got close enough to jump over, they raised the rope and clotheslined me on the asphalt. That's when my mouth started bleeding, and I lost my 2 front teeth!

Most days, I couldn't stay in the house because there were a lot of people over gambling with momma in the living room. I would have to squeeze past everyone just to go upstairs and pee. It didn't matter if I went through the front or the back door; the entire downstairs was packed with friends and family. It was the place to be, and people broke their necks to come to momma's house. I had to go and pee, and then go right back outside because there was nobody to watch me upstairs because there were too many men walking around the house for kids to be upstairs alone. After I peed, I ran back outside like always. One day, as I was moving through the crowd in the living room to go back outside, and I heard momma yelling and cussing. Everyone started getting up from the table, so I was trapped. While momma was yelling, she went to the closet that was 2 feet away from her and got that shotgun that I used to sneak and look at. Everyone started yelling and running out of the house when she lifted up the gun! My great grandma aint no joke! All I know is that I was running upstairs without moving my legs. Somebody was carrying me screaming get the kids upstairs. It was quiet over there for a couple of days after that, but it soon became the same ole.

I went to Camp Currant from momma's house, so I lived there for the rest of that summer. I got on the bus at the corner store across the street from momma's house named Shorties. Rumor had it that something bad would happen if you didn't lift your feet. So, the entire bus lifted their feet as we left Charter Oak, going to and from camp. We had our very own song that we sang on the bus! "Choke, Choke, Charter Oak, eat your boogers down your throat!!" We were singing about the dry peanut butter choke sandwiches that they fed us each day for lunch. I didn't like going to Camp Currant; I hated it. Every time I went, my clothes or shoes would get stolen out of the lockers! But I had fun all the time, and it was like a camp for bad kids, I think.

Mom found an apartment on Magnolia st close to homestead ave. My mom's aunt (whose three kids came to live with us in the projects) had a stroke and was paralyzed on one side. She needed somewhere to stay until they found her a place of her own; therefore, my mom moved her and her youngest son in with us. I'm sure it was to babysit because she was hardly home since she moved in. He was two years older than my brother, but he was my mom's first cousin. It wasn't long after they moved in; he would sneak into my room and put his hands in my panties while I was asleep. His mom slept at the bottom bunk of my bunk beds, and I was on the top bunk. When I woke up at night, he would run, and I thought I was having nightmares. However, after a few months of this, he would wait until I woke up, and then he would climb up on the top bunk and lay next to me and put my hand on his private part. I was so scared, and I would pretend to be asleep, but I think he knew that I was awake. One day as I was getting out of the tub, he was the only one home because my brother just left. He stole my clothes out of the restroom, forcing me to leave the bathroom with only my towel. He chased me around the house until he finally snatched my towel off. Then he grabbed me and made me fall on the floor. He got on top of me and kissed my private parts. I didn't know what was going on, but it tickled. That felt better than his hands when he would touch me in the middle of the night because it didn't scratch me. I kept yelling, telling him to stop, but he held me down and kept tickling me. I kept looking at the door, hoping someone would walk in and stop him. But they never came, and that day lasted forever. He pulled out his private and put my hand on it. He told me to kiss it as he put it in my face. I started crying, and I tried to get away, but where was I going to go? He laid on me naked rubbing his private on my private until he started shaking and rolled over on his back. I jumped up to get my clothes and ran back into the bathroom to get dressed and to wash the slimy snots off of me. Once I got dressed, I ran out the back door and went to see if my friends were outside.

I was in the second grade attending Vine street school, which was about 5 city blocks up the street and across Albany Avenue. I would walk to and from school with my friends with hardly any adult supervision for us kids.

My Great aunt found an apartment on Center street, so they moved out. However, it wasn't long before the lights were cut off and never came back on. The landlord lived upstairs and would keep knocking on the door looking for my mom, who was always missing in action. Unfortunately, mom went from selling drugs to using them. She would be gone for days and weeks. Terrance and I never knew how long she would be gone, especially since he's old enough to be in the house alone and old enough to babysit me. Sometimes we only had canned vegetables, or we just wouldn't eat. This was when Terrance started selling drugs for real. Within a month, he was buying clothes and paying rent. He had money coming in so fast, and he was only 13, but one day, he got robbed. Someone climbed into his bedroom window and stole all of his Buffalinos, Adidas, drugs, and his "kitty" with over a thousand dollars in cash. In attempting to make the money back, he caught his first case and went to juvenile! We had to move out after that since he was the one paying the bills.

Mom and I moved to Stowe Village with my granddad and his girlfriend. Granddad lived a double life where everyone knew about each other except for the 7 kids who lived 10 minutes down the street from each other. After my grandma had her 4th kid with the love of her life, granddad went and started working on his last 3 kids with the babysitter who used to be grandma's friend! Mom knew granddad's girlfriend, but she didn't know that they were together. When my mom had her first baby at the age of 13, she insisted on stopping in Stowe Village to let her babysitter see her new baby! It was shortly after that when she learned that she had 3 siblings by this woman, and everyone has been lying to her for years! Plus, I really think mom was just naive as her "Daddy" could do no wrong in her eyes. Anyway, it's been about a decade since she learned about the siblings down the street. Now she needed help from this woman who moved us into her apartment in the back of the projects close to Cleveland Avenue. We slept on the plastic couches that made you sweat and would cut and pinch you if you moved too fast. I hated those couches, and I got into trouble for saying so because it was rude, but it was the truth. My mom's new sisters would take me with them through Stowe Village to their boyfriend's house. Because these sisters weren't my grandma's kids, I didn't have to call them auntie and uncle like I did the uncle's that mom was raised with. My middle aunt Kim had a Puerto Rican boyfriend, so his family made weird Spanish food that I never tasted before. They had some food that was wrapped in paper like a present or gift but smelled so bad it made me feel sick to my stomach. They made me eat it all the time, and every time I opened up the gift-wrapped mystery meat, I began to cry. I knew that my auntie would be embarrassed, but that was better than eating whatever that mixed meat was in the gift paper. One day, Shelly, who was my auntie's mom, had a big fight with granddad. It was more than likely because my mom moved in. She started throwing all the dishes and glasses in the cabinets at granddad. He went out of the door, but she kept throwing the glasses screaming and going crazy. I had to get down on the floor and cover my face, so I didn't get cut. There were drinking glasses, mugs, and plates flying everywhere. Once she stopped throwing dishes, my mom grabbed me and ran out of the house. I heard my mom say she has glass in her head. As we were walking down the street, I kept asking mom if she is ok and if the glass was still in her head. She was mad and told me to be quiet and walk faster. The whole time I was remembering this was the same lady with the axe, chopping on our doors, and now mommy has glass in her hair!

That night we walked from the Ville to the homeless shelter on Capen Street. The shelter was called 'My Sister's Place'. I thought that it was another one of mommy's new sisters that we were living with. But it was a place that you could live only if you had kids. Everyone shared the kitchen and bathroom. This house had a bunch of cereal boxes and 4 tables in the kitchen for all the kids. I had to wake mommy up at night when I had to pee because the bathroom was on the outside of the room, and she didn't trust anyone there, she always said. Around the corner in the back of the shelter, we would go and get lots of free food bags! My mom would cry because she was happy to get those cans and other food that I don't like eating! But she was excited, so that made me excited too.

Mom found an apartment on Elmer street, which was right around the corner from the shelter. She had a boyfriend named Mark. He was living with his mom off Gramby street. He was weird, and they always had arguments about everything. One day they had a big argument in the car. Mom was yelling; telling him to pull over and let her out. He refused to let her leave and drove faster. I was scared because he was driving so fast and crazy. Mom opened the door to the speeding car and threatened to jump out of the moving car. I started screaming and telling mommy to close the door before she fell out and left me with this psycho. That's when she calmed down and closed the door. I knew that she would have jumped if I wasn't in the car. I saw it in her eyes as she was calculating the speed of the car and her landing spot. We finally stopped, and mom got away, but he was crazy and didn't stop terrorizing her. One day, he trapped her in the bathroom since her bedroom didn't have a lock on it. He was at the door, blocking her from getting out.

Terrance and I could hear her screaming and trying to fight to get out and away from him. We banged on the door and screamed, but it didn't work as he kept on fighting my mom. Everyone was screaming except Mark; he was like a serial killer. Terrance grabbed a butcher knife from the kitchen and kept stabbing the door, hoping that one of those stabs would reach this monster so he would release my mom! That must have scared this animal thinking that Terrance would finally get inside and stab him... He made my mom tell my brother to put the knife up, and if he did, Mark would leave. He put the knife up, and Mark left. But not for long. Mom told us that the knife was one inch away from Mark, and she didn't want Terrance stabbing anyone. We were safe for a week or so, but grandma came to stay a few nights with us so that mom wouldn't be alone. Sure enough, he was banging on the door! First, the front door, then down 3 flights of steps, up 3 flights to the back doors banging again. He was on the back porch banging on the Windows the door, everything. Boom Boom Boom! You could hear him yelling my mom's name and demanding her to open the door! We were all afraid of what he was capable of and therefore stayed away from the doors. We were all in the backroom, hugging each other to protect each other. Soon the banging stopped. We heard him go down the back steps. Ten minutes later, he came back up to the third floor and started ripping off the screen to the window. Mom and grandma told us to go hurry up and get dressed; to get our shoes and coats and put them on quickly. "Go! Go hurry up," they loudly whispered! "I was in a panic and couldn't find my shoes which were in my hands, so grandma helped me put them on quickly as we all lined up in front of the front door. Before I could put on my coat, we heard that the ripped screen sound coming from the back porch had stopped! BOOM!!! A big paint can flew through the window glass and white paint splashed all over the kitchen floor! We opened the front door and started heading downstairs. Before it was my turn to get out the door, I looked back and could see Marks' head and foot climbing in the window! The look on his face was as if he had planned on killing all of us that day and then himself. We ran downstairs to the first floor neighbor's apartment. I had nightmares about the paint can flying through the window for years. I think Mark went to jail, but he never came back after that.

I was attending Clark elementary school less than a block away, and in the 2nd grade, it was my second time getting enrolled in this school. During recess one day, I was playing double dutch with my friends when this 4th-grade girl came up to me asking me about my dad. She ran up on me, asking, "Is your name Sherrie Davis?" I said, yeah. She asked, "is your father's name, Joe Davis?" I said, yeah. She said, "that's my father too. My name is Sonja, and I'm your sister!" I was baffled because she was older than me, and I'd never heard of her, EVER!

My grandmother used to come to get me and my father's oldest son, Gerrard; to bring us to her house to play with my first cousin Chauncey, my auntie Kim's son. The boys would sleep in the bed, and I slept in Chauncey's old crib, which they had turned into a toddler bed by removing one side of the crib. I never met this girl before, and nobody ever told me that I had a sister too! She goes on to say that she is my sister and I won't have any problems from now on because she'll protect me! Now, I'm even further confused, because what problems? Where? Chile, let me get back in this game before recess is over! Plus, she doesn't even look anything like me or my dad. My brother looked a lot like his mom, but you could still see my dad in him all the way. This girl was an impostor, and I wasn't about to entertain this chick anymore. I mean it's like she's done research on me, how could she find me in school at recess. Who is helping this girl get information about me and my dad? She even knew where I lived and knew that I used to live in a shelter. That's CREEPY as hell. Now, I'm nervous as I think she has a motive, that's why I got the hell up out of there.

When I asked my dad about having a sister, he told me no, so I left it at that. I didn't think anything else of it. Even seeing her around school like she was watching my every move. Everywhere I went, I would bump into her. She was starting to creep me out after a while.

One day, I woke up on the couch at my aunt's house with her youngest son having his hands playing in my panties. I didn't stop him, because by this time, I was used to it. He had the TV on, and I heard nasty noises. He woke me up, telling me to watch it with him. I looked at the TV and saw a naked man and lady. The man on TV was licking the lady's private parts as my cousin did to me at my old house. Then the man put his private in the lady's mouth. It was like a lollipop, and she pretended that it tasted good. My cousin told me to kiss his private as he already had it in his hand outside his pants. I kissed it, but he told me to open my mouth as the lady did on TV. When I opened my mouth, I felt it slide on my tongue. It was slimy and tasted like salt, but he kept moving in and out until I moved my head away. He told me to climb on him with my legs across him. He put my hand on his private and moved it up and down and told me that I made him feel good. I was starting to wonder if this was my real boyfriend. I found myself doing nasty things with him every time I went over there. He would stuff me in the closet to touch me or make me touch him. Whenever I came out of the bathroom, he would push me back inside and put his private in my mouth. Now that he didn't have to wait until I went to sleep anymore, it was becoming a regular game to catch me and pull his private out. This caused me to go boy crazy. Anytime I was around a boy, I wanted them to touch and feel on me.

2

BUTTERFLY

Mom is 30 now, and she's having another baby. "How dare she try to replace me. I've been here all this time desperately waiting for her time and attention, and now I have to share her with somebody's baby. Who is the father anyway? I hope not that Paul guy with his big ass ears or that big black dude what's his name, George? I don't know!" My only job was to ask mommy for school clothes or some Christmas stuff when she comes home and pulls up with a guy. She wouldn't bring men around me, especially if it wasn't her boyfriend. Therefore when she did, it was time to hustle them out their money. I would throw tantrums when she says that she can't buy me new shoes, but this was all a game so the man can be her superman and offer to buy me the shoes or whatever it was that I was trying to hustle. The day she told me that I was going to be a big sister, I was in the back seat of Paul's car. He had a little money, but he was stingy with it. He would only do little things at a time, which was nothing compared to the money other men would give her. We pulled up at Kelis's house for the weekend. But before I got out of the car, mom looked back and said, "I'm having a baby, and you're not going to be the baby anymore." I'm now 10 years old and I don't even remember being a baby, but it's okay!

On weekdays, I was living in New Britain with mom's play cousin; Sage, her husband, Lenny, and their four daughters. I was now in the 4th grade at Lincoln Elementary and went without my birthday, and Christmas presents because of something called Jehovah's Witness. Why would someone want to go without gifts just to go to kingdom hall anyway? I'm being punished for no reason, and my mom is out making more babies; this can't be life! Turns out, no one was expecting this new baby, not even the very few people that were helping mom take care of her first two kids.

I'm not sure what happened, but it was probably the news of the new baby coming. Or maybe it was me telling their oldest daughter that Kelis's boyfriend Rick was her real daddy. Either way, we end up leaving New Britain for good and moving back to the South end of

Hartford with Kelis. She was my mom's first cousin, and their moms were identical twin sisters. However, Kelis's mom passed away when Kelis, her two sisters, and her older brother were very young. Kelis's mom gave birth to her son, first before her 3 daughters, while my grandma gave birth to her daughter first and then her 3 sons. For some strange reason, the twins seemed to be pregnant at the same time. My grandma would say that she and her sister were a mirror image, meaning they were identical, but they did the exact opposite of each other. I thought that was pretty cool. You know, being twins and all. I was somewhat infatuated with the idea of twins the older I got.

Nonetheless, here we go again moving back in with Kelis, who was also pregnant with no job, her boyfriend (who supported the whole family as a busboy at a fancy restaurant downtown), and Kelis her 3 kids; Tennille, Tommy and Shana. The oldest daughter was Tennille, and she never wanted to share her room or bed with me. She was only one year younger than me, and her brother Tommy was one year younger than her. They also had a 2-year-old sister by their mom's current boyfriend, and now they were about to have another sibling. Tennille hated me, though and rightfully so! I was pretty, long hair, skinny, and very popular. I was only 10 years old, and I already got titties and my period. My grandma always told me that once I got my period, I'm a grown woman, and I could have babies. So cousin was a little girl to me, you know with me being grown in all. None of my friends wanted her around because she acted so immature and goofy. I hung with older kids in the 5th and 6th grade. Cousin, the baby, snitched on us when we went stealing people's shit that one time by crawling under the porch and into their basement. We stole all kind of purses and watches, construction helmets, measuring tape, everything! Tony and Kam were our neighbors and were the thieving leaders. We didn't even know what the plan was, and this was my first time stealing, and I didn't like the anxiety that I had down in those folks' basement. We could hear them walking around over our heads since this was the middle of the afternoon. The older boys kept on stealing people's shit though, that life wasn't for me anyway. I can't stand a low down thief. One day we were all away from home at a family event, and the house was robbed. But they only took video games and little petty stuff, so we knew it was them but could never prove it. They were professional thieves before puberty, and they caught us slipping too.

We all went to McDonough Elementary all the way down Hillside Avenue. I went to this school two different times, before and after New Britain. This school was old as hell. They had old wooden floors that looked and sounded like it would fall through at any moment. I had a lot of friends in this school, though. I was 10 and badass hell just trying to get my mom's attention before she had this baby. The walk to school from where we lived was crazy. I mean, we had to walk a block from Zion and Summit Street to Hamilton street. All the way down Hamilton and then all the way down Hillside Ave. We walked to and from school without adult supervision. We got into all kinds of trouble during those long walks. One time, I had detention for a fight that didn't even happen at school, but as we were walking home from school. Whenever I got into trouble at school and had to stay after, it meant I had to do that long walk home all alone.

I had a boyfriend at the school; his name was Keon. He was dark-skinned with a high top fade, Deep dimple, and a pretty smile. He must have been the cutest boy in the school, so he had to be my boyfriend. We would hold hands as we walked to gym class, especially since the gym room was in another school 5 blocks down the street called Moyland. During swimming classes, they made us jump in the Deep end or fail the class. I already knew how to swim, so that was the easiest grade ever. Field day that year was dope, 3-legged and potato sack races.

We had fun with the rest of the school, but at some point during the event, I and Keon snuck off into the trees behind the school to kiss. I was so scared that we would get caught, so I ran back to finish playing. I kept thinking about that wet kiss though, especially since it was my first one. Sure enough, he told his friends that he kissed me, and soon the whole school knew. Gosh, I hate him for that. All of my friends think I'm too fast for them because I'm out here kissing boys in these streets. Now their mothers won't let them play with me because they think I'm too grown. I guess I'm a bad influence so I could only be friends with them at school and on our school walks. I knew too much for my age, and any mother could see that, but whatever! The boy that I really liked was Sam. He was the baddest boy at school and had a twin sister, Samantha; she was a bad kid too. They were in the 5th grade and had an older brother who was also cute, but he was in the 6th or 7th grade. I had to leave my cousins in order to walk home with them, but the two older boys didn't like me. I was still too young for them plus I didn't have nice clothes like the other girls in the school. They used to always laugh and joke about my old clothes that were dirty and how I looked homeless. But I didn't care either; I was still pretty, so what could they say about that! One night, Samantha had a sleepover, and her brothers were talking nasty to us girls, so she kicked them out. The girls kept playing with them, and we started playing hide and go get with the lights off. That's when someone grabbed me and started feeling on me. I didn't stop him because I knew it was Sam. He pulled out his private parts and put my hand on it while his fingers was inside my panties. He put his tongue in my mouth. He was trying to take my panties off, and that's when I started fighting him off. He started calling me a little girl, and saying I can't come back to his house to visit his sister anymore. I liked the fact that I was doing something that I wasn't supposed to be doing, but I was scared to have sex. All I knew is how it feels to have fingers in my panties. I just liked to be touched, that's all!!

A few weeks later, my dad's mother died. I remember she would always come to get me when I was younger. I would stay the night at her house with my older brother from my dad and my aunt's son, Chancy. Sometimes I stayed the night at my aunt's house too.

But anyway, I never saw that girl who said she was my sister at any one of these houses. Nobody even mentioned anything about me having a sister. Nonetheless, here she is at my grandmother's funeral. Nobody knew her until now, but I guessed she was my sister, or else what would have brought her here today? We started staying in contact after the funeral, but she didn't like me and made sure that I knew it. I didn't care; I had my father's last name, meaning I knew who my dad was from day one, so this mean ass bitch could never hurt my feelings.

That summer, I and my cousins would run up and down Zion street being wild and unruly. Me, Tennille, and her younger brother, Tommy had to leave the house at 8 am after a bowl of cereal, and we couldn't come back in the house until the street lights came on. That's a good twelve plus hours that we had to run the streets and surely the reason that I learned how to pee so well outside. I could damn nearly pee standing up. We even used to pick dogberries off the bushes to eat because we had to survive the full day out there. We called them dogberries, but I'm sure they had legit names, and I'm almost positive they were not edible. We would get extremely hungry every time we missed the free lunch hour in the park because we were too far away to make it back on time. We were little kids without supervision all day. We had to all stay together, and we would get in trouble if we ever split up.

Towards the end of the summer, we started going down to the little river for a private swim and knowing damn well that we were supposed to be at the public pool in Pope park with lifeguards and shit. We found the river a while ago but finally found out how to get there. We would walk right past the lifeguards at the pool and cross over Hillside Ave through the forest where there was a river with slippery edges that had lots of snails. The water was brown like the river that I fell in back in the day when they used to go fishing. One day, we went to our little private river and finally swam in it. It was fun not having to listen to the lifeguards. Tennille wanted to go straight home because we were stinking from the river. We smelled like sour milk, but instead of drying off, eating the free lunch at the park and then going home later when the lights came on like every other kid in the world, this chick wanted to go change clothes and stay in the house. Bitch, we all smelled like shit, what the hell did I bring her young ass for? She got us all in trouble with that smell. We always stunk once we got home but not as bad as we did while we were still wet. Kelis kept yelling at us, asking where we had been. "In the river behind the forest," Tennille replied! "What river? What FOREST?" Once she found out what we were talking about, she told us it was a sewer and we were swimming in shit water! OMG! What? We were so smart and couldn't even figure that out? All we knew was that we were tough kids, and we weren't following anyone's rules but, Shit Water? Gosh! What was even worst was the fact that we didn't have hot water at home. We were stealing water from our neighbor upstairs using water hoses that were connected to the hot water pipes in the basement. The kids had to share bath water every night. I never wanted to bath, I swear. I swam in shit water like a champ but couldn't bath in used bathwater. I would pretend that I took a bath if I couldn't get in first. I would sit on the toilet and splash the water around as if I was washing up. I got caught a lot because I would still smell so bad. I threw up after every bath that I was forced to take in dirty water even if nothing came up. I would still jerk over the toilet with dry heaves because it was traumatic trying to avoid someone else's dirt floating on top of the water. I would take a cold birdbath in the sink just to wash the second-hand bathwater off of me. Poor Tommy was last after two bodies were washed, but he was young and didn't really understand the sanitary aspect of it.

There was also a big pond in Pope park with a ton of crawfish in there! I never saw crawfish before; they are like baby lobsters. We would go fishing for them only to play with them! One day we found a big ass turtle in that pond! It was too heavy to carry. So we crossed the park street to get a shopping cart from Caldors. We didn't have to go all the way down into the shopping plaza because people would push the cart up to the bus stop, so all we had to do was leave the park, cross the street and boom, a cart. It took 3 of us to put the turtle inside the cart, though. We wheeled that bad boy home, and Kelis started yelling as usual! She's most likely scared of it the way she was screaming, "get that shit out of here!" The lil white boy named Mikey lived next door and was looking out of his second floor window. He wasn't allowed to play with us, and he didn't even go to the same school as us. He had a promising future in Amerikkka!

His father's name was Raymond, and he didn't like black people. The pack of ramen noodles that we ate a few times a week was from a brand called smack. So we called him Smack Raymond! Lol, we had no structure or discipline, so Mickey had to talk to us from the window so we wouldn't influence him! Anyway, he said that we had a tortoise, not a turtle! He was white, and we all knew that white people were smart, so we started calling it a tortoise. But the boys in the hood started saying 'turtties' as in 'titties!' We kept it for a few days in the back of Kam, Nee Nee, and Tony's building. That's also where we had 5 or 6 old mattresses stacked up so we can jump off the second floor porch! All the dust would fly up from the dirty beds with every jump. We didn't worry about getting hurt; we were just getting through the day waiting for the street lights so we can go and eat dinner. It was their house, but I lived with them for so long; I wasn't a guest anymore. I was the big cousin, yet they were always my lil brother and sister because they were all that I had. I would be mean to them sometimes, but that's what big sisters are for, plus, I'm already a troubled kid, and I think that's why my mom doesn't want me and keeps leaving me with other people. I can tell the real brother and sister don't want me here every day with them, but if it wasn't for Kelis, I know for sure that I would have been in child services.

My mom was not stable at all. In the last 6 years, she only had two apartments, and we only stayed in them for a few months. All we had in them were beds, but most of the time we made pallets out of blankets and slept on those. No house phone, no cable TV except in mom's room only. I remember seeing her throwing dirty dishes away and buying new ones because she always lived in the fast lane and wasn't the homemaker type of woman. Kelis was more stable probably because she always had a boyfriend unlike my mom who was always single and always lived a fast life. She was always on the go, and was caught up in the street life. But now mom is pregnant and depending on Kelis more than ever.

At the end of every summer, there was a big event downtown called the taste of Hartford. That's where all of the restaurants in the city would set up booths, and you could buy small portions to taste. We went every year because they gave away all kinds of free stuff like sodas, certs candy, and coupons. This year, Rick got us free meal and sods tickets and lots of other perks through his job at the restaurant. Grandma came with us this particular year, and she loved herself some free stuff! We ran through that event all day with the two pregnant ladies. I think they tasted food from every booth because they had different color stains all over their shirts. They kept separating from us so that they could sneak and eat because we didn't eat one bit on that day except the Cert candies the vendors were passing out for free. Even though there were hundreds and hundreds of people outside downtown, they let us go and wander around the whole place by ourselves. We always took care of each other because the adults were always busy doing something that didn't involve kids. It didn't matter, though we wanted to see the concert they had in the back of the news building.

We stayed at the Taste of Hartford until it closed, and the cleanup crew came. My grandma was sticking around to finish the rest of the free Zima coupons. Zima was a new beer that came out and tasted good too; I used to sneak sips of that stuff. I stayed with grandma while everyone else went home. What I didn't know was that grandma planned on walking back to Zion street from downtown. This lady was the walking champ; she taught me how to walk across town. We didn't live at the beginning of Zion street right off of Park street. We lived across from Trinity College, which is another 4 to 5 city blocks away from Park street. That walk took about an hour in the middle of a heavy thunderstorm. We didn't have umbrellas or anything, and I think grandma had enough beers to where she didn't even feel the rain. It soaked our clothes within the first few minutes of our walk. She made us raincoats out of garbage bags, but this rain was coming in every direction, and we were soaked. I had to pee, so grandma found a place between two cars close to Bushnell park, which wasn't far from the event. I pulled down my pants and peed as the hard rain was pouring on my back and down my butt, washing my pee off. We continued walking about 15 more minutes, and I had to pee again. She started yelling at me, asking me, "why did I drink so many sodas?" I was wondering why you drink so many beers, but I'm not asking you, grandma, am I? I didn't tell her that, but I was certainly thinking about it. She was mad at me for slowing her down, but I think she really was mad at herself about this long-ass walk that she signed up for!! She was cussing and fussing and screaming, hurry up your walking too damn slow. But if you saw how long my grandma's legs were, you could honestly say that I had to do a light jog just to keep up with them stilts. She told me to hold my pee because she's not stopping anymore. I started crying because I was about to pee on myself, and I told her that I couldn't hold it. She told me to pee on myself because she's not stopping anymore and she meant that shit. All this damn rain, "I can barely see where I'm going, and your pants are already soaked, so just do it god damm it," she screamed. So I did, I pee. OMG, it felt so good and warm in that cold rain. I peed a few more times during that walk home because, for one, I did drink too much, and secondly, this was the only time that I could get away with peeing on myself. When we finally made it home, they all were complaining about the pee smell saying I need to drink more water because my pee was concentrated. They didn't know those pants were a walking portal potty during my trip home. I damn sure thought the rain would wash it off. Nope, it just kept the pee fresh and wet. What a day!

My brother, Terrance, only stayed a few nights at a time with us at Kelis's house. First, there was nowhere for him to sleep, and secondly, he just spent the last year and a half in a group home for long term juvenile offenders, lastly, he had a big family on his father's side and was always with them. I didn't have anywhere to go but Kelis's. I've lived with her for the majority of my life. She was all that my mom could friend on since my grandma had been living with the Jewish family as a nanny for the past 5 years or more.

Kelis went into labor and was admitted into the hospital to have her baby on September 17, 1990. She didn't even have a baby name and was going to name her daughter Rickitta after the her father's nickname, which was Rick. I was like Nooo please "don't do that to the baby! Name her Kelisa," which was closer to Kelis's name! She loved that name, and I was sooo happy that I was able to name the baby! Grandma was at the house, helping babysit us, and Terrance was on his way over too because grandma had things to do other than watch kids though that's what she did for a living, but not on her days off. We were all chilling in the living room, laughing, being goofy, and joking around as usual—my mom, grandma, Kelis's 3 kids, and me.

Every time my grandma was around was a crazy fun time anyway. She was a natural comedian and made lil sarcastic jokes about any and everything all day long. We would laugh so hard until we cried. Gosh, that's a silly lady! This particular day I wasn't not sure if the joke was even that funny, but my grandma was laughing so hard that she started choking real hard. Everyone stopped laughing to check on grandma, who by this time was choking so hard and long that she fell face-down on the floor. I remember the look in her eyes when we all sat her up on the floor with her back against the couch. Mom was asking her if she knew her own name, if she knew her own daughter and if she knew where she was. Grandma didn't know anything, or at least, she couldn't say it. Her eyes were opened wide as if she saw a ghost while she looked around at all of us in her face screaming, but she couldn't hear us! This was the first time I ever saw fear in my grandma's eyes, and this was the last day that I saw her alive.

Everyone in the house was screaming and telling me to call 911. I couldn't even remember the number to dial. Maybe I could have saved my grandma's life if I was able to dial 3 simple numbers! I froze and went into a Deep panic as the yelling and screaming continued, I stood there in the living room, and everything started moving slowly, and the voices were going too slowly for me to understand as if someone pressed the slow-motion button on a movie! Then all of a sudden, flashes of still images took over as if my brain stopped video recording and started taking pictures for the next few hours until it powered off. Everything went blank after that day. I started losing track of time. I would wake up every morning and not remember what happened the day before. Like I was in a time warp or black hole. I don't remember the funeral either, I don't know where I was or how Deeply trapped I was inside my mind, but life was happening around me while I was still in that living room trying to help my grandma off the floor. I could hear my own voice crying out in the distance, "Grandma, please don't leave me!"

My mom, who was 8 months pregnant, slipped into a Deep dark depression after watching her mom fade away in her arms.

I remember coming home from school in mid-Oct and seeing my new baby brother laying on the couch. His name was Shanon. My grandma's name was Sharon, so that's the closest that mom could get to her late mother's name, who had passed only 3 weeks earlier. It was exciting to finally be a big sister to someone, but my mom looked lost with a new baby; almost like she didn't even know what to do with this little person. Her eyes were so empty that it was sad to watch her. She would hold her baby and cry all the time, and it made me cry too. I knew she was sad, and I wanted to stay away from her, so I don't make her more depressed and leave me again.

She was so lonely and depressed that she quickly moved to Chester Pennsylvania with her middle brother, his wife, and her three kids. My baby brother Shan, was only one month old, I was ten years old, and Terrance was fifteen. It was horrible living in PA trying to forget about the traumatic past. My mom pretended that she was okay, but she wasn't. She had slipped away into a place that even when she was around, I couldn't even reach her. My brother was destroyed too. He got into a lot of trouble in Philly. All of us were grieving the same thing but doing it separately, which caused us to grow even further apart! We all needed each other's love to get through this, but my mom was so devastated that she was like a sleepwalker! I could look into her eyes and see the disconnection from reality, but she was trying to pretend that she's okay.

Mom started going to church with her brother and sister-in-law. My uncle was the minister of music, so she decided that she wanted to sing in the choir. She was good at it, especially since she used to sing in the bars when I was younger! She found a crew from the church to hang out with. Sometimes, I would go over to her friend's house to watch the kids while they went out to the club. I would see her smoke, drink, and party and pretend to be happy, but I knew she was trying to mask the pain by medicating herself. She also couldn't let my uncle or his wife know what she was doing because they were too perfect and didn't do that sinning stuff, you know how them fake ass holy rollers are.

One morning, at Toby Farms elementary school, I fractured my wrist on the school playground before school even started. Some boys were racing, and I somehow stepped back without knowing there was a race behind me. I flew to the ground and used my hands to break my fall, leaving me with cuts and scrapes from the concrete. I wanted to cry but had to play tough since the whole school was watching and I'm the new girl. I went to the nurse who only put bandages on it and sent me to class. I had to stay in school the entire day and take the school bus back home. My mom was on the porch waiting for me as I carried my weak arm using my other hand to cradle it while I walked down the street. Once I got close enough for her to see me holding my arm, she started yelling, "what's wrong with your arm? Is it broken?" They didn't tell me it was broken! OMG, we need to go to the hospital now! She was so upset and kept repeating herself! The whole time I kept wondering why she didn't just come to get me from school when they called her in the morning. I went to the ER, and I came home with a cast and thought to myself, "*my hand was broken all day, I shoulda had this cast this morning.*" That school is horrible, especially since they threaten you with a strap or paddle if you don't do your homework... I hate this school!

I couldn't wait to move back to CT. I hated living out there! My 5th grade graduation was coming up. I was nervous because I didn't have anything to graduate in. I had a boyfriend, and his name was Erik, who had a twin sister Erika.

Remember my infatuation with twins? Okay!

I wanted to be cute at graduation since this was the last time I would see him I'm definitely not coming back to Philly or Chester, or whatever you want to call it here! I was going to run away when I would go to visit my dad for the summer like Terrance and I discussed.

At the very last minute, a day before graduation, my mom bought me a white dress with little blue polka dot flowers. We found some blue shoes at payless, but I didn't like them. They were so plain and cheap. I found 2 flower hair clips and clipped them on the top of my shoes. At this point, I was over this broke shit and hated being poor! My graduation theme song was the wind beneath my wings by Bette Midler. That song gave me goose bumps and reminded me of my grandma always telling me that I can be ANYTHING that I ever wanted to be, and all I had to do was dream! I had, by this time, become a daydreamer. I would imagine all types of fairytales with happy endings just to escape the sad and depressing thoughts that I often had. That song was the first time I ever believed in anything! I couldn't wait to grow up and get out of this miserable life. I'm only graduating from the 5th grade, but I'm going to be happy one day! If nothing else, I'll never put hair clips on shoes again! My shoe flowers came off a million times until finally, I kept them off. Fuck it! They were laughing at me and teasing me about those hair clips, but all I kept hearing was that song. It played in my head again and again and again, blocking out the jokes about being poor and not having my own things. Even when I get something new, it's not even new or real; it's just new to me. Whatever! I was getting out of here!

3

RUNAWAY

Summer of 91, Terrance and I took the Amtrak back to Hartford! We took lots of Amtrak trips to Philly, but this particular trip seemed to be the longest! I dreamed of a better life during this train ride. I went to my dad's house in Chappelle Gardens, where he lived with his wife Vicki, his 1-year-old paternal twins, inside his mother-in-law's townhouse. I tried to keep in contact with Sonja off and on with my mom moving around so much. However, without having a stable place to stay, it was hard to keep up with anything, let alone a phone number. I used to dream of how happy I would be if I had an older sister, though.

Once getting settled in with my dad, I wanted Sonja to stay the weekend with me so that I could get to know her. My dad spoiled me and gave me everything I wanted, but for some reason, he was hesitating to get her. I begged him over and over, so he finally went to pick her up! I've always wanted a sister so we could be the best of friends like in my dreams! This bitch was so resentful and jealous that we fought the whole time, I mean all day! She had an older and younger sister, and she had a younger brother, so she wasn't missing out on anything. No wonder she didn't care if we were close sisters or not because she already had two of them, so all she needed me was to take out her anger on my dad for being absent. It wasn't my fault that my dad signed my birth certificate and gave me his last name. I knew my dad for my entire life, even when he was away in jail. Big sis was the accident that my dad never acknowledged until she was 12, and now she's blaming it on me. I really wanted a sister! So when I came for that summer, I still wanted to be with her. She did me dirty every chance she got, but I would always find a way to forgive her because I loved her to pieces. She would let me wear her shoes and clothes because mine were always cheap and basic, but she would make sure to let everyone know that I was wearing her stuff. She would find ways to make me look bad everywhere we went, but she was my sister, and I guess that's what big sisters do.

Her mother was yelling at her one day and demanded that she told me that she was only over there with me to make sure my dad didn't buy me anything without buying something for her! At this point, I knew why she was treating me so horribly; she was using me to make my dad angry. She knew how overprotective he was about me. I guess that's why she was so angry; I think her mom was extremely angry too. I'm not sure whether she was trying to embarrass her or if she was trying to hurt my feelings, or both. I was sure that Sonja had been driven crazy if she had to grow up with that type of emotional abuse that hurt my feelings in just one day. I'm glad my mom left me rather than to having to hear this type of negativity all day. Even though I knew that her mom was telling the truth, the way Sonja was crying was like she couldn't believe that her mother told her personal business to an out-sider. I still forgave her for her actions and felt sorry that she had to live with someone so miserable. I allowed her to tell all of her friends that I'm wearing her clothes when they gave me compliments since that made her feel better about herself. It didn't hurt as much because I was used to getting teased about not having anything, I just wanted a sister, so I allowed her to be mean to me at times. I can take it now that I know why she is the way she is, and she really can't help it.

The summer was almost over, and it was soon time to go back to Philly. I talked to Terrance and told him that I really didn't want to go back in case he was getting cold feet about running away from Philly! He said "he didn't plan on going back anyway"! He said "it would force mommy to come back because I can't travel to Philly alone". It made so much sense, but I have to get out of my dad's house soon.

! He said "he was straight because he could stay with his grandmother or his aunt's house"! I know for sure that I can't stay here with my dad, this isn't even his house to say that I can live here. Visiting for the summer is one thing, but living there permanently is another! Again, I can tell they can't wait to get rid of Sonja, who has no sense of boundaries for people's personal space or belonging. She doesn't know when she has overstepped her boundaries. I was never comfortable in someone else's house, and always knew that I was a guest everywhere I went. Sonja would go in the fridge and ask for personal things that she shouldn't have seen if she didn't go looking for it. She'd be forcing people to tell her that she couldn't have it and make them feel bad for refusing her. It was so bad, and it made me feel uncomfortable the way she bullied people out of their things, throwing a guilt trip. Now they don't want any of us here, and I don't blame them at all.

My mom ended up moving back to CT with Kelis again, and I couldn't wait to get away from my sister from hell!

By now, Kelis had moved back to the North end of Hartford to Barbara arms apartment on Barbour Street. It was a big ass building full of lots of new trouble to get into, and I'm all for it! When school started, I was in the 6th grade back at Clark elementary. This was actually my third time going to the school, plus I already graduated 5th grade in Philly, and now I'll be graduating again in 6th grade! Good grief! To date, I've been in six different elementary schools on top of this being my third time at this particular elementary school. So basically, I'm always the new girl, and each time I hated that first-day new girl shit! Ughhh! That spotlight in front of the class was the absolute worst! That's when I learned how to be the class clown. I got tired of those death stares towards the new girl, and all of the other girls tried to avoid me. Therefore, I started making jokes during that new student introduction to let everyone know I could care less about this class or this teacher. Hello, class, this Is Sherry Davis. I quickly responded, it's SheREE. How would you feel if I call you Mr. Pain? I made the class laugh because his name was Mr. Fain, and now I'm a cool kid and had friends in my first week. I knew kids from last 2 times coming here, but I'm still the new kid to the other students who didn't know me from before.

I was super promiscuous by this time. After school, I would walk to my aunt's house on Center Street by cutting through the graveyard that sat between Barbour Street and Mahl Avenue. I had a crush on Ralphie upstairs in my aunt's building. He kinda liked me too, but everyone liked him, he was Puerto Rican with a curly afro! I snuck upstairs to his house one day, where we were kissing, and he was touching on my butt! I think he was a virgin because he didn't try to have sex or touch my private, and that's what all boys try to do. I didn't even have to fight him off of me like I had to do everybody else in life. He was the first boy that had a chance to but didn't try to put his hands in my pants.

I became friends with Brittany down the street who had an older brother named Justin. I had a crush on him for the 4 years that my aunt lived over here. Finally, after flirting with my young ass for all this time, he must think that I'm ready to have sex, so he took me upstairs to his room and laid me on the bunk bed as he started kissing and touching me. He got my pants off and started to kiss me slowly and for a long time. He tried to stick his private part inside me, but it was too big. It was hurting, and he asked if I was a virgin. I said yes, but he wasn't my first boyfriend. He told me that he wasn't my boyfriend at all, that he just wanted to feel inside me. He kept trying to stick it inside me until I started crying and got up and left. I left because I thought he was my boyfriend. I ran back outside and pretended that nothing happened as I walked back outside to play.

Back in Barbour Arms, I had a boyfriend named Tony. He lived with his sister and her girlfriend. He had a crush on this older girl, and I was jealous of her. I thought I was grown, but to us, little girls, she was. This Puerto Rican teenager who was ALWAYS in the parking lot for my boyfriend to see had to go. I kept talking shit to her, but I was show off for my friends and my boyfriend until she put her hands on me. I was sure that my friends and I were gonna jump this old ass trick once shit got real, but it was just me getting swept from one end of the building to the other. Everybody watched, but I kept fighting until my mom came picking me up off the ground, and I was cussing up a storm. I went a little too far, saying every cuss word in the book to the point where my mom had to stop me by yelling, "already, that's enough now!" Gosh, that felt good! I bet she didn't know I can cuss like that because I was good at it too.

My mom finally got an apartment on Earl street a few months before 6th-grade graduation. I was able to walk to school by cutting through Bracket Field on Westland street behind Parker recreation center. Not long after we moved into our new apartment in the 3 family bldg, my mom moved her youngest brother in with us from California. He was my favorite Uncle too. He was super gay with no kids. He made me feel special growing up, living far away but would always keep in touch with me and this time after all these years of being away from us he actually got to live with us, and I was so excited. Coming to find out he had HIV/AIDS, my mom didn't want him to die alone on the other side of the country. I watched him go from alive, well and kicking it to big sores that formed on his face to the uncontrollable reflexes where his muscles would just jump for no reason.

One day, my mom had a cold to the point where she could hardly breathe. Even with her asthmatic shortened breathes, she was still smoking cigarettes and was choking uncontrollably. I was screaming at her to put the cigarette down and stop smoking because she couldn't breathe between each puff. It was the same kind of choking that grandma did before she died, so I began to panic and screamed for my sickly and weak uncle who could hardly stand up but grabbed his cane and came in the kitchen where my mom was turning blue with the cigarette still in her hand. Uncle Randy used to be in the Navy, had CPR skills, and instantly jumped on her back, giving her the Heimlich maneuver to stop her choking! He was very weak and almost fell as he climbed off her back! It was a real-life dream as I saw him save my mom's life right there in front of me! I can't imagine losing my mom too. I couldn't believe all of the alcohol that I found in that house after that. This is when I realized that my mom didn't love herself or me. She left for a few weeks to go to a rehab center. Uncle Randy sat me down one day and told me that he was dying and told me not to grieve him when he died. He went on to tell me that he would leave me a house and some money after he died. None of that happened with the house or money, but he did die, though. I knew that he was dead when the teacher told me at school to go to Kelis's house after school instead of walking straight home. I walked to Kelis's house, and I saw all of my fake ass family over there, especially the ones who didn't even like my mom or Kelis. They didn't even have to tell me what happened, I just broke down to the floor crying, and I ran back out of the door. Why are all these people here anyway? They wouldn't even visit us because they thought that they could catch AIDS by a doorknob or clean drinking glass; they're all phonies. After the funeral, nothing, nobody, my mom was all alone again now mourning her baby brother and her mother. I would find more big ass bottles of liquor under her bed, in the cabinets, in her closet, everywhere! There were bottles everywhere! I would find smaller bottles that she would stash just so I couldn't steal all of her bottles. Once I did find any of them, I would pour them out and pretended that I didn't know what she was talking about when she asked me about her missing liquor. Plus, who's gonna watch her baby when she passed out? Definitely not me!

That summer of 92, I was 12. There was a concert at the civic center, and LL Cool-J was the headliner, so he came out last. It was my cousin Tennille's birthday in July, so we went to the concert alone, just her and I. However, all of my friends went to the concert too or at least tailgated outside the concert. After the show, all of us teenagers were outside of the hotel across the street because we could see all of the celebrities through the glass windows in the hotel lobby! I worked my way to the front of the window. I spotted one of LL Cool J's back up dancers and started banging on the window to get his attention. He was 15 and fine as hell! I've already had a few boyfriends by now, so I know what to do... He saw me and instantly walked to the window to see what I was saying as he read my lips. "LET ME IN!" I yelled! He didn't even hesitate to walk out to come to get me. I told him that my cousin is with me, so he took both our hands and pulled us through the crowd inside the hotel... Now I'm on the inside looking at my friends outside, going crazy on the window. It was like I was a celebrity now. They were screaming with excitement that at least one of us got in there! He brought us to the 8th-floor balcony, where we talked for a while until he kissed me slowly. None of those projects' boys ever treated me this nicely. He asked if I wanted to see the tour bus that he kept bragging so much about. My cousin screamed, let's go! So we went back downstairs through the lobby where my friends and other kids were still at the window. We went through a back door and a tunnel. BOOM, a big ass fancy bus... We got in and sure enough there was LL Cool J. I had the biggest crush on him since he sang "I'm Bad," but I acted normal as if I get on tour buses often! He asked our names and where we're from, and Tennille told him that it was her birthday. He gave her a BIG hug and kiss on the forehead, but as soon as he asked our ages we had to get off the bus. They didn't want any problems having two preteens on their tour bus. The dancer asked for my number, but my mom didn't have a phone, so he gave me his manager's number and hugged me again and walked me back outside to my friends who were still screaming. They told everyone that I was on his bus, but made it seem like I was a groupie. I don't care, Tennille and I were the only ones in Hartford to see inside of that tour bus! So whatever!

Back on Earle street, I now have curfews and shit. We got in trouble for staying out so late, but it was definitely worth it. My curfews were early enough so that mom could still make it to her happy hour! That was a joke because, by that time, I was having my own happy hour hanging in Parker recreation center between Stowe Villiage and Nelton Court. Parker was basically in my back yard on Earle street, so I was there almost every day with my friends Kelly and Tanisha. Kelly was my friend from Clark school and lived only 2 houses down while Tanisha lived right across the street from my house. After creating lots of choreographed dance routines to TLC and other popular new songs, I started feeling like an outsider because each of them had both of their parents in the house that they owned and grew up in. I'm a reject from a very confusing upbringing, and they didn't even understand my struggles. Going to Parker helped me find kids that were just as angry as I was and sometimes even worst. There were lots of kids from each project hanging inside and outside every day. I only knew the people that I went to Clark school with, which were mostly from Nelton Court area. The people that I knew from the Ville were people on my Parker basketball team and my friend Mudda that used to live in the Square, but they live in the Vill now. One day I saw my long lost cousin Val at Parker. She still lived in the Square, but every time I tried to call her, she was never home. Now living about fifteen city blocks away between two of the other projects, there was so much for a preteen to get caught up into. Val was able to hang out and get in trouble and still come outside the next day, not me! Even though my mom was an addict, she still didn't play that late night shit. One night, I called myself staying the night at Val's house, acting like I couldn't get home, but my mom came and got me in the middle of the damn night! I was on punishment after that, and now I have to find a different way to hang out with my cousin.

Some of my friend's moms were the functional type of fiends, the type that had apartments, but they didn't care where their kids were as long as they came home at night. When the party started on Friday nights, I made sure to be with one of those chicks who could get in the house at night, so that I have somewhere to stay when the party was over. They didn't know I was a runaway, but my mom sure didn't know where to find me at now. Since I didn't go home at curfew, now I can't go home at all. Especially not if I wanna go to the party tomorrow too. My friends had no clue that I haven't been home; all they knew was that I was always around when shit went down, but they just didn't know how I had so much freedom. I ran away at least 20 times that summer and mostly for just the weekend, sometimes I ran just to see if my mom even cared if I was missing or not. She never called the police each time she woke up in all of those mornings, but her twelve-year-old was missing. One day I stayed right across the street at Tanisha house and was looking out the window watching my mom play with her new 2-year-old son in the front yard. I'm out here as a missing teen, and this lady is moving on with her life. Wow! At that moment, I went from wanting her time and attention since she used to leave me, to not wanting to do anything that she wanted me to do. If she told me to go to sleep, I would be staying up. If she said no house phone and hide the phone, I would plug another phone up. If I couldn't go down the street, I would be going across town. I couldn't believe that I was finally seeing with my own eyes how much she cares about me, and I was damn sure wasn't into that little dude that stole my mom away from me.

I just ran and ran, and I kept running, I had a boyfriend in every project as soon as I break up with one, I'm somebody else's girlfriend in another project. I didn't want to have sex; I just wanted to be touched on. Most of the time, that's all that could happen since we're only kids! But my Lil horny behind would be down if one of my boyfriends could find a place to be nasty at. Boys are the only attention that I've ever gotten in life, so that's all the attention that I needed now.

Terrance was selling dope and was down with the 20 love gang. I would sneak up to Brackett Field and watch the meetings since most of them were from the projects anyway. Sometimes though, all of the projects got along, but most of the time, I was right in the middle of a battlefield living between the two projects. There were plenty of stay bullets flying over there. I was from Bellevue square. The Square girls would beef with Nelton Court girls all of the time. It's was all over a boy or two. We would risk gettimg jumped walking past their projects trying to get to Stowe village everyday. Sometimes I would walk all the way around to Clark Street just to avoid waking past that bodega on the corner of Main and Nelson Streets.

The Ville was where most of the parties were, and I guess it was worth the risk. The Square had house parties too, but Terrance's friends would be there and make us get kicked out for being too young. Sometimes, the Ville would help us fight Nelton Court. Everybody knew that you couldn't get a fair fight from any of the Nelton Court girls, that's a guaranteed jump. One day, 4 of us were trying to sneak through going to the Ville; we were sure that nobody was outside, and they weren't. Once we got halfway through the projects, these bitches came out like killer bees. They had knives, sticks, rocks, grandmas, brothers, uncles, and we were trapped. They caught two of us. The two that had the initial beef in the first place for fucking people's boyfriends and shit. Val and I ran, we saw that we were the only ones running and we had to turn around to help our friends. They are on the ground, surrounded. We ran back into the crowd to get them. I got clipped by one of the boys and fell, then came a few blows to the head by that older cousin. I ran again now; we're all running and still heading to the party in the Ville. "These chics were talking about how I let them get jumped."

I'm like, trick, "I got jumped too."

"No, you didn't help us. I thought we were all running together; you stopped to argue with all these people."

"Who does that when it's only four of us against a whole clan! My pants are ripped and dirty, my T-shirt neck stretched the fuck out, and I let you get jumped?" Anyway, we were the younger Square chics. The older Bellevue Square girls didn't really hang with us. They were on some big girl bougie shit, fucking with rich niggas and wearing designer clothes. However, those Nelton Court girls had the whole project down with them. Luckily for us, we had some help in the Ville if it came down to it because Maddy moved from the Square to the Ville. Also, Ericka is blood sisters with

Twyla from the Ville. The Ville had our backs unless we were beefing with them personally.

Sometimes I would run away in the Ville, and sometimes I would run away in the Square. But I only stayed in Nelton Court if they had a sleepover or something like that. They didn't too much deal with people outside of their project. I had about three or more places that I could stay in the Ville, so I was good there. Man, we were young and reckless out here smoking weed drinking Crazy Horse, Old English, and Private Stock. Basically, We drank whatever someone could steal from their house or get someone to buy for us.

I walked to the Square almost every day to meet up with my friend, who would most likely walk me back home later. One day, I got halfway to the Square and turned down Wooster street. I saw an older Puerto Rican guy in his yard. He started smiling at me as he watched me get closer. He ran to the fence and said hi, pretty! I said, hi.

He asked, "you gotta man?"

I smiled and said "no."

He replied, "Can I be, I'm Tito?

I'll take care of you."

I began to giggle because I knew he was older than me, but he looked like he had money. But he also looked like he had 7 teenagers chained up in his basement right then! The way he was thirsty for young girls. He handed five $20 bills and his phone number to me. He said, "call me when you need anything". I couldn't believe it. He gave me $100 dollars just for walking past his house. He must be rich! I finished my walk and didn't even tell my friends about Pito. I didn't want them to take my future money. I don't know why he gave me that money, but he knew that I would come back for more. After all, anybody can see that I'm a street chick with no guidance, but it seems like Pito wants to upgrade me, and I can't let anyone get in the way of that! I'm going to get out of this hood one day! I just don't know how!

On this particular day, everyone was at Tina's house, who lived in the high rise building of Sand's Projects. They were practicing a new dance move in the hallway in front of the elevators. All of my friends were dancing machines, but our passion was dancehall music. It's the classic roots reggae and hip-hop mixed with an up-tempo rhythm created to make you dance.

Whining is when you twist and gyrate your waist like a belly dancer but slower and more circular movements. I recently learned how to whine upside down on my head, doing a headstand. It took lots of practicing, but we had to be prepared for these house parties. The square girls had to represent, no matter what! By this time, my mom had gotten in contact with my dad, who was obsessed with his twins. They were the apple and his eyes. He loved those twins more than life itself. All of his cars and motorcycles were personalized and monogrammed with twins. It was like he didn't have three older kids, well two and a possible.. But whatever! I was the youngest of my parents children, now both of my parents are preoccupied with their new toddlers.

I ran away in the Ville one night, then I ran into a girl who told me that my dad was looking for me. "your father came looking for you earlier." In my mind, I would think "you don't even know my dad. You just mad that you don't get any attention every time I come around, so you must want me to leave." I didn't give it a second thought other than jealousy because she didn't like me anyway. The next night, there was another party in the Ville. The next day, a dude started yelling across the street at me! He said "yo, you better go home, yo! Your father is looking for you, saying that you ran away." By this time, everybody in the projects knew that I was a runaway, and now I didn't have anywhere to stay for the night. So I waited a while and finally went home, I was tired of running.

My mom told me to call my dad and that he's... I stopped her in mid-sentence and finished it for her, "I know he's looking for me." She said it like I'm really about to dial his number. I wasn't about to call him; what, do I look like a dummy? At least, I came home, damn! I'm home, isn't that what you wanted?

She ended up calling him herself. That mofo was there faster than he ever ran from the police. He banged on our god damn door as if he lived there. Mom let him do it because she was still in love with him, I guess. She instructed me to open up the door. We sat there and stared at each other for a minute as the fear consumed me. Fear stepped out of me and walked to the door to die. As soon as the door opened, my feet lifted off the ground, and instantly I had my back against the wall in the room behind me. It was like magic. My adrenaline was so high it felt like I was on a Slingshot rollercoaster. This dude mushed me into the following week. He was already crazy and almost killed me that day. Needless to say, that was my last time running away.

My mom scheduled surgery on my ankle that had, by this point, grew into a clubbed foot. After I broke my ankle back when I was seven, my bone didn't heal, and my muscles did all of the work in my foot. Eventually, the muscles had gotten so tight that it caused my foot to grow into a claw foot. My arch was so high, and I couldn't straighten out my toes like a bird claw. This was from extreme neglect. Nobody paid enough attention to me to know that I've been nursing my weak fractured ankle since I was seven, and now I have a disability! After my surgery, the doctor told me that I'd never be able to wear high heels! It's a good thing that I'm a tomboy and 5 feet 9 inches. This whole surgery thing was a distraction that my mom came up with to slow me down a bit! This August at the parade, I was in crutches with 3 screws in my foot. That didn't stop me from walking up and down that parade with my friends!

Val and her friends danced on stage each year on Community Day! Community Day was an annual block party celebration for the community. It's held in the Sands school parking lot right in between Bellevue

Square and Sands projects. It was celebrated on the same day as the Jamaican parade. The parking lot would be packed with people from everywhere but mostly people from Bellevue Square and Sands projects. This is where you get to see all the people my mom and grandma grew up with. It was like a project family reunion! People you haven't seen in years but love them the same! I hated this part. This is when everybody tells me I look like my mom and OMG! You've gotten so big! Do you remember me, Sherrie? Most of the time, I do remember them, but I still say Nooo!!!! The parade ran from downtown all the way down Main Street and ended at the West Indian Club at the corner of Main Street and Tower Avenue. That's where they had another block party for the remainder of the day and night. You could walk up and down the street all day for endless fun! Cast on my foot and all! We did just that!

4

PROMISCUITY

I started 7th grade at Fox middle in the Fall of 92. My cast was still on, so I was on crutches at school. Once the snow came, I took the short bus with the disabled kids because I couldn't walk to the bus stop on the ice with these screws in my foot. This short bus would pick me up in front of my house. I got teased at school; the kids were calling me Ree-Ree. But I didn't care because that bus had heat and the regular buses were cold ass hell. Not to mention walking to the stop and standing in the cold, waiting for the bus to get there. I wish I could ride this bus all winter long, to be honest. Once I was finally free from my cast and had my eye on this cute light-skinned boy named Byron from Westbrook village, the same projects that my dad grew up in. He had a girlfriend named Tonya, who always had nice clothes and new shoes. He also had a crush on Nikki with the braces, who was another fancy chick who stayed fresh every day.

I got his attention with my own little style, and swag, plus I was prettier than both of them put together. We started dating instantly, and I fell in love with him. I was able to stay over his house every day after school and all day on the weekends. This was the first time someone showed me real love and loyalty. He had a paper route job where he delivered newspapers at night, and he gambled in the dice game every now and then. Well, a little more than that, but nonetheless, he spoiled me rotten. He gave me anything that I wanted. He bought me sneakers and outfits, he paid for my lunch and dinner every day and every night respectively. We would break up almost every month so he can cheat, I think. He was one of the cutest boys in the school and damn sure one with mad paper, so all the girls wanted him, even most of my friends.

He did all kinds of nasty freaky shit to me. He was much too experienced to be this young. We're only in 7th grade, and he's a whole man already! He would have me climbing up the walls! I was so in love with this boy. He was his mother's youngest kid with 2 grown sisters who had kids a few years younger than him. So he basically had the house to himself when his mom was working or at the casino. I was there every single day and all day. My parents let me go and stay all day since at least they knew where I was at any given moment. They were happy that I was in one location and not all over the city, getting into danger.

For some reason, Byron loved the attention that he got from girls, and I suffocated him by trying to fight everybody who I thought he liked. He would break up with me over my actions. One day, I threatened to stab him with the knife that I was holding to his throat in his hallway. I saw from the look on his eyes that he wasn't sure if I would slice his neck or not, for wanting to break up with me. He would always forgive me because he knew that I had personal issues from my past. He would even walk with me to the children's village to my appointments with my therapist after school. He would wait for me to finish, and we walked back to his house, where he would tear my ass up in his bedroom.

I started going back and forth over my brother's girlfriend Callie's house on Townly street on the west end of the city. She was pregnant with my niece, and I was super excited. I was now 13, and my brother was 18, and his baby mom was like 27 and already she had 2 other kids. I met a girl named Dana, who lived down the hall from Callie. She was my age, and we became friends. She was also the only girl and just a gangsta as

I was. She had an older brother, two younger brothers, and a cousin brother that her mom raised. Her cousin's name was Bags, and of course, he became my new boyfriend on the west end. He was very immature, but I had fun over there with him. His cousin was also my friend, so I got a boyfriend and a best friend in the same household! They all were going to Quirk middle, and all of my square friends went to Quirk too. I would often walk down the avenue from Fox Middle to Quirk Middle to hang out with them in different crowds too. There was a corner store across the street from Quirk called Little Montego. The store had arcades, food, and a jukebox, so they turned it into a teen club. It's like I knew so many people because I moved around so much. I also had a big family and a lot of friends who had friends. We played nothing but dancehall music, and we danced and danced and danced. At least half of the kids had West Indian descent from all of the islands. However, we all knew how to whine our asses off. The funny thing about the hood is that it's so diverse, and you are forced to learn other cultures.

On Townley street aka Tside, there was a whole team that was already established since elementary. My friend Dana, her brothers Boo bang and Funka, her cousin Bags and all of their friends. However, Henny and Gee were like their brothers too. In total, there would be at least 10 to 15 boys over there at any given time. She was usually the only girl, so I couldn't let that happen, I had to help her out. With so many boys, HELLO! Are you kidding me? Of course, that's my new favorite place to be. I was boy crazy! I don't know if it was a result of how much my cousin used to play in my panties whenever I tried to get the attention that my mom wasn't giving me or because I missed my dad since he was always in and out of jail. I just knew that I wanted to find a way to get the attention of boys without being loud and ratchet. Bags and I were flirting around, but we weren't having sex. All I wanted was Byron though, but he didn't have time for me then. Of course, whenever Byron beeped me, I would leave whomever I was chilling with every time. All he had to say was "call the cab," and he'll pay when I get there, and I would bounce on anyone. That was my real love, no matter what he did to hurt me! I knew he wasn't traveling or having games every time he told me he was. I didn't ever imagine him being that good in basketball honestly, but he was my boo forever!

One Afternoon, my mom and I were at Kelis's house, who now lived in West Hartford. I wanted to leave because I was bored hanging with those little kids. I walked to the store, which was only half a block away. I just wanted to get out of the house because there was nothing to do over there. When I came out of the store, a blue Honda Civic pulled up on me with two guys in inside. The driver who was about 16 years old asked me, "what's your name pretty?"

"Why?" I replied.

"My name is Tony, but you could call me Tony. I'm just trying to get to know you and see if you would like to hang out with me" he responded. I looked at his passenger who was also staring at me.

"Oh no! I don't do shit like that!"

The driver said "I'm about to drop my boy off, can I come back to pick you up in 10 mins? I got weed and drinks!" He said with an innocent smile.

I heard weed and almost jumped into the car right then. I responded, yeah I'll come back here too in 10 mins. I went into the house and dropped off my bag, and ran back to the store to wait. When I got there, he was already pulling back up alone. I hopped in with no problem or second thoughts. We got some beef patties because I was hungry. We pulled up to Ashley and Garden street behind a building to smoke. We talked and smoked for a while, and all of a sudden he said he had to get something upstairs. As he was getting out, I heard him say "come with me, it will be quick." I said "Nah, I'm not gonna steal your car," because that's why dudes won't let you stay in their car with the keys in it. I said, "take your keys, I'm good." "Nahhh," he said, "I just don't want my family pulling up and asking you questions while I'm upstairs." That was enough to get me out of the car and upstairs with this older guy in his late teens. He knows that I'm not only 13 but that I'm young. Once we got to the 3rd floor, I saw a glass table in the kitchen where I sat. He kept pacing from room to room like he was looking for something, but each time, he would look straight at me as he walked by. Finally, he stayed in the room and said, "come here, let me show you this before we leave." When I walked into the room, he pulled out a gun and slammed it on the dresser and said, "take off your clothes, baby." I don't know if it was fear or shock which hit me first, but survival took over. I took off my shirt sleeve by sleeve, pretending to struggle over my head to stall for some time. Then the pants; I tried to struggle with them over my feet, but he sat there and watched every part of the show that I was putting on almost like it was erotic. Finally, he had enough. "Hurry up and lay down," he said and I did just that. He grabs the Vaseline and puts on a condom. Rubs the Vaseline over me and started to penetrate me. It was the worst pain ever, especially because I was so afraid of what he would do with that gun; I pretended to like it. I started moaning and even touching and rubbing his back. This made him do it harder, faster, and rougher as if he was stabbing me with his penis. This lasted at least 10 minutes with him flipping me over, sticking his finger inside my butthole while he aggressively took my body. Once he was finished, I jumped up, and I immediately started getting dressed. He said you're rushing back; we can smoke another piece. I told him that I had to get back because I told my mom that I would be back in 30 mins. He asked, "did she ask who you were with?" "Yeah, I told her my friend Tony was picking me up from the store with the blue Honda. You said your name was Tony, right?" His eyes got bigger, and he didn't say anything else while we walked back outside to the car. Silence all the way back to West Hartford, where he dropped me back off like nothing ever happened. But it did, I could barely walk; I was in so much pain. I couldn't take a bath until I got back because we were only visiting Kelis's house. I had to wait until I got home to take a bath, so I had his dirt on me for hours. I'm never jumping in a strangers' car ever again! I'm so afraid of strangers. If someone I know doesn't know them already, I don't want to know them.

Since Byron broke my heart, I started having the biggest crush on Roame on Baltic street. I started kicking it with him heavy, while Byron was busy playing basketball or so he said! Roame had a different type of swag. He was fascinated with those New York chicks though. Although he liked me, he would still flirt with them when I was around. He kept talking about how he knows their whole family. It was just sickening to listen to, especially coming from someone that you wanted to be crazy over you like Byron is. He thought I was average because I wasn't from NY. But his friends didn't think I was a basic bitch. I don't know if he normally talked about that sex he had with me to his friends, but they were on it. I could tell from the way they looked at me that they all wanted me. Also because Roame made me feel inadequate, I needed to be validated. We would all hang out together because his boys wouldn't let him spend quality time with me, without them. I would come over and sit with about 4 of them playing video games. He didn't have an opportunity to do anything too freaky because he always had someone in his house. He had two younger sisters and a much younger brother in the house. So we could barely even sneak a kiss in, let alone anything else. I couldn't really get into him like that because he always talked about the NY girl and always made me feel like the second best.

One night, we all were at Antoine's house watching a movie in his room. Now Antoine was probably the sexiest of the crew because he had a full beard and mustache in middle school. His swag was crazy too; he was really laid back and so much different than other boys. After the movie, Roame had to go home because it had passed his curfew, and the cab was taking forever to pick me up. He couldn't stay and wait for my cab with me, so it was just me and Antoine alone in his room which was upstairs in the attic. He never made any passes towards me in the past, but that night for some reason, I felt his energy! It was so hot in there that he was about to go up in flames. He was my homeboy, and he was my ex-boyfriend's best friend. However, the hormones in that room were already having sex with each other. I don't know what I was still doing there after everyone had gone home, but my fast ass wanted to find out why! It was about 1 AM and no sign of a taxi. I kept calling the yellow cab, and they kept saying 30 minutes for the past 2 hours. I leaned back on the bed and pretended to dose off like I was tired, but I was wide awake. I felt him building up the courage to touch me. He reached over and started by hugging me. Then he pulled my body closer in a spoon position. Then kissed my neck and rubbed on my boobs, which were already a 38DD in 7th grade. He slipped his hand under my shirt and pulled the titties out... He turned me over on my back and looked at me with those pretty eyes and hairy face and kissed me. It was slow and soft and the longest kiss ever. During this kiss, he had climbed on top of me and started dry humping my pants. I felt how hard that thing was, and I wanted it so badly! I started sweating and getting nervous because it felt like a monster was in his pants; that thing was jumping so much. He slipped my pants off and then the panties. His pants damn near melted off. Once he slowly started sliding inside me, my eyes rolled back, and I started shaking. I knew that I was wrong, and that was turning me on even more. It made what we were doing feel so good even though it was so wrong! The passion in the room came through the roof.

I ended up staying the whole night with Antoine holding me and making passionate love to me all night long. After that night, I knew for sure that he was a grown-ass man. I knew that I was wrong for doing this, but it felt so right, I swear! I took a bus home the next morning like nothing ever happened! I didn't have to take a cab anymore because the buses were running again.

I still went back to the rec on Blue Hills sometimes, but Roame wouldn't talk to me. I wasn't sure if it was because of those girls or if his boy told him about that night we had! I still kept riding my bike from Earle Street to the corner of Blue Hills and Tower Ave. All of the kids at fox middle that were from blue hills went to that Rec center, and that's exactly how I met Savage. I only dated him for a little while though. He was weird and dusty, but he had a Lil bit of money, so I wanted to see what was up and what he could buy me. His bedroom was in the basement of his grandmother's house. Even after a few months of dating, I still wanted to keep him a secret. One day we walked to Mr. Pizza, ordered a pizza and a soda, then walked back to his house, but the nosy bitches from the Rec saw me with him. I didn't care because I wasn't messing with Roame anymore. On top of that, I wanted them to go back and tell him so he could feel jealous like I was when he wanted those girls from New York. Especially that new one who just moved here with the big butt! He would forget all about me when she came around. I don't even know her name but I hated her. She wasn't even prettier than me, she only had a bigger butt.

When we got back to the house, Savage went through the house from the front door. I went to the back yard and into the basement. He opened the basement hatch door, and there it was. Cold, dark, molded with bootleg electricity by connecting a million extension cords and running them to the ceiling with nails. There were two beds, a TV and Nintendo. This boy has his very own apartment down here. I wanted to see what it was like to have sex with him in his own apartment. I did it, and it was horrible! He never got hard enough to get it inside me, so he kept humping his little soft self on my leg. I was disgusted and mad at this little slugger over here. Next thing you know, he started bragging about having sex with me in school. To the point, Byron and Roame heard about it. Damn! These little boys like to kiss and tell! Why didn't she tell them that all he did was hump me. Roame was pretty much done with me by now, but we stayed very good friends afterward. I kept going up to that Rec. The boys weren't too concerned about the rumors, and the girls damn sure wasn't going to say shit about me; not to my face anyway. I told Savage's sister and her friends that I was pregnant with his baby. I did this in efforts to get him to admit that he only hump me, but that only made everything worst.

Usually, after the Rec, the Baltic crew would walk down to Aron's house, who lived past the town line in Bloomfield. I used to think it was dope to walk into another city, but it was really down the street. One night, I stayed over Aron's house for the whole weekend because we all had so much fun that I didn't want to miss anything, plus I couldn't go home, but they didn't know that. When Roame saw that I was staying over, he gave me a look like, Bitch, you're about to fuck my other homie too? That night I stayed over, Aron took me in the back room that was past the laundry room and caressed the shit out of me. He made slow love to me all night in multiple positions. We had so much fun knowing that we couldn't tell anyone what we were doing with each other all night long until the sun came out. Again, the thought that it was a secret is what turned me on. Now I've fucked two of Roame's friends just trying to get him jealous, but now I'm nothing but a hoe, I guess. Aron wanted me to stay over another night, so I was like why not, you're already wrong. That boy was chocolate all over, and the way his big ass hands touched my body was worth whatever rumors that will come out of us being together like this. The next night, we went upstairs and slept in his mother's bed, that shit was crazy! It was fun and so risky all I kept thinking about was getting caught, and that turned me on even more! Especially knowing damn well we ain't supposed to be in love like this, even if we don't take this any further. I stopped coming over after that because I felt like shit after fantasizing about having an open relationship with Aron. I wanted to stay friends with all of them, so I had to cut the passion out of it. How the hell I'm in love with all 3 of these friends! I used to imagine having all of them at once, just touching every inch of my body. I mean, if I'm a hoe, I might as well be the best one, right? Nah! I have to get back to my true love Byron. I miss him like crazy, and to be honest, nobody can reach the pieces of me that he had touched. So, I'm never leaving him alone. Ever!

By 8th grade, Bags and Dana all moved to the south end right off of Park street on Babcock street. My mom also found a south end apartment on Zion street, and we moved off of Park street too. I was able to walk over to my friend's house often. I had to catch the city bus to school now, but it was cool.

Dana's house was now my second home, whether Bags is my boyfriend or not. One day, my mom said that I couldn't go over to Dana's house, and I'm thinking to myself, here she goes with these silly ass rules again! But this day, I needed to go over there. I think I was feening for some weed or something. I assume it was because I was so angry and frustrated that I took the house phone and brought it in my room as if I'm about to use it. I locked my door as usual and opened my bedroom window on the second floor of the six family apartment building. I looked down and thought to myself, I'm getting the fuck out of this house! I must have been on one! I sat in the window for a second and thought to myself, the ground looks farther than what I had imagined. My anger took over, and I slid out slowly as I held on the ledge with my legs dangling outside the window. I looked one last time at my room doorknob, thinking I should probably ask her one more time, but I'm a savage, and I do what I want to do! I kicked off and let go of the window. Boom! I hit the bottom so fast that I was still looking up at the window when I landed. I sat there frozen for a while, still looking at the window and how far away it was from the ground! Here comes the pain like whoa! OMG! My foot is throbbing like a heartbeat! I tried to stand up but my feet were numb, so I sat back down for 5 mins. I limped to the steps on the back porch and sat down again. I was able to move my ankles back and forth, so nothing was broken, but something was wrong with it. Of course, that didn't stop me though, I limped 4 blocks to my friend's house. The boys were all laughing at me because I was in so much pain, but I was still trying to hang out like nothing was wrong! I took off one of my shoes to relieve the pressure and my foot instantly puffed up like a balloon. Everyone started freaking out, and Dana's mom said that I had to go home and so I could get to the hospital. I called my mom, who still thought that I was in my room and asked if she could come to get me and bring me back home! She started yelling, cursing, and screaming, "who jumps out a window? Those are Joe's crazy-ass genes! Bring your ass home the same way you got there! That's what the hell your ass gets!" Dana's oldest brother and the middle brother walked me home like human crutches. I had my arms around their necks and hopped on the foot that still had the shoe on. My mom just kept laughing like... Jumped out the window? For real? She told me to put my feet up and then she gave me pain pills, but she was NOT bringing me to no damn hospital! That's Out!

One night, I was at my brother's house, who had at this point moved to Sisson Ave right off Farmington Ave. I asked my brother to bring me to Mcdonalds 6 blocks up the street because I didn't eat all day. He said no that he didn't feel like driving. He just got into the house from hustling all day and night, so he was tired. I was hungry as hell and waited hours for him to get home so he could bring me food, and now he's tripping! I asked him to let me drive since he was too tired. He laughed at me, you don't know how to drive. I begged and begged him, he finally got so annoyed with me that he started being mean, calling me names and laughing at his own jokes about me driving his car. I got angry that he was hurting my feelings because all I wanted was food. That night, I waited for him to fall asleep so that I could steal his car keys. At 3 AM, I started my mission. I woke Callie up to help me roll his fat ass over so I can get the keys out of his front pocket. She was with the bullshit too because she saw how bad he treated me last night, so she helped me get even. I slowly slid those keys out of his front pocket and crawled back out of their room on my hands and knees. Now, my heart is beating faster, and I'm nervous. What now? I proved my point, plus I don't even want any food this early in the morning. I went to the back room where I slept and put on my shoes and coat. I creeped out the door and out to the back parking lot! I sat in the car for about 30 minutes, hoping that he woke up and caught me, but nobody came outside, so I pulled off! Down Farmington Ave to Woodland str. A left on Homestead Ave and straight to West Brook Village! Byron was home but didn't want anything to do with me or my brother's car. He was like "hell nah, that nigga ain't coming looking for me! I'm sick of this scary mother fucker! He's always pushing me away too! He just mad that I'm driving and he's not! He sees these skills, though!" I left and went through Bowles Park, where my friend Tamika lived. She was black and Puerto Rican and somewhat bad too. She came outside but was not getting in the car with me! "What is wrong with people? Why is everyone scared to hang with me?" I pulled off and drove to the square to get Val. She was my roll dog and always reliable when it came down to getting in trouble! She couldn't believe that I stole Terrance's car. But it didn't stop her from getting in that bitch! She was screaming with excitement as we were driving down Main Street We cut through Nelton Court, but it was too early in the morning, and nobody was outside yet. We rode through the Ville and Chappelle, but it's not even 10 AM yet. So we drove to the Capital Hall parking lot. I pulled over and got out! Ain't no way I'm going to know how to drive and not my partner in crime! Come on Val, let me teach you how to drive! She was nervous at first, but then she did it! Circle after circle all over the parking lot, she drove that damn car like I knew she would! She should be my sister because we're so much alike, and both can learn how to do anything once we teach each other what we've learned! We drove a little longer, and I brought her back to the square early that afternoon. I've had the car for about 6 hours now and forgot that it was stolen. I drove everywhere except Blue Hills because Terrance's family was up there, and they might see me. I made sure that everybody else in the world saw me driving, though. I went back to Westbrook and let one of Byron's friends drive because I was tired of driving. Pat drove for about an hour around 6:30 pm before we went back to Westbrook. That's when Terrance was following us through the projects. Pat jumped out of the car and left me in the passenger seat. I tried to hop in the driver's seat, but my brother opened that door. I jumped back in the passenger seat and hopped out. I ran around a few buildings, but he couldn't catch me. I was fast as hell. I finally lost him as I ran to my friend Marshalene's house. She couldn't have company and definitely not any drama, so she sent me to the back hallway where I stayed and waited for about 2 hours to make sure my brother was gone! That was crazy! They were calling me crazy for that! Terrance told everybody that I stole his car and to call him if they see me. I had to stay low for a few weeks to let big bro cool off a bit! He wanted to kill me, but now he knows that I'm not the joke that he tries to play me to be!

My behavior was spiraling out of control. Nobody could tell me anything. The only person that I was scared of was my dad, but that nigga stayed in and out of jail, so I'm straight! By the time he gets out the next time, he won't remember any of this.

Also nobody knows that I've been molested for years and now I've been raped too! Even though it wasn't a forceful rape, it was still a rape because he pulled out the gun and forced me. I kind of blame myself for being so grown and getting in that car with him!

My mom went on a trip out of town for the weekend with her baby daddy. I told her that I was staying over Dana's house, but I already told Byron that he could stay with me for the weekend, and he did! We had so much fun pretending to be grown and living together. We took showers and baths together. I loved him so much, and if he didn't put basketball before me, I would have never been with anyone else. Nobody could make me feel the way he did, maybe because he did more than have sex with me and hold me. He studied every part of my body and mind and knew everything about me. I loved that about him, he always made me feel loved. I knew for sure that I wanted to be with him forever! All of that unsupervised sex we had all weekend long, I got pregnant! I didn't even know that I was pregnant, I just had a cold that lasted forever. One morning, my mom woke me up from my sleep and told me to piss in a cup that she dipped with a stick. I went back to sleep. A few minutes later, she brought me the positive pregnancy test and kissed me on my forehead and said ok, I'm heading out, I'll see you later! Just like that, nothing else! I stared at that stick for hours, thinking of how embarrassing it is to be pregnant when I just turned 14 and only in the 8th grade. When I told Byron about the baby, he was nervous. He pretended to be grown, but I knew he wasn't ready for anything like that, neither was I! Over the next 2 months, we made up baby names. If he was a boy, he would be a Jr. If she was a girl, we would name her Bryesha. I saw the baby on the ultrasound machine and heard the baby's heartbeat. I can't believe I have a baby inside me and now I can be with Byron forever! Everyone at Fox knew that we were having a baby! They looked at me like a circus freak though, especially the teachers! Byron was scared to tell his mom, and I was almost 3 months pregnant. I called her myself, scared to shit, but she had to know! She was not thrilled with this news. I told her that this could've happened last year when I was in his room all day; every day being dicked down in your house Hattie Mae! So chill. She kept saying that we were too young and asking why my mom was letting me have a damn baby? My dad was losing his mind over being a grandfather. He kept saying you're not having a fuckin baby! You're not having no mother fucking baby! Period! Between him and Byron's mom, I was stressed out and depressed to the max! If nothing else, now everybody knows that I am out here fucking up a storm because now, I'm busted!

Now, I have an appointment at the hospital, which seems like the long drive ever. I was so depressed that I was about to kill my baby. I never had attention from anyone, and now they want me to kill the one person that would love me forever, MY BABY! Nobody wanted me to have it, and I can tell that Bryon was scared shitless too. He just didn't want to hurt my feelings. When we got to the hospital, I saw an older girl that I knew since I was a kid from Main Street; even my mom knew her. She was with her boyfriend. This made me feel a little better, knowing that she was about to do the same thing, and she was at least 7 years older than I was. When I woke up in the recovery room, I couldn't stop crying. I instantly knew that I was no longer pregnant because I didn't feel nauseous anymore, and I felt like my old self that nobody wanted. My mom knew that I was sad and she cried with me. Maybe because she was able to keep her baby; she was 12 years old when she was pregnant with my brother Terrance. I went home and went straight to my room. I climbed onto the bed and continued to cry. It was a heavy pain that I felt Deep in my soul. With no strength in me to make a sound, my voice painfully whispered... "I KILLED MY BABY! I KILLED MY BABY!!" I repeated those words like a broken record. My mom came and laid on the bed with me and held me so tight. I was shaking in a total panic as my tears soaked the pillow. She knew that this abortion destroyed me! I couldn't eat nor sleep for weeks. I couldn't even talk to Byron because he made me think about the baby. I should have run away from everybody and kept my baby. FUCK EVERYBODY! That was MY BABY! I hate this world. I want a new one! Why did they bring me into this cold world? I'm still a kid and don't know what happiness is! Who wants to live in a miserable world?

Soon after the abortion, I became numb and had checked out of reality. My mom signed me into Mt Sinai hospital mental rehabilitation adolescent psyche Ward. She said she put me in there to get me the help that I needed. She told these people that I needed help and was depressed and uncontrollable. I was locked in that place with crazy kids for real. They needed medicine just to calm down. All I needed was to see them getting their meds, and I was calm as fuck now. I followed all the rules. All of them! Just get me outta here man. I did all types of mental evaluations with flashcards. They wanted to see what I saw. In each picture, I saw multiple things. They never tell you if you got it right or wrong, they simply move to the next card when you finish naming shapes.

I also found out that would lose track of time, the doctor called it blackouts. During the blackouts, I couldn't recall what was happening around me. It's like I'll be there, but mentally, I'm somewhere else. The doctor said that I learned how to do that after so many traumatic events. My mind automatically finds an escape during a stressful event. Sometimes, I would blackout from anxiety as well. That explains why I can't seem to do well on tests even when I master the coursework. Anyway, a few weeks in this hospital calmed me down for sure. Especially, after they put me in the safe bag inside that paddled room. Yup! You heard me, A SAFE BAG! The staff makes you step into a big duffle bag and tie you up inside of it. I found this out the hard way. The padded room was all white, and the floors and walls were made of super soft gym mats. You have to be physically out of control to get locked up in there. I thought that I could escape the ward one day. After taking those daily medications for few weeks, I was becoming crazy, even trying to fight the staff. That was the first time that I wasn't in control of what I did, and the drugs made me even angrier because I didn't feel like myself. Nobody has ever been able to control me, and now these white people are handling me any kind of way in here.

I was still in Fox middle, and Byron would walk with me to my follow up therapy sessions at the children's village at least 3 times a week. He knew that I had problems; however, he still loved me no matter what! He was the only one in the world who saw me for me and not my issues or behavior! But since we got pregnant, I could no longer be in his room with the door closed. We had to stay in the living room or keep the room door opened like normal 8th graders. Lol, the adults were not about to let us make the same mistake twice, so they had their eyes on us.

I started going back to my brother's house after the mental hospital. He forgave me for stealing his car, but he didn't trust me anymore. I think he feels sympathy for me for being in a psych ward for a month and a half. He made jokes and teased me about it, of course, but he gave me a break about the car incident. His baby mother was pregnant with my nephew now, but since my brother would be hustling all day and night, she let Dana and I throw big ass parties at her house. Nothing but teenagers, so it was LIT in there. We threw Gin and Juice parties almost every weekend. She was in her mid-twenties and didn't have friends, so she made friends with me and my friends. She introduced me to Dana and her family, but even still, she had no business hanging with people my age. She's already 9 years older than my big brother.

Dana and I both had older brothers who were rappers. We would take our brother's songs and rewrite them with our own words and create new songs. We would put on private shows and freestyle lyrics off the top of our heads. It's been almost 3 years of knowing her and we were good at raping like our brothers but better because we were girls. We started getting a little fan base and would start a rap cipher almost anywhere we went.

Then we started going to the night club around the corner called the trill on Walnut Street adjacent to Quirk Middle School. The tar on that floor was sure to fuck up anybody's shoes and outfit, but it wasn't stopping the line wrapped around the corner to get in that bitch. Lots of fights, shootings, underage drinking, and other crazy shit was happening in there, so it wasn't a surprise that it was over. We were still throwing parties at my brother's baby momma's house, but we're about to turn up the heat and invite more people now that the trill is shut down.

5

THE TRAP

The summer after 8th-grade graduation, Dana moved back to the West end on Ashley street across from Sigourney Park. It was already a trap spot before her mom moved there. We had already started selling weed to our friends, but now, they lived on the block. The Lil weed that we were trying to flip with each other wasn't gonna move fast enough, so we started moving crack. Just enough to buy more weed and more liquor. We connected with them niggas on Huntington street that we already knew from back in the day, and they put us on to the block, letting us know who was who. We were flipping little 8 balls, to make our re-up money, and the rest of the pack was profit! I could make at least $250 off one ball if I didn't take any shorts. I was coping the balls for $70-$90 and sometimes $100 if the cheaper plug wasn't ready as fast as the pagers were coming. We called them crackheads pagers because they used to page you on your beeper back in the day. Now we call them licks or Jays. It didn't take long before Dana, and I were one of the homeboys over in Sigourney Park. They saw that we weren't about that fucking or sucking shit, we were here to make money, that's all. The majority of the block was smoking wet like the Wu-Tang Clan though. I was like wow, they're smoking what these celebrities were talking about in their songs. I would sing their songs about getting wet, but now I know people living that Tical life for real! We already knew what sniffing powder, and smoking crack did to that generation before us, which didn't turn out good for the younger generation who had to suffer the consequences, but this was different and I didn't have any bad news about it since it's the new drug out in Hartford. Actually, it wasn't even sold in Hartford yet, we had to drive to the projects in New Haven to buy the bundles of Wet. Wet is a mint leaf soaked in embalming fluid, PCP. We rolled it in a cigar and mixed it with weed. Sometimes, we would smoke it straight without the weed. I would geek out so bad. I was able to escape reality without being in the hospital. That felt so good. I just didn't know what was happening on the outside in the real world. I was a total mess on the outside and causing so much destruction and chaos. I didn't feel anything because I was numb. I could feel it moving through my body as I inhaled it. Once the smoke hit my lungs, the rest of my body turned into an armor suit. Nothing can hurt me after I smoked it. Any fears that I had before taking a hit were extinct.

Bags got shot in the leg. The girl that helped him when he got shot was a younger girl from sergeant street. I didn't know her, but she knew so much about me. Bags fell in love with her for saving his life, but she was worried about me for some reason. I haven't been close to Bags since 7th grade, but he keeps telling her that I'm his ex. I'm sure it made her feel uncomfortable with me practically living there, since I was there every day and all day. He was a little boy to me now that I've been with Byron, who was a grown-ass man trapped in a teen's body.

One day, I was at their house using the phone when someone called on the other line. I answered the phone because I was on a call.

"Hello," I answered.

"Put Bags on the phone!"

"Who are you talking to like that?" I responded.

"You! This must be Ree!" She said.

"Who is this?" I said with a frown on my face because I had no clue who knows my name.

"This is Lisa, put him on the phone!"

This isn't my phone, so I had no right not to give him the phone.

"Bags!" I yelled over the music and several other conversions going on in the house. Everybody was over there chilling either in the hallway or in the house. Bags yelled back, "WHAT YOU WANT?" I said, come get this phone with this grown-ass Lil girl before she gets hurt.

He grabbed the phone and instantly started arguing. "Don't tell me, tell her!" Yelling at his girl on the phone. "Ree, what happened?" He asked me. I said nothing, "she's just talking funny out her mouth like she wanna do something." Apparently, she did. He said "she's here right now, come tell her to her face." After a few back and forth words, I said to tell her to meet me at the corner of Ashley and Huntington, and she can say what she wants then.

So the whole house and the guys on the block started walking down the street. It was about 15 people behind me as I walked one block to go and handle this lil girl. I'm singing gangsta songs, getting my adrenaline up so I'd be ready before I get there.

We made it to the corner, and there she was walking up with her 2 cousins and 2 big ass pit bulls barking and going crazy. The little girls couldn't even hold the dogs; that's how strong they were. I said "hell nahhhh!" I'm not fighting her with two adult dogs that she feeds. It's not like they're someone else's dogs, they were her dogs. The dogs are already too strong for any of them to hold if something went wrong. You can tell by the way the dogs are wilding out pulling them around. I'm not fighting unless they take those dogs back. Everybody were saying the dogs are not going to bite you. These dogs are trying to bite everyone because it's a big crowd, and I know once they see me touch their owner, they were coming after me. I have a phobia of dogs, and I've seen what pits can do to people! I'm not touching her, period!

Here she comes walking closer to me talking shit. I backed up. "Girl, I promise you that I'm not going to lay one finger on you with those dogs here so you can do whatever you came to do, but I'm not touching you." She came closer and smacked me. Okay, you got that, I'll see you again. I'm not worried about a slap. She swung again and missed. All I hear is dogs thirsty for blood like the movie Kujo! She kept running up on me, and I kept backing away, still insisting on not fighting. I tripped and fell on my ass, I was scared to

make any fast movements, so I stayed seated on the ground hoping that she would see that I've surrendered the fight since I'm sitting on the ground with my head down not even looking up at her. Plus, I don't have a point to prove when two dogs are waiting for me to swing. While seated on the ground, she ran up and kicked me in the head, leaving a timberland print on my forehead. I didn't care about being kicked, and I didn't care about not swinging on her one time. They can call me a punk for this one, but I've put in so much work on these streets that it still didn't affect my street credit. I was totally fine with losing this fight. However, I wouldn't call it a fight if I never swung and let her slap and kick me. She knew that those dogs would save her. If not, she would have come with straight hands to prove a point. She had two weapons, and I didn't have one, so it is what it is. The fight was over once they saw that I wasn't going to swing on her no matter how badly they wanted to see some action. We walked back to the block, and everyone was talking about it. Why didn't you... you should have... What the fuck ever! I thought to myself! Y'all muhfuckas were scared of the dogs too, and neither of you was their target. I wasn't doing shit with 2 dogs around, PERIOD! I don't care what they think!

Fall of 1994 was Freshman year of High school. I got accepted into Prince Tech, but those students were weird. This was a technical high school where we did half classes and half shop. Freshman year shop time exploratory phase was where we would explore every shop and switched shops every couple of weeks. I took apart from an engine in auto mechanic's shop, I built a brick staircase in masonry, I made a steel baseball bat in the machine tool class, and I wired a whole closet in electrical, etc. The shop that I chose was cosmetology aka hairdressing. It made sense because I always had a passion for hair! I was high as a kite going to classes and shop floating on air because the dust was controlling my life. I'm still in love with Byron, but he's knocking these bitches' heads off left and right at Weaver High! At least that's what the rumor was. I heard he was messing around with a girl that I knew, and she knew how I felt about him. She was pretty too, but she was a girly girl. I was sure I would lose him for good to her if she got close enough to him, after all, that's my baby daddy. One afternoon, I left Prince Tech early and took the bus over to Weaver High because this pretty bitch is trying to steal my soul mate!

As soon as I got to Weaver, I saw all of my old friends from middle school. They were getting ready to go home, but once they saw me, they already knew that I was on some bullshit. They knew how close I was to Byron, and they also knew that he had moved on and couldn't wait to get away from me. Somehow the whole school came over to where I was waiting for him just to be nosey and see some action. Messy motherfuckers! I never got a chance to see him or her because someone went to warn them that I was up at the school! What a wasted trip all the way across town.

Anyway, Prince Tech was kinda cool to a certain extent. I didn't like that freshman underdog shit that the older bitches were on, but other than that, it was straight. I got into a super beef with the juniors and the seniors. I was down for whatever smoke they wanted because I stay sucker free. They tried the typical bully the freshman bullshit, but I wasn't hearing that noise! These bitches had to show me how tough they were because all that loud shit didn't scare me at all. Where I'm from, the loudest ones are always the weakest! So try me! I'm smoking a couple of dust bags a day at this point. I'm upstairs in the English class, fallen out on the floor when the teacher told me to leave his class. I was straight tripping for real, laying there in the middle of the floor kicking and screaming in the front of the whole class like a toddler tantrum. The teacher eventually got me out in the hallway, where I had an even bigger dust head explosion. They should have called the ambulance, but they didn't even know that I was on drugs. The only drugs they knew about was weed, and weed didn't make you do crazy things like that. They just sent me to detention. They knew that I was a kid who always showed out, but I was passing my classes, so I wasn't a complete idiot. I just had behavioral problems throughout my school years.

A few months went by, I was in class when four junior girls came to my class looking for me. I went to the hallway to find out what they wanted because I knew that they didn't like me. However, I wasn't going to let them intimidate me either. I wanted to show my nervous freshman classmates that they didn't have to be scared of these weak ass chicks. I didn't know them personally, and that was the main problem. I've been all around this city with the best of them, and I never ran into any of these chicks. So I was confused at why they think they're tough? In the hallway, one of the junior girls asked me if I was the one who called her a bitch. This particular girl had no prior issues with me and just wanted to initiate the conversation.

I responded Nooo! In a confused tone and a puzzling frown. I went on to make it clear that it wasn't her that I called a bitch. I actually called you a bitch, I said, pointing to the other junior named June who had apparently psyched her friends up to think that I had a problem with all of them. She was the only one who was mad because her freshmen boyfriend liked me. She was the main one trying to bully us freshmen, and she was the main one that I had problems with over this little boy. She must have been the ringleader because after I made sure that everyone knew who I called a bitch, they started all got vexed in that hallway. They were asking her why she was letting me call her a bitch to her face. She said, "don't worry, I'll see you," and then she repeated it, "I'll see you" so that her friends knew that she meant business. OK, bitch! you'll see me. I responded.

I went back in class, and everyone stared at me, asking if I was scared of what they were going to do? Whatever! I know a tough bitch when I see one, and these chicks ain't nothing close to being official. They're too worried about getting suspended, which further lets me know that they are not about the thug life! Later that day, all I heard throughout the whole school was how she's going to fight me after lunch. Freshman girls talking about we gonna roll on these bitch's if they touch you. Ain't nobody gonna touch you watch! We're going to do this, we're going to do that, and ain't nobody going to do shit. After lunch, at least 30 of us freshmen walked down the Hall, and there they were! All of the upperclassmen in full effect at the end of the hallway, it was enough to scare anyone away. As we proceeded down the hallway, we had to pass by the staircase, and most of my friends must have hit those steps. I was the only girl to make it down the hallway to face off with the older chicks! When I got there, I knew that she didn't want to fight based on the look on her face. She was hoping that I didn't come down there, but here I am coming to get my ass beat like she promised. Her friends were yelling beat that bitches ass... I stood there, sizing her up, and waiting for the first hit. She wasn't moving, and I think her friends thought that she was going to back out of the fight, so they pushed her into me, and that's when I lost my damn mind. I fought like my life depended on it. Soon I was being touched from behind, from the side. Hands were coming from everywhere and from every direction. I couldn't believe that these love taps felt like I was slap boxing. I wasn't about to let them get me down on the ground, and honestly, between all of them, they couldn't even if they tried to.

The principal came, bear-hugged and carried me away. I wondered why he grabbed me when I'm the one getting jumped. What I didn't realize is that I turned into a complete animal in that hallway! I took out all of my frustration and past trauma on them. The whole school laughed at the upperclassmen because so many of them jumped in, and nobody was able to get me down. Neither were they able to leave an impressionable scar that would show the freshman class that they meant business. So it was a big ass joke to everyone!

All that they did was give me more power and respect at school, at least to the freshmen class. But what's the key to life? I liberated us! Fuck them weaklings. We were now safe from upperclassmen's verbal abuse because they only wanted me, everyone else was safe! The principal kept asking me who was fighting me. I told him that I don't know. He started naming names. I told him that I don't know them. He did his own investigation and wanted to escalate the situation. I didn't want it to go anywhere close to the law because I knew that I wasn't finished with these chicks. I was going to get revenge soon, so I didn't want them to get kicked out!

I started talking to a Senior Tim for a little while. He was quiet and sneaky. Sexy as hell with good hair like he was mixed or something. He was in the Machine tool class. Tim had a job at coastal tools right across the street from my brother's baby momma on Sisson Avenue. Tim would come over there after work to chill with me. Nobody at the school knew that we knew each other and certainly didn't know that he was knocking my socks off on the regular basis. Plus, he didn't want anyone to know that he had the hots for a freshman.

I started acting too immature for him, so he started avoiding me after I was exposing him at school, bragging to my friends that I pulled a senior and one of the cutest ones at that! Ha! That's why them upper freshmen were mad at the girl!

Then there was Tyson, he was chocolate and had a bodybuilder body. What's up with these young boys built like grown ass men? That's probably how guys viewed me as a young girl stacked up? Tyson was my boyfriend for a few months until we found out that we have the same distant cousin. He still wanted to fuck around, but it was kinda weird to me even though we weren't really cousins.

I started getting worse on the dust. I was like a superhero for the freshman class of 1998, and you couldn't tell me shit. My dust habit was up to 3-5 bags a day. That's $30 a bag. But it cost me to get suspended for the rest of the school year. By this time, I'm not in school anymore, but I still talk to my Puerto Rican homie, Mari. She was from charter oak and down with the Solidoes, one of the two Hispanic gangs on the south end. She brought me into her crew. I was the only black over there, but they all loved me and accepted me as one of them. Somehow, one of them hating ass bitches got mad that I was coming around all the time. Then I started talking to one of the park street captains who lived in my mom's building. He looked white, but he was Puerto Rican. Once the girls found out that I was talking to one of the cute guys, they started saying that I was falsely repping their gang. I could get into some serious trouble if I wasn't initiated into their gang but repping their colors. Word got around that I was going to be the next target for the girls to jump on. I had to chill out from going over there because they could kill me for dumb shit like that.

That summer was crazy! We had Gin and juice parties at Callie's house almost every day. A bunch of young kids packed in a living room and a dining room. Our parties got so popular over this last year that older people started coming over. Especially South Marshall dudes. They were so close to Sisson ave, that sometimes they walked to the parties about 7-15 Deep. We had big bottles of liquor and mad blunts passing around. Dance contest, rap battles we had so much fun! One day, Tina got so drunk, which is normal for her (she was an alcoholic already), she was drinking a lot when we were younger and running away. Most of the time, she got too drunk! Yeah, she just liked that attention she got from the guys. This night was one of those nights, and she was yelling at everybody about her ring missing. Because she's from the square, she got most of them in here shook. But I'm from the square too, and I'm not having it, so I let her talk to them as long as she wasn't talking to me. She had them going in their pockets and everything, it was kind of funny to see her play the tough guy. After about 15 minutes of her shenanigans, she comes to me saying, "somebody stole my ring, so I'm just checking everybody, let me see your pockets." I replied, "Yo Tina leave me alone yo, don't nobody want that lil cheap ass ring from Raphaels!" Raphael's was a cheap Chinese jewelry store downtown. The gold they had was made out of 10k blends of paper-thin gold! So if she did have a ring on tonight, it would've been worth about $20-$30. By this time, the whole house is laughing because they know how inexpensive this imaginary ring might be, plus nobody saw her with it on all night like she made the story up just to start trouble with everyone because she's an alcoholic. She started to raise her voice, trying to regain control of the situation and trying to check me. She and I had one argument back in the day while she had around 5 of her friends at a sleepover. The argument was that I didn't have PJ'S to wear to the pajama party, so I wasn't going to go. She volunteered to let me and another girl wear her Pajamas for the night, so we could all go to the party! They started having a ketchup and mustard fight, and she got mad at me for letting them put mustard on her sky blue Pajamas. She got pumped up to fight, but I decided to back down that night. For one, we would have gotten kicked out of the sleepover in the middle of the night with nowhere for me to go after that. Secondly, I was there with my cousin Val who would have helped me if they rolled on me, but there were still too many for us to fight. Not to mention that they were all Val's friends who didn't like me to begin with. She would have to go against them for me. I thought about all of the possibilities before I reacted and decided to peace it up. Tina and I were cordial ever since then.

But now her ring is missing, and she remembers me backing down when we were younger. She starts walking towards me yelling. I'm like girl... You better leave me alone before I wax you on this floor. She was offended because I'm supposed to be weaker than her, especially in front of all these people. Everyone stood around waiting for shit to go down because nobody liked her like that since she was so loud and obnoxious. She said Sherrie, I would run your pockets right now. I said I dare you to check my pockets bitch. As soon as she started walking, I knew she wasn't going to stop, so I punched her on the cheek. Nothing major, I didn't want to fight anyway and was hoping that she left me alone after that. Nope, she came and dug her nails into my face, that's when I lost it on her. We're on the bed, on the floor spinning, banging against walls and furniture. I tried to mop the fucking floor with this bully bitch. They started pulling me off of her. She started yelling, you ain't do shit tho, you ain't do shit tho. Maybe not, but why are you walking toward the door? Are you ready to leave the party so soon, trouble maker? It's still early, and we're just getting started. She's had enough for the night because now she's mad at everyone yelling in the crowd, "y'all not my friends!" I was just happy to catch a win around the same people and so close to the fight that I had to forfeit because of the dogs. Now I don't have to hear about me not hitting that girl and letting her kick me in my head like that. Lol

By sophomore year at Prince Tech, I was trapping in smoking so much that I barely even went to school. When I did show up for school, I would always make my way to the track field in the back of the school to smoke weed. One Tuesday afternoon, I was sent to detention for disrupting the class and being the class clown. In detention, there was a substitute teacher. For whatever reason, I decided that I was going to smoke some weed right there at the desk in detention in front of the whole detention classroom. The kids were like Yoooo!. She's smoking weed in school! The teacher called the cops, and the cops made everyone line up to walk across the hall to the lunchroom and empty their pockets. Nobody snitched on me because they know what happened between me and upperclassmen last year; they had respect for me, I guess. After 2 rounds of not finding anything or any suspects, they started interrogating these kids, and someone broke and snitched on me. When the officers came back into the room, they pointed me out from the back of the class. Young lady, come here, one officer yelled. They had a lady cop now, and she frisked me. That's when they found not only the weed. I had some crack and a big long machete that I had inside a piece of cardboard that was wrapped with duct tape. I could barely walk with that thing in my waist, but I was going to gut the next bitch who tried me. I went straight to Juvenile, and I got expelled from the school indefinitely.

It was the winter of 95, and we were floating off that purple tape by Raekwon the Chef, entitled only built for Cuban links. Most of us on the block were rappers anyway, so we all would be rapping in the hallways, banging on the wall beat boxing and everything. We would have a whole talent show on the block while we took turns catching sales. My homeboys Polo and Tall T were the most experienced rappers! We would go over there and have rap cipher too. They taught us how to freestyle off the top of the dome. Dana and I became very good at it too!

Back on the block, a few of us were smoking dust one night and were tripping for real. Everybody was out that night in the hallway doing an all-nighter. We were rapping, drinking, smoking, and catching sales all night. This particular night we were smoking straight dust blunts. Most days, we would mix it with our weed, but tonight the entire blunt is all dust. These blunts were rolled smaller and thinner than a regular joint because the mint leaf is smaller than a marijuana leaf. It only takes one puff to get high, therefore, you don't need to roll a lot of dust. One small blunt piece went around and got everyone high. The only other dust heads in the city were them dudes up on Blue Hills Avenue. Them dudes were straight wilding up there for real though. That's where my brother's family is from.

We stayed in that hallway all night, which was a normal thing. We trapped all night and slept during the day. That next morning came, and we were starting to get restless. People were now outside across the street waiting for the bus to go to work and to school. The building that we hung out in during the winter or rain was right across the street from the bus stop. I looked out the small window in the hallway door where I could see the people standing at the bus stop. I immediately started crying, screaming, and yelling, telling them to get me out this hallway because it's the end of the world. Everyone started laughing as they tried to console me. They kept asking me what's wrong and telling me that I'm blowing everybody high because I'm scaring them. This bitch doesn't have a face! I screamed. They were wondering who I was talking about. I started to point out the window at the lady.

They were four ladies out there waiting for the bus at the time. One of them didn't have eyes, a nose or mouth just a blank face. They told me that I was tripping out and that I needed to chill. At this point, I was crying real tears because I'm losing my mind inside this nightmare, and I can't get out! I started repeating myself, "I'm going to knock this bitch out, where is her face?" "Where is her FACE??? What is happening?? Where is her face??

As they were all holding me back, preventing me from leaving the hallway, the bus came to pick up the group. As the bus pulled off, they let me go, and I ran out of the building and chased the bus for a half block until it got away. I came back into the hallway, where they were all clowning me calling me crazy. They know that they saw that shit too! Somebody was even in agreement with me during the whole commotion. I heard them say that they didn't see a face either. Whatever! I know what I saw.

One afternoon, I was out there getting it! I don't know if it was payday or what, but money was too fast for me to re-up sometimes. I could literally write my own paycheck. It's enough money for everyone to get paid comfortably. One minute, I look up and guess who I see walking up to the porch? It was Terrance! What is my brother doing on my block?

Ree-Bee! "What's up monkey girl?" He yelled into the crowd where he only knew me and about 3 others. I started smiling as he walked up on the porch! "What's up Tee?" I screamed with excitement as I gave my brother a hug. What are you doing over here? I asked him. I came to see my little monkey! He responded! "I see you're over here getting money!" "Shit, I'm trying to survive out here! You know I don't have anywhere to go!" I sadly replied. "Yeah, I know Ree! You doing your damn thang though! I see." He said with a smile as if he had an agenda for being here. "Sis, I'm fucked up! I just need a couple of dollars!" He said as he looked desperately into my eyes. I knew something like that was coming because I know my brother. He will try to talk you out of a house and home if he could. He was good at it too. If he wanted something from you, he would take it from you. However, not by force, though! He was so good at what he did that you would be handing him money you just told him that you didn't have. It was kind of like Danabo! So if you weren't prepared to beat his ass, you were going to give him whatever it is that he wanted. Anyway, just so it happened that I recently had a re-up, and I had nothing but work on me. I know Terrance didn't smoke crack, but I knew that if I gave him some crack that he could go and flip it for some cash. I handed him a 6th of crack. He can flip it quickly for about $100, but if he did it right, he could make over $150. He practically started crying when I put the work in his hands. He was expecting to come and get about $20 from his little sister and ended up with the whole cheque!

During this emotional exchange, somehow, we knew that each of us was also smoking angle dust! I don't know how it happened. But we starred each other in the eyes, and after a minute or two, I asked him if he wanted to smoke a bag with me! His face lit the hell up like a Christmas tree! You could tell that's what he needed the money for, and now he got work to flip, and he can still smoke a bag right now! He was in full bliss!

Now I could see tears drop from his eye. I can't believe that my little sister is putting me on! He whispered in disbelief because, in his mind, I saved the day! Terrance convinced me to leave the block and go with him. I needed a little break anyway, and plus now, my big brother wants me to hang out with him! Hell yeah! My brother gets into a lot of trouble, but those escaping death adventures be LIT, I swear!

We got in his half of crack car. I asked him how long he had it. He told me that he just got it and wanted me to drive, especially because he knew that I could drive, after stealing his car for an entire day! We were driving everywhere, but stopped Off Blue Hill's Ave on Euclid. This was where Terrance's grandmother lived. He knew that all his cousins would be there. Sure enough, the majority of them were there. His Aunts Piggy and Meme, Uncles Wendall, and BumBum. His cousins Fly Ty, Tasheena, Trakia, Lori, Little Man and Teoni! It appeared to be some kind of family reunion, but this was simply a typical Saturday afternoon at his grandma's house. His family is so dope! This is the family that he grew up with whenever my mom couldn't take care of us. He was over here getting treated like a king, and I was at Kelis's house, eating the left overs that nobody wanted to eat.

Anyway, we stayed over there for about 2 hours before we got back on the road. We stopped 2 other places before we finally got stopped by the police. When the officers came to the car, they knew Terrance! They said Ma'am what are you doing with Mr. Copeland? I heard a chuckle.

"That's my little sister! Cowboy, leave her alone man, she's with me!" Terrance started laughing!

I'm trying to wrestle with my heart so that it won't pop out of my chest, and now the officers seem to be friends with Terrance.

It turns out that the car was reported stolen. But because we had the actual car keys and the fact that they knew Terrance personally and knew that he wasn't a car thief, they told us to get out of the car and let us walk away. They know a half a crack when they see one, these are street cops who spend every day in the hood. Like forreal, these half a crack cars are the drug dealers' rental cars. It's a well known tradition for the struggling crack head. I don't know what just happened or why I'm walking back to the block and not in handcuffs. I'm 15 years old with no license, driving a stolen car under the influence of PCP, with a half ounce of crack in my panties, and now I'm walking away. My brother has been getting into trouble since he was 12 years old. These cops watched him grow up and realize that he's not a threat and won't hurt anybody, but just trying to survive. I had to separate from big bro, he now got some work to flip, and so did I.

Back on the block, I have the major hots for this little wild dude named little Ty. He was 17, so he was 2 years older than me. He was the youngest of the older dudes on the block. His name was little Ty because there was already a Ty on the block who they renamed Big Ty. He had cornrows in football shoulders with gold Teeth from Steve's in NY. You weren't a real hood nigga in my city if you didn't have permanent custom made gold teeth. Ty was like the perfect little gangsta. He acted like he didn't like me, but he would sneak me to the hotel room at times. He likes the fact that I know how to get money, so I guess that's why he liked me. One night, he didn't even have a 1/2 a crack car, so how were we gonna get there tonight? A half a crack is a car that we rent from crackheads in exchange for crack. They'll give you their whole damn car, all you have to do is get them high! Anyway, Lil Ty needed a ride to the hotel in the meadows. It was only 15 minutes away right past downtown.

One of the old head on the block gave us a ride in his half a crack. His name was Robert. He was on the Marine Corps and went to war and Desert Storm and then decided to come to the block after living a sheltered life. It was kinda funny to us watching this old corny nigga try to learn how to be on these streets when we did this our whole lives. He even looks like he doesn't belong, he was always laughing all the time, and at everything like it was a nervous reaction. What the fuck is so funny, and how are you so happy? It ain't got out here. He thinks this is a game, it's like he's having fun out here! Nonetheless, he gave us a ride to the room with no problem.

When we walked into the hotel, little Ty got super comfortable and undressed down to his t-shirt and boxers. He rolled up about 3 blunts and pulled out a bottle of Henny. During this smoke session, this dude also pulled out some crack and a box of sandwich bags. I know this nigga didn't bring me here to help him bag up his drugs. I think he's trying to play me, but I really liked him, and clearly, he saw some value in me, even if it was my street knowledge. He was my little block boyfriend, so after we got finished bagging up all of his crack, we enjoyed each other that night and went back to the block the next morning!

Anyway, after that particular night, Robert started acting like a bully on the block and pretending that he didn't like me. He's trying to diss me, talking about me dealing with a little boy. At least he's in my age group, in fact, he's older than me, so he's not a little boy to me, you're just an old ass man. One night, he saw me on the block in the middle of the night. He was on the porch of that corner apartment building at Ashley and Sigourney. Dana and I walked past, minding our business and catching sales. He was up there with Roc and another side, he shouted out, "I should snatch your chain from you." Referring to the big ass herringbone necklace that I had on that night. It was my brother's chain, but I told him it was Lil Ty's chain just to piss him off and let him know that I like Ty and not him. He replied, "Ohh, now I'm really taking it from you." Let him come get it back from me! Ha! Ha!"

I'm closer to Sigourney street now, and in my mind, I'm thinking this cornball who is still on the block with us little kids ass nigga has some nerve bothering me. He is always talking about how he went to Desert Storm, he went to war but now you're on the block with us, so what happened to your life? Talking about you're a killer! We're teenagers 15, even Lil Ty was only 17, but this old ass man was like 25-26. He looks silly as hell coming to the hood at this age, that's so corny to me.

Once the fall came and stayed, it started getting chilly to stay outside all day, so we tried to find other things you do. I never had a best friend, but I'm pretty sure that Dana was because, honestly, I've never been this close to any chick that wasn't my real family!

Anyway, Robert invited all of us over his homeboy Tee's house, so that he can record us free styling. He pretended to be a DJ, and I acted like I gave a fuck because we needed to record. That recording session was dope, and it was honestly my 1st time recording ever!

After this, Robert was infatuated with me. He would give me weed and buy me bottles of Hennessy. He would invite me and Dana to his private parties at his house that he shared with his girlfriend Chris and her son Tyson. He was rude as hell flirting with me in his own house right in front of his girlfriend. Before this, I thought he was lame, but the way he's showing me attention is like he was determined to get me. He was slick because he got in cool with my homegirl so that he could get close to me. And he did just that with his old ass manipulation and the 11-year leverage he has on me. But this old dude ain't even worth my time. He just wants to make Lil Ty jealous. But Lil Ty had more hoes than he did. He had the suburban type of good girls chicks that all the guys are into. He only fucks with me because those prissy chicks that he really likes, can't help him make any money. So I'm winning in the Bonnie position for any Clyde out here, it just happens to be him for the moment because I'm as thorough as they come!

Later that winter, the block was getting hot. The police were down the street, spying on everything moving out there. We were all outside that day, and I'm talking about everybody. This was a nice and warm day to be in winter. There were at least 300+ people outside between Sigourney Park, the block which was on Ashley street, and the neighborhood package store and drug store Pierce Pharmacy. The police jumped out on us and started frisking us. I wasn't worried because my pack was in the backyard. Then all of a sudden, they pulled out one dime of crack from my jeans pocket. I'm screaming historically because I don't even carry crack in my pockets. EVER! Let alone having it in the tiny little pocket, the pocket that 2 fingers can't fit in. You wouldn't be able to move fast enough to throw it if you got rushed by the boys. I had 3 dimes in my mouth that

I swallowed immediately they jumped out on us. Why would I have just one dime in my pocket? I told the cop that he planted the drugs on me, and that made him even more pissed off. They found drugs on Dana, was it planted too? Her older brother Boo Bang was in handcuffs with us, and he didn't even sell drugs. They brought us to a little substation down the street where they processed us and took our fingerprints. They were mad that Dana and I were minors and couldn't prosecute us as an adult, so they took and decided to charge Boo Bang with possession even though he has never been spotted selling drugs. That wasn't even his thing, he was a rapper. We went to juvenile, but he went to the real jail. I think he got charged for being around minors too.

I went to juvenile for 90 days for possession of narcotics. That little bid was cool though, I found a boyfriend in there to pass the time. Plus, I got locked up with my best friend Dana. I didn't miss much time on the street because my homie was locked with me, and she was my roommate. My Juvie boyfriend's name was Steve. He knew how to rap too. We spent time together every day at lunch and at rec time after dinner. When we get out of here, I knew I wasn't really into him like that, so I don't plan on getting too close to him. He was something like a little boy. Gosh! Cute as hell though, his smile, crooked teeth, and the whole good boy has gone; bad thing he had going on was the shit. Just wasn't made for this life out here, it's like he had too much love inside him. Damn sure he made the best of our time in there, I can't lie. It was him, my friend Dana and a couple of other kids from the hood that we knew. It was more like a camp in Juvie. We were Deep up in there, representing each of our blocks and hoods. We convinced the staff to host a talent show since we used our lunchtime to battle each other. One of the young girls from Bedford street was with us, but she couldn't rap. She was a Lil thug though, and was a couple of years younger. I knew her from the outside, she was a young girl out there with her big brothers. I asked her about some events in her life, and I wrote her a verse with that knowledge. She was on the girl's teams, so we had to win, and we beat the boys hands down! It was fun, and the winning team gets to have an extra hour of TV for a week.

Before my release, I was able to write a letter to my dad, who was in prison doing Federal time. They let me write a letter from juvenile because it was my father, so they allowed the juvenile to Jail inter-correctional transactions from daughter to father only.

I told him that I hated my life and wanted to die. I didn't ask to be in this fucked up world that they brought me into and that all I ever wanted was to love from someone, anyone, and especially him. I told him how he dissed me after the twins were born and how I waited so long for his quality time, and now I'm old news after he had twins. I went on to explain how I've been suicidal now since my grandma died because I knew that life would only get harder without her. I told him that while he's supposed to be protecting me, he's out here chilling in jail. I say chilling because he never has a problem going back inside. In fact, he spent more time in jail than on the outside. In closing, I told him that if I ever had kids, I'll love and support them more than him or my mom ever could have loved me!

And after my release from juvenile, I was on probation and house arrest for another 6 months. I couldn't use my youth offer because I already used it, so I had to do that time. I wore a big ass monitor on my ankle and can only go 100 feet away from the box that they set up at my mom's house on Zion Street. The leg monitor was as big as a deck of cards and so bulky that regular sock couldn't fit over it. I had to wear men's large tube socks. It was an electronic device, therefore,

I couldn't get it wet, so I had to wrap a plastic bag on my leg just to take a shower.

My mom enrolled me into an alternative school called Woodstock in West Hartford that had nothing but crazy kids enrolled. They subscribed to me with Zoloft for depression and would bring my meds to my class during meds break. This was the real deal! I'm really in trouble now! The best part about this school was I went Tobogganing down a steep hill for the first time! I've been sledding all my life but never on a toboggan. 97% of the students were white, so they were used to activities like this.

I was like a celebrity in that school, going by the way those students and staff would stare at me! It was embarrassing because they didn't know what I went to jail for, all they knew was that I went, and I'm walking around with the proof on my ankle! I hated that bracelet! I hated my life and I don't know why I'm so sad.

I'm looking for love in all of the wrong places. I'm a little horn dog and want to have sex just as much as the boys do, sometimes even more.

6

REHAB

Dana and I were supposed to refrain from communication until our case was over, but still she called me one day from a different number going crazy! She started telling me that Robert just landed a brick of cocaine when Tee got busted and went to jail. She was like, "Yo, you know he got the hots for you too. All you have to do was flirt with him, and we could get rich too!"

I was like "What? That old ass corny nigga yo? Why don't you do it, he likes you too!" She said, "girl, you know he's only trying to get closer to you by calling me his little sister. I'll have him drive me over there, and we can all chill and get on a bottle or something, just hear him out Ree! See what he's talking about!" Next thing you know, Robert came over a few times a week with Dana. He started calling her his best friend to manipulate me into trusting him. "That's my fucking best friend nigga!" This dude is starting to get weird.

I couldn't smoke weed because my P.O. came out to my house with a cup for me to pee on the spot. I had no time to plan or alter a piss test with them making home visits. Therefore, when Robert and Dana came over, they had big bottles of E&J VSOP and 40 ounces of Old English. We got drunk as hell every time they came over, and I saved the bottles under my bed to remember the fun I was still having even though I was trapped in the house. Robert was not giving up his flirting. He was chilling with two little girls that he now knew were only 15, and went to package stores because he's going on 26. One night, we got so drunk; drinking bottle after bottle in my bedroom. Finally, Dana passed out, and that's when he grabbed my thigh. He seemed more nervous than I was, but he kept moving it up and down and said, I want you to be my girl, Ree. Let me take care of you! He kissed me with those weird-ass lips. He was in a motorcycle accident years ago and had scars all over his face and half a lip. It made me nervous when the lip touched mine. I jumped away from him. He asked me if I was scared of him. I'm sure he was thinking sexually, but yes nigga you look scary as hell. He made several attempts to get me to relax because I wasn't feeling him like that. It was about 3 am and Dana had been asleep for a couple of hours; so by now,

Robert's groping me and humping on me. This is the part of sex that I liked, the part where I felt nothing but hands and fingers on my body. It got hot in that room as the radio just kept playing hit song after hit song. We were already having slow and passionate sex when the LL Cool J song came on "doing it and doing it and doing it well." It was the perfect song to hear when you know you're a little girl but have this grown man going crazy in your bedroom at your mom's house! I was doing it well, and I secured the damn bag. I had him hooked instantly! He became possessive and controlling and didn't want anyone to talk to me or even look at me. Dana said "Yo Ree, what you do to the homie?" "Bitch, you told me to get him; so I got him, and now he won't let go!" Every free time I had, he was digging in my little young guts! Even at his girlfriend's house during his parties, she would be entertaining the guest, and he would have me locked up in their bedroom kissing all over me. He was in love with me, but I just wanted the money! I didn't care about his relationship because he didn't care about his relationship. I knew that I didn't want him, especially the way he's been mistreating her. Nonetheless, she couldn't beat my ass, so what was she going to do or say about any of it? Robert, Dana, and I were cool on the business tip, and I showed him how to make the real money by cutting his dub sacks into dimes since he was selling them for $10 anyway. He was giving the product away! This made all the crackheads come looking for him only, and now he has all the loyal customers by way of robbing himself and giving them double the product, and the crackheads knew it. I also helped him see that he needed a loose bag of rocks, for when they come with short money, you don't have to turn them away or give away credit. Therefore, we were catching every last sale that came around. We even caught $4, and $5 sales and all! We had the block locked down because we had the best work and the best prices. My cousin Trauma was around the corner with those Sargeant Street dudes. Robert didn't believe that he was my real cousin and didn't like how cool we were. He didn't like any guy around me, and his jealousy was showing up all the time. When he found out that Trauma's real name was Byron too, he thought trauma was my ex-boyfriend. Robert walked right up to me and punched me in the eye! That was the first of many black eyes to come, but I was too young to know any better. He thought that this whole time my cousin Byron was my first love from middle school. Therefore, he assumed that I was playing him for a fool this whole time. He thought we were pretending to be family to trick him. Dana's mom came and got me from off the ground in the parking lot across the street. Robert walked away once I hit the ground. I've seen him knock out grown men before, now he just hit me like one. They all helped me walk back across the street and into the house. By the time I got in the house, my eye was already closed shut! Aunt Deb was already screaming, "I'm calling the police!" That fat ass old bastard wants to put his hands on a girl and a little girl at that! That nigga better not come back over this way or he's going to jail. Fuck That! Aunt Deb yelled, "You better not ever talk to that nigga again, and I mean it Sherrie!" She was HOT! She couldn't sit still and was pacing back and forth through the kitchen, yelling and fussing.

Dana and I were begging her not to call the police. Not because we wanted to protect him, but because she didn't know that we were as Deep into the drug game as we were, and we didn't need any extra heat with the police on the block. She told me that I better stayed the fuck away from him or he will end up killing me some day! I wish she would have used her authority to keep him away then, but instead she made me leave and go home.

Kelis was staying at my mom's house because at the time, she was having some personal issues. She was finally able to run to my mom for help, which she was never able to do in the past with my mom's instability. Now, she was able to get away for a minute, and she had my mom this time. When I walked through the door, Kelis instantly saw my eye. She started screaming and yelling. I begged her not to wake my mom up to tell her. She was getting so irate and loud that I had to leave the house before my mom saw my eye; she would have tried to kill Robert. My mom thought Robert was our rap DJ and didn't know that I was fucking with this old man. I mean, why did she think he was coming over every day anyway, to rehearse? LOL.

Eventually, I violated my probation when my urine test came back positive for marijuana. I was heading back to court for the judge to decide if he was going to send me to Long Lane as he told me he would the last time that I went to court for a previous drug charge. Long Lane was Juvenile detention for long term stays and will usually lead you right up into the women's Prison called Niantic! Juvenile was more like a camp lock up, while Long Lane was where kids did the harder time.

Next thing you know, I'm pulling up To Blue Ridge drug abuse facility on blue hills avenue. Now I'm thinking, "What the FUCK is going on here?" My mom was saying that she rather lock me in a drug program than to send me away to Long Lane. I didn't like anything about this place nor any of the addicts and alcoholics who were locked in there too. I knew about two people out of the group of over 50 adults. Well, I didn't know them, but I'd seen them in the hood before. And this was the place for them, not for me, I don't do real drugs. I just smoke a little dust here and there, nothing too crazy and not enough to get butt naked over. As I sat with my intake counsellor, I tried to find out what the program was all about?

"Why am I here?

How long will I be here?"

That's when I found out that I'd be staying there for at least 3 months... "What? Are you fucking serious? Like staying the night for 3 whole months?" So my mom replied, "You wanna stay here or go to Long Lane?" That's when it hit me. I'm not a real addict, I'm just avoiding jail time. I don't know if I believed it, but it helped me get past the intake office. Mom left, and there I was with a bunch of strangers for the next few months. After the intake process, the next stop was the detox unit. OMG! Detox was horrible!

You just lay in bed all day reading books and looking at the wall. You hear all the screaming and vomit and dry heaving noises coming from other rooms. The heroin addicts had it bad, and I felt sorry for them. All you hear was painful cries and weird sounds as if I was listening to a horror movie all night long. I only had to detox for 2 days. However, the dope fiends had to stay in the detox wing at least a week or more depending on how bad their sickness was while detoxing.

That third morning, I got up for breakfast and they gave me my schedule for the day. WTF is this? Between twelve and eighteen meetings every day? A different schedule each day, good grief! I got to my first meeting, and they were all kids. I was one of the 7 oldest kids there and the only black kid, period! These kids did real drugs though! The youngest of the group was a 10-year-old acid tripping zombie. He didn't even know he was here. He was spaced out in a zone like the walking dead. He touched his fingertips with both hands as if he was doing the itsy bitsy spider hand dance. He looked like he had one last trip and never came back. It was sad to see someone younger than me in this condition. The older kids were using homemade drugs that I didn't even know were drugs. They had all types of kid drug addicts such as glue sniffers, paint sniffers, mushrooms, pain pills, muscle relaxers, ecstasy pill, acid tabs, meth, all white people drugs I guess! All I knew about was weed, cocaine, crack, pills, dust, and heroin. Here I am on angel dust, and they are looking at me with a side-eye. It was crazy in there! Katie (a very pretty 16-year-old) was from Groton; she told me all about ecstasy pills and her super sweet 16 lifestyles. I had no clue what ecstasy pills were before I met her. She was cool, and the bitch was crazy rich. Her dad laced her with a bunch of snacks, food, money for the payphone and vending machines, 10 cartons of Marlboros in the red pack and new socks, as well as sweat suits, because she didn't want her good clothes in a place like that. At first, I didn't believe it until she invited me to her room to get some snacks. This girl had her room set up like the college kids on TV. She had EVERYTHING in there. All the different perfume, fancy deodorants, scented soaps, matching socks, everything! Lots of pink and girly glittery shit in there with furry pillows and rugs! We can certainly be friends now Katie, she's like a movie star or something. She got me in with the boys. They were the tough kids of the suburbs. The ones that start fires in cars and spray paint stop signs on park benches! They looked like they have been cussing their mothers out for years! One of them even had white boy dreadlocks and tattoos. For some reason, everyone smoked cigarettes. Kools, Virginia slims, and Marlboro, but not one Newport in sight! The Kools were the closest alternate, so I started smoking those. I still smoked Marlboro because I didn't have cartons of cigarettes like my new rich friends did.

The adolescent program at Blue Ridge consisted of 2-3 meetings a day, and was designed to keep the kids together and safe at night away from the adults while we slept. The remainder of our daily meetings were with the general population. The evening meetings were held in the auditorium and held at least 500 people each night! Friday night meetings were like a party! Those were public nightly meetings where people from the outside came to do either AA or NA, but it was a combined meeting, so everyone came. Most of the attenDanas had already done the in-house program and had since been released to come back for follow up meetings. Some never did an overnight stay in this program, and some were part of an outpatient court order. Even the veterans who are what they called sponsors, were present in these meetings. Sponsors were the people who have worked the rehabilitation system successfully and now responsible for helping others do the same thing. In these meetings, sponsors talked about how many years, months, and days that they've been clean. They brag and boast about it like they're better than us, and we're little peasants stuck in the mud. They called us babies, and they are the adults because they had grown over their addiction, but we're still learning to walk by crawling. Good for them, but fuck them too. They make you feel like shit; it's supposed to be okay because they too were once a piece of shit like you. They want to be viewed as saviors and like appear to try to help us come out of the shit hole. They give us these long testimonies of how horrible life was for them before they found a rehab. We should be grateful that we are at the baby steps of their journey too. They were like the celebrity addicts, everyone knew who they were, and everyone wanted to be like them when they finished the program. You should see the new folks begging them and fighting each other to have these sponsor celebrities as their personal sponsors rightfully so though; in order to discharge from this program, we needed to have a certified sponsor from their list of veteran sponsors.

The last meeting for the day ended between 9 pm and 10:30 pm, and bedtime was 11:30 pm. There was a game room close to the detox unit, and that was the late-night hang out. There were a lot of activities to get busy with in that very room. The older guys were playing dominoes and spades, and the younger kids were playing UNO, video games, and connect four. No matter what, 11:30 pm is bedtime, which means; get into your private room and don't come back out until breakfast.

Over the following weeks, I learnt how to play spades and dominos with the old men. I had a portrait drawn of me by a 3-time recovering crackhead named James. He was in his mid to late 50s, and here he was staring at me across the table at 11 pm as he drew me with a weird smile on his face. I bought that picture for a pack of cigarettes which I got from Katie. She also blessed me with some quarters for the phone. James didn't take all the cigarettes for his drawing, he just wanted half a pack.

I couldn't get visits for my first 2 weeks; although in the third week, mom came to visit me along with Kelis. I don't quite know why she brought Kelis over. Could it be because Kelis knows me more than she does? They brought me some cigarettes, though just 3 packs and not a carton like everyone else. Man, we smoke cigs after every meeting, so that's close to a pack a day, although I wasn't as rich as Katie and these other addicted kids, since my mom didn't have it. I had the least amount of supplies of all the other kids by only having the basic toiletries rather than the luxuries. I never knew that people used all these things anyway, so I wasn't deprived at all. Mom bought me some crossword puzzles, word search, and other little things to keep me busy. She remembered my request from being in Juvenile and all those other places, so she didn't have to think about what I liked. It was a good visit, and I was happy to see familiar faces for a change. Although the gifts they left were everything! I sold one of the books for a pack of cigarettes though. Just saying I needed more cigarettes.

My mom didn't let Robert get on the visiting list; in an attempt to keep him away from me I guess. Although I used my quarters to call his house. He lived with his girlfriend and her son, but she didn't have any rights because he took care of her by himself, he said. She let him do anything he wanted, including fucking with me. So I would call the house and ask to speak to him. She had to put him on the phone because he would wait for my calls at 10 pm each night. He would talk to me for the whole 20-minute time limit that I had on the payphone! He would tell me about all the plans he had for us to get some money together and I already proved that I knew how to get it; so now he wants to join forces. He'd be talking like that at home in front of his girl, so I knew it's real. He would tell me he couldn't wait for me to come out so he could take care of me. I believed him, I knew he loved me more than his girlfriend, and he kept on telling me that he was going to leave her. It was enough to keep me sane in there, besides it was nice to dream about something; anything other than these addicts.

The staff had to split up Katie and I because we were caught fantasizing about our drug of choice inside a rehabilitation facility, which was against the rules! We still saw each other in our teen groups, but they wouldn't allow us to have a private conversation. We were only talking about how much fun we had doing our drugs on the outside! Gosh! Katie's drug seemed better than mine though. Her stories were filled with parties and sex, while mine were mostly nightmares and crime. After lunch each day, we all had about 1 and a half hours before the next meeting started, so we would hang out in the garden inside the courtyard, which was in the center of the building. In the courtyard, we would chain smoke cigarettes and play hacky sack! It was a game using a little rice-filled ball that you have to kick to each other and catch with any body part except your hands, and do all of this without letting it touch the ground. It was mad fun, especially when that's all that we could do until we could get to the game room at night! I met an older lady named Monica from Hartford, who was addicted to crack cocaine. She would talk to me and tell me to change my life so that I don't end up like her. She was like my mom inside that place. She saw how those old men looked at me, and it was like she wanted to protect me to make sure they didn't try anything funny. She would come inside the game room on a late-night to send me to my room because there was nothing but grown, substance-addicted men in there looking in my young and pretty face. I didn't trip on her though, she seemed very genuine and always said she has a daughter around my age. She was in her late 20s, dark-skinned with a big butt and very pretty; but you could tell that drugs got the best of her. She transferred to a long term facility after her first 4 weeks. I was getting closer to my discharge date, and my mom was trying to make me stay longer, so she signed me up for an outpatient program where I get to go home at night and return in the morning.

I was discharged on a certain Friday night. That night Robert came to get me. He booked a room on the Berlin turnpike for the entire weekend! I didn't even have any clothes to change in and out of. He brought me home that Sunday night after a long weekend. I only told my mom that I was going to the corner store that Friday night. She was tired of my bullshit, or tired of her boyfriend yelling at her about how she needs to control me. He would catch me stealing her car while she was asleep. He came home waking her up to let her know her car wasn't outside! Fucking hater! He was my little brother's father and was a big-time drug dealer who didn't like me hanging in the streets.

Nonetheless, she broke a broomstick over my back while she was beating me, then she grabbed the mop and broke that stick on my thigh. She finally beat me up that night, leaving me covered with black and blue marks all over my body. I was trying to hold her to tell her to stop hitting me, but that just made her more angry and violent. I was screaming! She was crying the whole time, so you could tell that she was fed up with me! I was so angry that she put her hands on me like that and I couldn't fight back because she was my mom! I was looking at her little short self, imagining the damage that I would've done to her if I hit her back, but I just couldn't do that to my mom, so that made me even angrier. I went back to rehab the next morning as scheduled. I could hardly walk straight as my whole body was in pain. My friends asked, are you ok? I said yes, I'm just tired. By the afternoon, my body looked like it's dying with all of the dead marks. I was now limping pretty hard because my legs got it the worst. In the group, the kids would ask me why I am limping after being out for a weekend. They were jealous that I got to go home. They were coming up with all types of sceneries for me limping and being sore! Since it was rehab, of course they mentioned drugs. I started yelling in frustration, "I wasn't out getting drugged up! I just didn't come home, and my mom beat me with a stick! OKAY!" I screamed!

It was quiet for a minute and an awkward silence. I think they were processing their thoughts.

Finally, they called the Administrator to descalate the situation. He sent me to the nurse. The nurse asked me, "where did your mom hit you?" Still in a loud, defensive, and aggressive state, I replied

"EVERYWHERE!!!" She asked, "can you show me?" I only showed her the smallest bruise on my wrist, and that was enough to start the process! A detective came and spoke to me briefly about the physical event between my mom and I. They then called my mom to explain that they are removing me from the program and placing me in custody. She was cussing them out, telling them that I'm a manipulator, and I'm playing with their intelligence. She explained that I'm a troubled and uncontrollable teen who can't be fully trusted. She advised them to find out the whole truth before accusing her of abusing her kid. Nope! They saw those bruises and packed my shit up and brought me to 999 Asylum Ave. This was the Department of children and families' headquarters. By the time we got to the office building, it was late in the evening around 8:30-9:00 pm. The police walked me up to the second floor in a big room full of mostly empty cubicles, and only a few people were working that late at night. Some lady there picked her head up and smiled. Hello, "Sherrie, I'm Ms. Vasquez. I'm your intake worker, please sit down." The officer said goodnight to both of us, and went about his night. It was just she and I. You could hear voices on the other side of the room not loud enough to be understood what was said, but enough to know that others were in the room. She smiled and said, "It's ok, you're safe now, and nobody can hurt you again! We will keep you safe until you're 18 and able to take care of yourself!" In my mind, I screamed 18? That's almost 4 years. I just turned 15 a couple of months ago. I responded with confusion, "Where will I be until I turn 18?" "You will be going to Stamford tonight. They found a bed for you out there, once you're admitted, you'll be on the list for family placement." "You mean, I can't go live with my own family? Are you bringing me to live with strangers?". She replied saying, "If you have a family that isn't connected to your mom, we can consider that, but if not we will give you a new family!" "A new family? What is a new family? Like foster care?" Yes she said, "We will place you with a foster family. Is that ok with you?" I smiled to mask the fear in my heart. I might never see my real family again if they bring me 2 hours away. I went along with the whole thing, even pretended to be excited to be leaving my family and to be safe from harm and danger! She was off guard completely as I was spinning her with my quick wit and manipulation that my mom warned them about. I'd be telling her about my fear of my mom coming up here to steal me away from her! Especially since she was pregnant and wouldn't be able to protect me if my mom was to come to steal me! This was when she got to tell me about the building's high tech security with that one security guard at the front door. The old man who was reading the paper and listening to music looked like he had about 2 hip replacements. I thought for sure that she would mention the police, even the one that transported me there. Nope! So all I had to worry about was the old man at the bottom of the steps? As we sat another 20 minutes or so, she advised me that I only had about another hour before the van would come to take me to Stamford. She also informed me that she had to use the ladies room and that I shouldn't worry that I'd be safe while she's gone! Oh yeah, I had her hooked! She thought I was really afraid!

She even pointed to the restroom door, which was all the way across the room, away from the steps!

I inhaled deeply and exhaled to show her that I had enough courage to stay alone until she returned to her cubicle! She started walking, and my heart started pumping. I knew that I would only get one chance at this, so I had to carefully calculate this next move. I piqued my head up while she was just about to push the bathroom door, then she saw me peeking up at her and looking suspicious. She paused and stared at me, looking at her across all of those empty cubicles. That's when I took off running! She started screaming and jogging to follow me, but she was too big for the chase and I was already at the staircase! She started screaming at the top of her lungs. Once the security guard finally figured out what was going on as they heard her scream. I was already flying down the staircase. He had to walk around his desk before he could get to the front door to block me. Once he finally came around his U-shaped desk, I was flying out the front door! Now I'm running into traffic about to get hit by the oncoming cars on Asylum ave, trying to cross the street! I could hear the guard yelling and chasing me, but by the time I got across the street, I jumped over that big ass black metal gate at St Francis Hospital parking lot which was directly across from child services. That hospital parking lot had so many exits that I had to run to the one closest to Atwood and Townley Street. I kept running up Townley Street to a big cube-shaped building that connected on each end like a square. You could walk down the hallway and take 3 right turns and end up where you started. I knew two crackheads in that building and was sure to be able to stay there, as long as I had some crack. I didn't have any, but I knew that I could call Robert and get some. I knew about four people who lived in that building, but nobody was home to answer the door at any of the apartments. I went back to Barbara's house, a crack head whom I've known the longest and treated her like she's my real auntie. I sat at her door for hours before she finally came home. Once she let me in, I was relieved. Now I knew they would have to knock on every door to find me if they saw me run in this building. I was sweaty as hell though. I had on a light grey sweat suit and some old ass new balance which I wore for a whole month. I'm now a real fugitive and can't go anywhere.

I stayed with Barbara for about 3 weeks but I had to leave because she was smoking crack in front of me as if it was weed. I saw this lady pour out the liquid that collected inside of her pipe into a plate and set it on fire. After the fire burned down, she scraped the black residue off of the plate and put it back on the pipe to smoke it. That was too much to me to see and to be inhaling but I literally got nowhere else to go right now so I'm stuck breathing second hand crack smoke.

Child services are like the feds, and nobody wants them investigating them in efforts to find me. Everyone turned their backs on me once agents started showing up to family and friend's houses looking for me! I had nowhere to go and nobody to turn to. Dana would tell me to turn myself in because her mom didn't want me over there getting caught at her house, since she'd be charged with harboring a fugitive and risk of injury, with all kind of bullshit involved. I had to lay really low. I dyed my hair and only came outside at night to hustle up some money. I wore hats every day and couldn't let passing cars see my face.

I left Barbara and moved in with Niecy who lived in front of Pearce Pharmacy. This allowed me to still be on the block making money but inside and out of harms way. Once Niecy's friends found out that she had a plug at her house all the time, they started coming in groups who are wanted their own personal sack. She started having friends that she didn't even know that she had. She didn't mind because as long as I was there, people would visit her and she would get high for free.

I slept in the back room on a pissy mattress that was on the floor. I paid her a twenty dollar rock each night that I stayed there so it equaled out to be around $150 a week to rent her room out. The worst part about being over there was that it was a bonafide crack house. It was just like Barbara's house but times 10. I really loved Niecy though, I wish she didn't smoke crack because she had a good heart. I can tell that she came from a good background because she was filled with joy and always had a smile on her face. But I'm sick of breathing this crack smoke and I'm scared that I may start liking it after a while. A crack pipe was being lit up over there almost every thirty minutes or so. If they weren't smoking, they were geeking. Crackheads all have different geeks. Meaning one of them would get naked and that's their geek. Another one would pick up all of the lint in the carpet or everything white on the sidewalk. The most common geeks are paranoia, super hyperactive behaviours and mouth twitches.

It has been over a year out here in these streets. I'm tired of running and Im ready to turn myself in. I need someone to take care of me but Robert is taking care of a broke bitch when he should be taking care of me. I moved around the corner upstairs from Dana with Lucy and Chicko! They were an older Puerto Rican couple, though Chicko was always in and out of jail for stealing or other petty crack crimes. Lucy would work for her dollars by walking to the store for us, selling things that Chicko stole, and other small odd jobs to earn a dollar or two. She was loud and annoying and spoke thick Spanish, so you could hardly understand her. She was about 4ft 9 and 90 pounds soaking wet, yet she would fight anyone and over anything! She was always getting into crackhead fights, but anytime another addict got tired of her aggressive behaviors and tried to fight her, we would never let them touch her. She was our block grandma or something like that. We all couldn't stand her because she could easily piss you off by invading your personal space and forcing you to either talk to her or yell at her to leave you alone. Either way, she just wanted to hear your voice, it seems. She would insult you for no reason and laugh hard in your face. The way she laughed was even insulting. So it was a double insult. She would say what she's saying and then end it with a laugh "Ahh Ha mommy or Ahh Ha poppy" lol. I'm not sure if that was her culture, but it sounded very offensive after an intentional degrading remark.

Anyway, I stayed on her couch for a few more months. She had a mice infestation; the whole building had tons of mice, but the other apartment on the third floor was empty, which made all the mice play on the third floor for some reason. You could see them running back and forth under the front door between the two apartments like a mice playground. Twenty mice were running in at the same time while 25 were running out! It was a mice circus. I was scared as hell, but I was even more afraid of getting caught and taken away into custody. I lived in that nightmare at Lucy's for months. That was my only option until I could figure something else out.

It was New Year's Eve. We got an invitation to Roberts' sister's house to celebrate. Her name was Canice, and she was about 2 years younger than him. She had a one bedroom apartment on Asylum avenue at the corner of Gillette Street. She was doing big things, especially since we were homeless. His whole family was mad at him for leaving his last girlfriend and his apartment to be with me, who didn't have anything going for myself.

Anyway, Fruit was cool, I knew her from the block, and she knew my dad too. The party was small, just Fruit and her boyfriend, Robert and I and about 3 to 4 others. We had a ball that night! We drank and smoked so much that Robert and I ended up passing out on her living room floor! When I woke up the next morning, my throat was swollen to the point that it was closing up, making it hard to breathe. Since the hospital was only a block away, Robert walked to the ER with me. During patient enrollment, the representative looked up at me and asked for parental authorization. Robert looked at her and asked, why would you need parental authorization? The lady responded, "Because she's a minor" and needs permission to treat her from a parent or Guardian! Are you her Guardian? Robert looked at me with anger and disgust and yelled, "You're a minor?" How old are you Sherrie? He asked in a loud and stern tone. I replied, "Don't worry about that! That doesn't matter! Can you authorize them to treat me?" I asked him desperately as I could barely talk, and my throat was almost sealed shut! "Don't worry about that? This lady is telling me that you're a Minor! What do you mean, don't worry about that Sherrie? Nahh, I'm out of here yo!"

He got up from the enrollment station and walked out of the Emergency Room. By this time, everyone is looking at me, and the poor lady is sitting there confused and not knowing what to do at this point. I asked if she could call my mom with the number that she had on file. My mom was able to give permission over the phone, telling them that she would come and sign the papers. They gave me antibiotics and sent me on my way back to Lucy's house upstairs from Dana. Robert disappeared for about 2 weeks. I couldn't get in contact with him at all. He just popped up on the block one day and told me that he was going to get me an apartment. I guess now it made sense to him why I was down so bad out here. It's not like I'm a real bum wasting my life away, I'm just too young to do anything other than sell drugs! It seemed like learning about my age made him love me even harder because, if I'm that young out here surviving on my own, imagine what I could do once I get old enough to make some real moves?

After being sick and throwing up for days, I found out that I was pregnant. I was scared to tell Robert, who would come upstairs to chill with me every day but went home most nights. Sometimes he rented Lucy's bedroom for the night, so he could have room to sleepover. That love seat in the living room is where I slept most nights. Anyway, I told Lucy that I might be pregnant, and I was scared to tell Robert. I told her that I'm only 15, and I can't go to the clinic by myself. She covered my mouth as if to tell me to stop talking. "Ok, mommy! I'll take care of you now mommy! Ahhh hah! I'm going to help you! Mira, trust me, ok?" She knew I was scared, so she gave me a tight and long hug! "Mommy, that lil baby, (pointing to my belly) is no more! Ahhh hah!" She yelled! Then went to the fridge, got three eggs, cracked them into an empty glass, opened up a Malta drink which is a Spanish soda. She poured the whole bottle in the glass with the eggs, then grabbed another soda but didn't open this one. She opened a bottle of castor oil and poured half the bottle into the mixture. Then she gave me about 6 aspirin to take with the mixture. As I drank the concoction, I felt sick instantly. I started sweating and cramping up. Next thing you know I couldn't walk, I was in so much pain. I laid on the couch, crying for a few hours until she gave me warm Malta to drink with a couple more pain pills! Before that night was over, I thought I was going to die from the extreme cramping, cold sweats, and fatigue. I dragged myself back and forth to the bathroom with diarrhea, heavy bleeding, and vomiting! My pants were soaked in blood. I just knew that I would die soon. When Robert came and cleaned me up and asked what happened to me, I told him I didn't know. He knew right at that moment that I was pregnant and that I was having a miscarriage. He blamed me for losing the baby, so he left me there and pretended to be madly in love with his girlfriend again. It was a relief getting a break from him. However, it didn't take long before he was back on it again.

7

THE BLOCK IS HOT

I'm so tired of these mean streets and all of the ripping and running. All of these boys of my age bracket still living with their moms, but I've got nobody to take care of me the way I need to be taken care of. By this time Robert left his girlfriend for good and moved me into a studio apartment on Sigourney and Sargent Street. I was still selling crack, but only in the house and only to regular well-known customers. After a few months had passed of course, I was getting too comfortable. First of all, I'm 15 years old; with my first apartment. Well, at least I own my own kitchen, bedroom, and bathroom. Robert wanted to domesticate me, so he taught me how to cook everything except fried chicken breast, it seems. Whenever I served that man the best piece of chicken and he bit into it, all you saw was blood. He was convinced that I was trying to poison him, so that night I got my 3rd black eye. It wasn't close tight like the other two were, so I guess it was a little love tap. He only did it because he wanted to show me how much he wanted to help me learn how to take care of a man. He made the best love to me that night too. Surely I was convinced that he didn't mean it. I got pregnant again that night. Again? OMG! This nigga is trying to trap me. All he does is beat me up and knock me up. How in the hell did I get this Deep with this old ass man? If I leave him where do I go now? I don't have anything without him. He does a good job reminding me about how much help he offers to me and how he is the only one in the world who loves me. He makes sure I never forget that I was a bum on the street with nothing before he saved me. I'm not even old enough to do anything legal. I had to drink another one of Lucy's Puerto Rican abortion potions so I may some day get away from this old man without having his damn baby. I can't imagine him being the father of my baby. I mean, he has two other kids with a possibility of another, yet he's out here trying to be my damn baby daddy!

A few months went by and since we were on the corner house, anyone could see the building's activity down any of the two streets. I had that motherfucker jumping with an easy three to five hundred a day in sales. I have the best loyal group of crackheads, all the private smokers who didn't want to get served on a street corner were knocking on my door. These were the ones who had jobs and had lots of disposable money to spend. They had too much to lose to be getting caught buying crack. The dudes on the block were getting mad because I was making a lot of bread in the house. Robert was out fucking other hoes while I made the money. He took me off the streets so I guess I owed him a few cheats. I mean honestly what can I do about him cheating if I'm not financially stable enough to leave him yet.

On a certain day, one of the crack addicts tried to get back the ring that she pawned to get some crack a couple of weeks prior. It was a big ass ring too. She damn near wanted to fight me to get that ring back. I'm pretty sure she understood that she couldn't leave it with me for longer than a week. Bitch me and that ring became one, and it's mine now. The lady must have been seriously mad that she left my house without her ring. Within a week, the police came knocking on my door. It was crazy how it all went down though. First, a knock, knock, knock, knock, but at the moment, I was cooking in the kitchen which also had a door connected to that same hallway. I could hear multiple sets of steps walk up to my goddamn door. It was clear that I heard more than one person out there. "Who is it?" I said. A male voice on the other side of the door answered "it's Pat." I replied, "Pat who?" Pat said "I need a six." I replied again, "get the fuck away from my door with that dumb shit, there ain't no drugs here!" It sounded like they left, but I still wasn't convinced. That scared me and led me to hide all the crack inside the lotion tops of every lotion bottle. I didn't have a lot of crack but if I got caught with it, they would make it become a lot.

I had to pee now. However, I had to go across the hallway outside of the apartment to my private bathroom that had to be opened with a key. I wasn't still sure if they had left yet, and so I grabbed a large cup that we normally keep from McDonald's, who doesn't save those cups anyway? I peed in the cup and poured the piss down the drain in the kitchen sink. Over two hours had passed. I finished cooking and got to bed. Watching the TV, I heard; knock, knock, knock again. "Who the fuck is it?" I asked. "It's Richard from downstairs." I completely forgot about the previous knocks that had me paranoid earlier. Nonetheless, I opened the door for the familiar voice of my homie downstairs. BOOM!!!! I fell back on the bed. "Freeze! Put your hands up!" All I thought to myself was, these motherfuckers have got me! And that snitching ass neighbor is getting his ass fucked up. They searched high and low through the rooms, trashing the whole place. These assholes thought they were coming for some big weight, so they didn't even bother to open any of the small containers that I had strategically split up the crack into. They called me all kinds of bitch names for neither telling them where Robert was nor where the drugs were. Fuck them! They needed to have a search warrant and they didn't even find drugs though. So what the fuck did they want? I still went to jail that night. That was crazy because all they found was the weed that I was smoking. When I got out of jail, I came back to the apartment to find out that it had been kicked in. I wasn't sure whether the police came back or I just got robbed by my neighbors. Of course, we had to move out, the landlord wasn't fooling with any of those drug activities in the building.

Robert moved to live with his mother and wasn't leaving me out in the streets without him, so he begged her to let me stay too. I turned sixteen years old in her house, where her son and I slept on the floor in the second bedroom of her East Hartford apartment. We stayed for a few months, while I served as a babysitter for his eldest daughter who came to visit for the summer. She was 5 years old, and he had another daughter as well, who was almost 2 years old. I saw a portrait of a little boy of about 5 years old whom he denied wasn't his son. I don't see how he's not because that little boy in the portrait looks just like him. Anyway, his 5-year-old daughter arrived from California for the first time to stay with her dad. When she went back home, I had to leave too.

I was back on the streets, but this time my mom came up with a plan to go to the court office in order to emancipate me. Since Child Services could not process me into their system before I ran, my mom was not prosecuted, and therefore; I was still under her custody. I found a gap in the system and used it to my advantage. My mom got my dad's signature from jail, went to court and filed a paperwork for me to divorce my parents and become a legal adult. You cannot get emancipated before the age of 16, but once you do file the paperwork and both parents sign their rights away, you become legal and will no longer require a guardian to make decisions for you. My parents knew that I was able to survive on my own, and wanted me to stop having to run, duck and hide every day.

Now I was able to go back and stay with my mom and a month or later Robert started working with his cousin, not far from his mother's house! He still called me every day, though he knew that his mother didn't want him to be with me, simply because I was too young for him. He started becoming busy after work, saying he was hanging out with his buddies from work. This happened more often than not and I started getting suspicious. He didn't have a car, so we both were riding the bus and it was always difficult for us to see each other. I would call him and he wouldn't answer, and would even send me to voicemail sometimes. He sent me to voicemail so many times that I started trying to crack his voicemail code. He wasn't too smart, so I knew that the code had to be easy to break into. Sure enough, it only took me about 3 hours and I was in! I heard all sort of messages from several different females, yet he didn't even call me back that fateful night! The next morning, I called while he was heading to work. He then told me that he overslept the previous night, and next he said that he had to hang up so he could clock in. On his lunch break he told me that his company was having a party for the employees so he will be home late again. I knew he was high on some bullshit, especially after hearing the messages from other females. He was good at lying and getting away with it, so I had to wait until I could catch him red handed before holding a valid case of cheating against him.

I had to wait until he got off and turned his phone off before I could check his voicemail, otherwise he would see me calling during business hours and get on high alert. My predictions were on point. It was just 10 minutes after 5 O'clock and then his phone switched to voicemail. I entered his code and the first message was a young lady who didn't even have to mention her name. She was basically following up on a previous conversation about meeting him at the bus stop on Burnside Avenue at 5:30pm. That bus stop was just one block from his mother's house. I jumped up and got dressed. I requested for $5 from my mom because my pockets were down bad. I ran to Park street to catch the bus, I wish I could fly out there. It took me 25 minutes to get downtown where I could exchange buses. The buses for East Hartford were all the way in the back of the Pavilion and so i had another five-minute walk to get on to the next bus stop. I then waited 20 minutes for the bus to arrive and another 20 minutes before I could travel to that very bus stop which I heard of on the voicemail.

Of course by the time I got to that bus stop, it was about 6:30pm already. His mom's building was then secured so I couldn't get in. I walked round the building to the window of his room upstairs where I used to sleep on the floor and I noticed the lights on. I went back to the front door to keep on waiting for anyone to walk out, so that I could get in. After 30 more minutes, I was in. I listened through the door and I heard music and voices. I started knocking on the door and immediately heard footsteps walk up to the door, but then those footsteps soon walked away. Soon, I heard the music turned off and then I began to bang on the door like the police. It was loud enough for the neighbors to open their doors to see what was going on down the hallway. After about 10 minutes of banging nonstop, I heard a voice on the other side of the door saying "Sherrie! Stop banging on my mother's door!" That's when I lost it! I began to pound that door. Who the hell does he think he is? "Open this mother fucking door!" I screamed as I turned around with my back to the door and started kicking it with the sole of my feet! "Robert, I'm not leaving until you open this fucking door! You trying to play games with me! You really think that you can eat your cake and have it too? After this I'm done with you, but this time I'm going to make sure that you're done with me too!" That moment, I pulled out my keys and started carving into the wooden door. You Dirty Dick Ass Nigga!! Fuck You! After all of that carving, It just wasn't enough to make him open it though. That's when I started covering the remainder of the door with more carvings, leaving not one inch of the door untouched. I kept going in, Deniseper and Deniseper and finally the door opened up. He grabbed me and pulled me inside this dark apartment. I started fighting him and knocking down plants from the table. He put me into a bear hug and held me so tight that I couldn't move and then he yelled out to the girl telling her to run out the door while he had me restrained. This big black fat bitch came running out of the room!! I went crazy trying to get lose to catch her but he held me even tighter!! She got away!! I kept struggling to break free and started head butting him. He finally let me go and I ran out the door! . His mom's building was made up of about 8 different buildings which were all connected to each other, forming a big ass square, and so there were at least 8 exits out of this building. She could actually be anywhere, but the first thing I thought of was that she would rush back to the bus stop, and that's where I was heading too. At this moment, I'm running up the street and he's running down behind me. I really don't know why I'm chasing this girl, I think I only just want to see whom he thinks is better than me, I thought to myself. As I get to the end of this long ass building, I see her down the other end. I start running towards her and she runs even faster. By this time, it's already dark outside and this bitch is so black that the only way I could find her was by the bright color of her shirt. I just think she was too big to keep on running, because I was actually able to catch up with her. When I walked up to her, she started explaining how she didn't know that Robert had a girl already.

"What's your name?" I asked the lady, while panting hard for breath. "Monica," she said in a loud whisper. She went on to ask "Why are you beefing with me? I don't want to fight; you should be beefing with him." Just looking at her made me angrier, because I just didn't know what he saw in her with those big ass lips of hers'. There was nothing about her which was attractive, and all I could think about was the fact that she probably had a job or something like that. However, she did have a bigger butt than I did. I just got jealous that she was just in there jumping up and down on the old man's dick that trapped me. How on earth are we fucking the same dick? This bitch must know how to do some tricks or something. Either way, I have to learn how to suck some dick, or something! She was almost twice my size and it was very possible that she could beat my ass, though the way she ran made me think that I might have a chance too. Before I could swing on this chick, here he comes grabbing me. I'm crying only because he didn't let me get a chance to touch her, this means that she might be back! Ughhh.

I took a bus back to the south end crying. Now, his mother had called my mom to tell her about how I carved the door, but mom was less interested in involving herself in any of my shenanigans. Again, I hoped they didn't think of me or my mom paying for the repairs of that door.

Soon, Robert and I moved into a sublet apartment on the corner of Sargeant and Atwood streets. We rented one of the three bedrooms and shared the kitchen and bathroom with the two other bedrooms. We had a two-burner portable electric stove where we cooked complete meals on. I was done with hustling for good. Within a few months, I got pregnant, and within a few weeks of learning about the pregnancy, I was bleeding and having a miscarriage. Robert made me feel so bad about losing the baby, that he told me I couldn't have kids at the time, because I had done too many abortions already. I'm only 16 years old and now I can't even have kids because I terminated two pregnancies and miscarried one. Oh my God, what have I done to my body at such an early age?

I started getting depressed again as Robert used this as another reason to cheat on me all over again. Fuck him! I can have kids. I'm just glad it's not by his sorry ass. Sure enough, I was pregnant again before my next period came. I was amazed by how the human body worked, to heal and gave me another chance to reproduce; after being so disrespectful, reckless and treating my body like shit. That became the first pregnancy which I could finally celebrate. I was so excited that my organs were still intact. I made sure that I did it right this time.

I started going to Adult Ed and also began to take double classes in order to catch up, because my baby was warming up to come into the world by February 98. It was still fall 97 at the time. I would go to morning classes and then leave the school for the next 4 hours, before returning to school for night classes. It was difficult, but it was worth it. Robert would go missing almost every night even still. He always found a manipulative way to make it up to me. Not to mention the fact that I was still a little girl and he knew how to take advantage of my vulnerability. He would cook a big seafood, feast in that one room to celebrate his failure and distract me from it. I'm talking about lobsters, king crab, scallops and shrimps, everything seafood. He did all of this on those two hot burners. We had 2 of the portable stovetops; the equivalent to a traditional stovetop. He would use all 4 burners at once and like magic I had a restaurant-style meal right in my bedroom at the rooming house. He would do all of this monkey shit, and then a few days later he would disappear and start coming home late. This just went on for months and months.

We came to find out his sister Candice was pregnant also. Her pregnancy was about 2 months ahead of mine, but she was just now saying something about it. I'm not sure of what she told her brother about her pregnancy. All of a sudden, this man began to question the paternity of my baby and my loyalty to him. "Is that my baby?" He asked. "Are you fucking serious?" I responded. "First of all, you track every move I make, so you know the only way for me to get fucked would be a 2-second quickie behind the dumpsters at the bus stop, and if that's what you think of me, you might as well send me on my way right now because you're already stressing me out."

At this point, I wasn't aware that his mother had told him that he needs to drop me because I'll be fucking out of every hole in my body by the time I turn 18 years old. I have never been so insulted before in my entire life. These people are extremely older than I am and this is how they mistreat a little girl, all because he is committing statutory rape. He has been super possessive and controlling because he had believed that I must be a whore, simply because I was a pretty girl out there in the streets.. Fucking out of every hole in my body? Gosh, this lady must think that I'm some type of street animal. These people have no clue of what I'm capable of becoming. I'm not even that old, enough for anyone to count me out. I could be a little more skeptical if I was over 18 and in this position, but people aren't even giving me a chance to see who or what I could become before judging my situation. If you can't help me, don't try to degrade me; "is that not so?". I can't wait to grow up and get the fuck up out of these slums. If I can survive on these streets, I know I definitely can survive in the real world. I just got to get there first! I'm going to show the whole world that I'm coming to get the life that I should have been born in.

At this point, I still wasn't old enough to work yet, so I started calling hair salons to ask if they needed a shampoo girl. One of the largest ads in the phone book was up on Blue Hills Avenue. After school I started working for Regina, the owner of Turning Heads hair salon. I was the shampoo girl making $5 for each head I washed, $10 for color and also for relaxer base preparation. Gina was extremely busy and had clients back to back. I would make an easy $350-$600 a week but the hours were super long and crazy ridiculous for a pregnant young girl. Robert had so much time to cheat on me since I left home at 7 am for school and came back well after 10 pm of the day. While he was cheating on me he was also terrorizing me and interrogating me about the idea of me cheating on him even with pregnancy. He didn't care about the money that I was making, he just wanted me to quit my job and go to school only.

We had more fights in that one little room than ever before in our 2-year adventure together. Now I have to constantly validate my pussy to help this man's ego or whatever insecurities that he had. We ended up getting kicked out of the room because the other tenants kept complaining about the loud fights every day. They were tired of the constant screaming and wanted us out. We found a real one-bedroom apartment on Farmington Avenue right at Woodland street. There was so much privacy for the loud physical abuse, because the new neighbors were either too far away or minding their own business. Although I wished they wouldn't have, I needed someone to save me from this monster who now had a safe environment to beat me to death if he wanted to. With this big ass belly that I'm carrying around, I can't fight him off me anymore. I was 8 months pregnant and my pelvis had fallen out of my ass at this point. I didn't know what to expect as this was my first successful pregnancy. Robert was the big man now because he did have a job and I didn't, and he'd got his first real apartment. He kept on talking about how much he took care of me and how he's the man and this, and that, and blah, blah, blah! I'm so big that my belly is about to explode and he's over here complaining about taking care of me, and now he wants me to quit my job.

My mom was giving me $75 in cash assistance and $100 in food stamps because she still had me listed as a dependent with social services. Now she had added my unborn baby to her household benefits list and had started giving me more with the increase of assistance. However, those extra cash and stamps were not enough for me to survive and to keep Robert from cussing and fussing about food and bills and everything. I'm about to have a baby for him soon and that is about to become another thing for which he'll begin to complain about. I can't do anything right and he thinks so too, so I don't just know why he won't leave me alone.

This man came home from work one day and he didn't have money for his daily 40 oz. of Old English. As soon as he walked his grumpy ass into the kitchen and saw a plate and a fork in the sink, he lost his damn mind. He grabbed me by my neck and threw me against the sink where the plate was quietly resting alone. My belly hit the sink so hard that my body went into shock immediately, after which I collapsed on the floor. Afterwards, I couldn't walk on my feet for 2 weeks, then i thought that my hips were broken. He was extremely apologetic for injuring me and the baby especially, after realizing that I was completely debilitated for weeks. He did all the cooking and cleaning until I had the baby. Not because he wanted to, but because I was hurt so bad that my hip bone seemed dislocated and I needed help with everything including going to the restroom, bathing and getting into bed.

My mom bought me a crib for my baby shower. Robert took a lifetime to even open the box. I begged him for several weeks to put the crib together. As soon as he finally started removing the pieces from the box, my water broke. I was limping over the half-assembled crib (that was dismantled all over the living room floor) headed to the bathroom when it happened. That second step over the cribs' pieces caused me to pee on myself. I guess I couldn't hold it. Robert started yelling at me, saying how disgusting I am to piss on the floor. Especially because I'm a street animal, right?

I paused in shock though he screamed at me; of course I couldn't believe that I'd be peeing on myself either. I looked down to the floor to see milk coming down my legs and on to the floor. I was now sure that he was going to beat me up for peeing on the floor.

"Oh your water broke, I thought you were pissing on the damn floor." He exclaimed. I didn't know what exactly was happening, and this started to scare the shit out of me. I called the hospital and told them what was going on, they replied that I should rush down immediately. The hospital was just 6 city blocks down the street, but our broke asses couldn't even afford a cab or taxi. I put a towel between my legs and we went walking slowly down the street, stopping every few steps because I was still hurt from the edge of the sink and from the collapse. I was admitted in the hospital right away, and this time; I was so nervous. As soon as they told me that they were going to induce my labor, I immediately asked for an epidural. That's what all of the other teenage moms had told me to ask for when I got there. I wish they didn't give me that shot because the paralysis of the lower half of my body caused a delay in my labor. Thirty-one hard hours in labor before delivery to be exact. As soon as the time to push was at hand, Robert asked the doctor if he could cut the cord himself. This was his third baby and apparently, he had never had the opportunity to do that. He and my mom finished that liter of Hennessey which they snuck in the hospital. Every 2 minutes that passed had me pushing, while Robert held my legs, and my mom holding my hands, helped me breathe. It's been over an hour into this pushing shit and I'm about done with the whole birth thing. This time I'm tired as hell and I'm passing out between each contractions because I don't feel anything except pressure, and after all these 2-minute intervals my endurance is completely gone. I was actually knocked out to the point that they had to watch the monitor to tell me when another contraction was on its way, so I could wake up and push. "This little baby is stuck inside me," I would wonder. He'd been haunting my dreams since the 2nd trimester, having me thinking that I'm carrying a reptile or dragon or something scary. The way he would move in my body had me dreaming of crazy shit like too many limbs or heads. Gosh, this labor is taking a lifetime. I wondered if it was right to tell someone in the hospital of my domestic violence injury and my inability to walk prior to the child delivery. Maybe that had something to do with why my baby was so stuck inside me.

Finally, they saw the head crown through. I began to think to myself, nobody mentioned to me that the child birth took so long. It's been three hours now, and how many two minutes' segments does it take to have a damn baby. I could care less if the baby came out since, but not at this point, I'm so tired. But here comes another contraction, so wake up and push! The nurse was over it too; she was ready to go home already, it's way past the end of her shift. She whispered in my ear and told me to push like I'm taking a dump. "Huh? What do you mean?" "Use that same muscle" she replied. I'm overwhelmed with the whole delivery process, the pregnancy, the old mans' dick, this fertile little vagina, this young ass student doctor, everything! Now I went ahead to defecate on the bed though they cleaned it up so quickly that I didn't even know that anything had happened. I kept up the same momentum and what do you know? A head was finally visible and Robert's punk ass was about to throw up, either watching me shit or watching how wide I'm stretched. It was at that moment that I should have known he was a weak bitch. He could put his hands on many women but couldn't watch the birth of his first son, yeah okay! My mom at this point switched over positions with him, so she took charge of my legs. She was so dramatic and extremely nervous that It was written on her face, though she hid it with this giant fake smile by locking her jaws with a grin. Her eyes were popping out of her head as she looked down there at the baby's head. She really needs to control herself and chill out before I began to panic in here. "Can I get a real doctor in here, I'm done with this!" I yelled. This doctor came in with the welfare package plan or something. She was from the school of medicine and they have had her in here alone delivering my baby. Who signed off on this experimental childbirth anyway? I finally pushed this boy's big ass head out of me. They were excited, but they then got quiet and started doing everything faster. I looked up wondering what was going on? My mom said to me "just relax for the next contraction baby! Huh? Relax?" "Why are they moving you out of the way, mom? What is happening with my baby?" There was a short moment of silence, and a bunch of moving and shuffling around which seemed like forever! He said "push." I got back into a good position and kept on pushing. My mom smiling yelled "the shoulder out baby, the shoulder is out!" I'm like only a shoulder? But of course, I didn't have the energy to talk shit, so I pushed a few more times and it was over! I didn't even get a chance to see that baby until he was about 5 hours old when they woke me up for more meds, food, breastfeed, or whatever they woke me up for; because after that last push, I went straight to sleep. When I finally woke up, my mom was on the couch cuddled up with my baby and Robert over there; passed out like he just had a baby. "Give me my baby!" I said to my mom, letting her know that I was awake. That's when I first saw this little 7 pound 2 ounces, 22inch long cone headed baby! I thought to myself, this is a crazy looking baby. I was sure that my genes would dominate but nope. I started asking my mom about his cone-shaped head, but then I felt bad for talking about my newborn baby that way. My mom said it's common and that I have to mold his head into shape. Anyway, I'm just glad he had his father's eyes and eyebrows as soon as birth, so at least the paternity issue was resolved. Good grief!

8

MOMMY IS A BABY TOO

Everything started getting better for me. I was growing up and mentally maturing much faster than a lot of my peers. I soon began to make my own decisions, and whenever this man fought me, I got something bad for his ass. I named our baby Robert but we both called him Tre at home. He was the third, and it was perfectly possible for me to disassociate him from this lousy man as much as possible.

I was still in high school (Adult Ed) and most times I didn't have anyone to baby sit, so I often brought the baby to school with me. It was against the rules though, but my teachers saw how determined I was and helped me get through those last 3 semesters more easily by doing most of the work at home and coming to school just for the tests. I finally graduated from high school and Tre was about a year old at the time. The graduation ceremony was held at Buckley High School. As I walked off that stage with my diploma, I was so excited! I ran and grabbed my son out of Robert's hands, and began to shed tears as I squeezed my baby tight in my arms. He was the reason I kept on going, and with a strong purpose in life. I had never felt so accomplished before; not in my entire life, and I owe it to my son who was my motivation. Guess who else I saw at the graduation though? Yup, it was him...'Byron', Oh my gosh! He was there to see me graduate too. My soul mate was there; I couldn't believe it! That day for me was the best! The truth is; he was there with his baby mama who was one of my good friends in middle school, or so I thought. I couldn't believe he had a baby from her, let alone date her at all. This bitch used to listen to all of my sex stories about him. She must have been fantasizing about him the entire time. I would have never in a million years put those two together. You just never know these days. She seemed so... well, not quite his type, with her little sneaky ass. It's always the quiet ones. A lot had changed since we left middle school though. His baby mama had this strong beef with me, as if she just found out that I've been with her ex-boyfriend and that I had a baby for him. She was lucky that I didn't put my hands on her slutty ass. At this point, Byron sighted me from a distance and spoke out to me instantly. "Hey stranger!" he said, while I was holding my baby and he holding his. It was actually funny how we both had kids of same age, although mine wasn't from his friend.

Now, I was a little jealous and for no reason at all. She could be rich though and still have nothing against me. Ha! Now this was Robert's first time ever seeing who Byron truly was though. He knew how I felt about that boy and he knew that boy was crazy about me. After graduation, oh my goodness; Robert couldn't stop talking about me bumping into my "little" boyfriend. He swore up-and-down that I invited him there. I haven't talked to this boy in a few years, but this nigga already gave me a black eye for thinking that my cousin Byron was him.

My cousin Tennille was having a lot of problems at home and she asked if she could come over to live with me and my baby daddy away from her home. I didn't hesitate to help her because she was like a sister to me and if for nothing else, I needed her help with the baby just as much as she needed mine. These next few months were a little different for me, my plate is completely full. I wasn't in school anymore but I still had this part-time job at the telemarketing place which my cousin Val told me about. I kept busy hands making good money here. I worked 4 hours a day at $7 per hour with commission, and I would bring home over $400 each week. That was pretty good money for the number of hours that I was working. Let's just say my hustling skills were still on point. I wasn't selling crack anymore, I was now selling home improvement materials including windows, doors, vinyl siding, cabinets & countertops. These were big-ticket purchases that I earned commission on. Who the fuck sold windows the way that I did? I was so hungry for money, all I had to do was get these salesmen into these people's homes and BOOM they knock them in the head and take their wallets. At least you would think so the way my closing rate was set up. Each lead was a complete cold call to people who weren't even thinking about home improvement. I get to catch the fish, real them in and then the salesmen close the deal, it was a win-win situation. I knew I was a hustler but that was a whole different type of hustle. Cold calls from the White Pages phone book, C'mon son, where do they do that at? Most of the people hung up on me, I was prepared for it, but after someone stayed on the phone with me for more than 40 seconds that's when I banged them in the head. "Listen lady, take this appointment here, we're coming over to sell you windows, honey; whether you want them or not. My favorite line to tell them was "just take this free appointment and let our sales guy come in and give you a free estimate." "Also you can hold on to them for up to 10 whole years before you cash out on it and it's all free whether you want to use the service or not." Who wouldn't want a discount certificate that they can have for the next 10 years? Call me the home improvement Queen, master of estimates, I was good at what I did and I made a killing doing so. My cousin Val got me into this telemarketing thing. This was our second telemarketing job together. She was dope with it too, especially because we knew how to talk with our white voices. We were kids ever since we started practicing our white voice using a valley girl accent. "Like... we should go downtown... huh... yeah like... I was totally thinking the same thing!" "That's totally like... awesome!" We spoke in these accents since we were about 12 years old and we did it so often that we actually started talking like that for real. LOL Like, OMG!

When Tre turned six months old, we went on to New Jersey for the weekend. Robert didn't want to come with us, and honestly I was glad to get a break from his possessive and controlling ass. I was finally able to show my new born baby to my family in New Jersey. This was pretty cool because we met my mother's grandmother's sister who was my great-great-aunt. Her name was Aunt Puga. She always did speak in the softest of voices; indeed, she was one of the prettiest people I'd ever met. This was my first time meeting her as an adult. We would always like to go visit the family in New Jersey when I was younger, though all I remember is catching the fireflies in the big old backyard with a garden and lots of squash at midnight. I don't quite remember what the reason for our urgent visit was, but we had fun with family that weekend and I was able to get a picture of Tre with my dear Aunt Puga who was five generations senior to him.

When I returned from New Jersey, Robert got nicer to me than ever before. This man made us breakfast, lunch, and dinner round the clock. I suspected something fishy was up, though I couldn't quite point my finger to it. Now, here comes the constant crank calls on the house phone all over again.

Hello click, hello click, hello click. This went on for about three weeks. Some fateful day, he decided to answer the phone, and in the bedroom. He began to whisper in the phone and quickly hung up. The phone rang again, this time he said the call's meant for me. "I'll get it," I said while I snatched the phone off of the hook in the living room so hard that the cord fell over my head. What on earth did I hear at the other end?

"Please don't call my house anymore; I don't want to deal with you. I'm over here with my family." He said.

She yelled out. "Oh, you have a family now Robert?" I heard enough. I almost jumped through the phone yelling "Hello!

Oh hello, Sherrie how are you? She replied

Who is this?" as I continued to reply. As I listened, I heard a lady say "This is someone extremely close to your baby daddy. So close that I've been all over your house and even slept in your bed." I became silent as she continued to speak and soon I felt my whole body get numb as I couldn't even feel my hand holding this phone anymore. I had to play tough and pretend that this bitch wasn't killing me with her song-and-dance. Then I said "sweetie, please don't call my house again, do have a good night my love." I hung up the phone and this chick called right back. This time she's laughing all over the phone and telling me how dumb of a little girl she knew I was. To make matters worse and to make sure that I believed her, she told me that she had left a gift for me under my mattress. Then her last words on the phone were "By the way, your

African art hanging on the walls are very cute. However, you should get a new furniture set because those mixed match couches in your living room are tacky." Right after those moments, I still held on to the phone, up by my ear but couldn't hear anything anymore. I guess this was due to my dumbfounded stare at the tacky ass couches and the black art on the wall which we bought from the art show parties. The love seat was black with polka dots squares and the sofa had some dumb-ass blue flowers on a dirty ass cream backdrop. I was numb and in shock. Whoever this was, she had been in my house and now she's mad that she's not able to come back.

Robert walking out of the bedroom into the living room watched me hold this phone up to my ear. The phone kept making this loud beeping sound. The put me back on the hook because the call is over kind of beeping sound. As he came into the living room, I got up and quickly ran past him into our bedroom. I feel like I flipped that mattress over with one sling, I was so hotheaded. There they were tucked away in a corner close to the wall. Red thongs, O my gosh! If finding them wasn't enough, they were actually pretty and sexy as hell! Lace and ribbons and they were cut from the finest panty fabric in panty heaven. I never had anything close to those types of panties. All of my panties were cotton with little girl flowers on them. All of which covered my whole ass like pampers pull-ups. Maybe that's why he kept cheating on me? Maybe it's because I didn't wear sexy drawers? I was so devastated. At this moment, I began to cry out, but this poor good-for-nothing man was over there crying too. He must have known that this was the last straw for me, because I was done with all of his fat bitches. This would be the last time I'd be fucking behind this nasty old ass dick. I didn't trip though at all. I just sat there silently as the tears dripped down my face. I watched my world falling apart around me. The family that I promised my son was somewhat over. If he's not cheating on me, he's beating me up, or both. The next few days were very quiet as I plotted my escape. I took my baby and a small bag and moved over to my mom's apartment. For some reason, I wasn't too devastated because that same night I was able to call Byron who came down to get me and took me to a hotel. I knew he was good at making me forget about anything negative in my life whenever I was with him. He made the most passionate and sensual love to me that night. I began to cry again with the dick inside me. I wasn't aware if that was happening because I was finally with my true love, or because this boy was a professional dick slinger, or because my heart was broken, or because this dick was still the best I'd ever had? I didn't know why, but there were tears which he wiped all away that night. Within a week I was back home after getting stretched out, I finally got even! I stayed with my mom for about two more weeks to get my mind right and to have at least one more session with Byron..

I finally had to return home though to get some more clothes with a thought that I could run in and out before he got there. Nope, there he was in the living room, right on his knees asking me to marry him. That was a little bit weird because this sorry ass nigga was proposing to me with a ring that I already had on my finger from the crackhead lady. I'm just 18 years old, what do I know about love or having a family? Nothing! But I knew that neither my mother, nor my grandmother were ever married and that was my chance to break that curse. Maybe one day I could change the way my son views life knowing that his mother was a wife! Robert was already divorced with two older kids, now he wanted me to be his what, second wife? Since I already had a son for him, so to at least have his last name would validate his love for me right? Haha! That's funny as hell. Robert knew that he was a piece of shit though and so didn't want to stretch the wedding date out too far in case he slipped up again, so he could trap me for good. He sure had his hooks in me! He cooked a big meal the night that he proposed to me and It's like he'd been planning all this the whole time I disappeared. However, here was the control. I had to marry him the day before my 19th birthday which was in less than 6 weeks. Not only was I not getting a formal wedding experience from this cheap bastard, but I was going to be giving up my next fucking birthday. This man was the epitome of bad ideas. I just wanted my son to be able to say that he wasn't some teen pregnancy mistake.

I chose pastor Powell to officiate our marriage. He was my paternal grandmother's pastor. Pastor of the Holy Trinity which was right across the street from Bellevue Square. Now, his new church name was Latter Rain and was located at Main street. He agreed to marry me after we completed his marriage counseling sessions. Robert's mother was a member of the African Methodist Catholic something church on Main Street, where they sang hymns out of hymn books. She had also wanted to be a part of this so she wanted us to have marital counseling with her pastor as well. We were bankrupt as hell, trying to plan a cheap-ass last-minute shotgun wedding. We got married in the church at 'Latter Rain' with about 15 immediate relatives to witness and a big ass ghetto (cookout) reception at riverside park, in the meadows by the river. It was a hot ghetto success though. Most of my family came around because I had my reception in the park with a massive cookout, but whatever. Most of the fun about that whole quick ordeal was that we didn't have enough time to even change our minds.

We had our honeymoon at the Poconos resorts. They had so many recreational activities from fine dining to horseback riding, to zip-lining, to jet skiing, though we didn't do any of that shit because those activities cost too much money. The truth is that we can only afford what's included with the all-inclusive package. We did do the fine dining because it was part of our package. Our honeymoon suite had a private pool, massage table, sauna, and champagne glass jacuzzi inside of this luxury three level suite. It was super romantic, and with mirrors all over the place including the ceiling. From the living room in front of the fireplace, you could view the 2nd-floor level at the top of the champagne glass. It almost looked like you were sitting in a giant champagne glass; so dope! You could lie down in the heart-shaped bed and see the pool as well as the living room downstairs through the ceiling mirrors. With such numerous mirrors, it wasn't hard to miss the fact that I had gained close to a 100 pounds since meeting this asshole. That was when the thought of how he would wake me up in the middle of my sleep to eat ice cream and pound cakes with him dawned on me. This bastard stole all of my beauty and wanted to make me less interesting to other men. I guess he wanted me to be so unhappy with myself until I had no choice but to depend on him for his half-ass emotional support. I was hideously fat and obviously miserable, even in my honeymoon. I became so depressed and began to feel like I was tricked into marrying him, because I now realized that I legally belonged to him. I started skipping meals for the next few weeks after the wedding until I found out that I was pregnant again. Even though I was obese, I was now a married pregnant woman. Somehow that changed my thought about being fat, I think or maybe, it didn't matter at all because the baby is a girl this time, and now I've finally got my full set of kids! I actually don't know how I got in so Deep with this man, but he wanted to trap me and that's exactly what he did.

9

MAJOR CHANGES

It my annual recertification for receiving my welfare benefits, my worker informed me that in six more months I would be cut off of cash and food stamps if I didn't participate in any welfare to work program. All of my friends knew about these new requirements and had already signed up to do a CNA certification. This was a 6-week program which was enough to satisfy requirements until the next annual review. My worker gave me a list of all the different programs which I could choose from. So, if I didn't want to go get a job at the time, they already had programs that could help me get a better life for my future. As I looked down the list of approved state programs from the workforce, I noticed that the Goodwin College was one of the selected certification programs. My anxiety rose beyond the roof as I had my very first thought of going to college. It was like a fantasy, something only lucky people; who had the best lives and upbringing got to experience. Certainly, it was just a fantasy for someone like me; a high school dropout who only got her diploma from the Adult Education program. Wow! This lady actually helped me entertain the idea of college. "Yes! Yes! Please sign me up! I'll do college. When can I start?" I enrolled in the Information Processing Specialist program. At the time, I didn't know that Goodwin College was a private school and did not receive state funding. I had to take out eight thousand dollars in student loans which was mandatory to be paid back at the end of my enrollment. 'Information Processing Specialist' sounded so sophisticated and educated, I was so proud of myself. I never knew that this major was only fancy for data entry, though I knew that it had something to do with computers which I was good at. I actually didn't see this career pathway going beyond becoming a receptionist or an executive assistant, but I'd never known anyone who had gone to college and graduated to own a real career; so I didn't know what field of study I should even venture into. However, I knew that this was 1998 1999 and this is the wave of the information highway, and I want to be a part of that growing market.

I'd been in school for a couple of months now. Tennille had been helping me a lot with cooking and household duties while I went to school and work. The next semester had begun and one of my classes being 'Introduction to Accounting'. There were about twelve students in this classroom and none of us found it easy to grasp the concept of this dumb shit. What is accounting anyway? Not one of us chose this as a major, so at the moment, we only needed the credit and then get out of this class. We were almost halfway through the semester, close to midterms and none of us were going to pass this class. That teacher was horrible and I wondered if that was her first teaching gig. I remembered the fact that this was a privately funded school, and so all of this might just be a joke. Am I ever gonna get a job after leaving this fake school? This is a horrible way to get introduced to college. I had been in college for only about four months in and I was already failing. "I can't fail this class," I thought to myself, "I need these credits." I started getting obsessed with the fact that I was failing, so I started studying harder, trying to find a new way to learn this accounting stuff. At the same time, I had to cook and feed my husband and my son.

Finally, after the midterms; I got the whole thing right, though after receiving the fact that these simple numbers were enough to destroy my hopes of one day making it out of the hood. I was Deeply determined to understand these concepts. Once I did, I was able to help my classmates understand what this bitch was trying to teach us too. I helped everyone to pass the class that we were all failing. I couldn't believe it! We all did it, not just me. The teacher came to me at the end of the semester to suggest that I change my major to accounting. Accounting? Man, I don't even know what this is. She said "you really should look into it." I went home that day to tell my husband how that my teacher suggested that I change my major and how she showed me that it might be a good fit for me and my family because of my analytical brain. This monster started laughing hysterically. I mean serious gut-busting, knee-slapping and hearty ha-has! He then begins to yell "If you don't stop letting that white lady set you up to fail. Look at your family. Look at your mom, your dad. I found you on the block selling crack, you're not an Accountant Ree! Haha!" The Accountant pulls up at my job in a brand new Mercedes Benz every single year, yet Robert yells "Now stop playing around being a rebellious little girl like you did to your mother. That's your problem... You think life is a game! I'm a grown-ass man Sherrie! You need to grow the fuck up, and stop playing little girl games, and hurry up and finish school so you could help me pay these bills. I'm tired of taking care of you. I have to feed you, clothe you, buy your fucking tampons and maxi pads while you're out here playing around in school trying to learn a job that you can't even do! Stop playing with my life, stop playing with my kid's lives and do what you need to do to finish this shit!"

I felt humiliated at the fact that this nigga didn't even believe in me. Am I a dummy or something? Or is he the dummy here? Damn, I cried so hard that night. I pretended it was the baby girl moving around in my belly hurting me. But I couldn't catch a wink of sleep that night. I laid there watching him sleep all through, just wondering how I could actually love such a monster. I'm gonna do this shit. I'm gonna show this hater that I could do it because I'm smarter than he thinks I am. The choice of what world or family that I should be born into wasn't mine. I didn't create my past. I didn't have control over that. But I could do whatever I wanted to do no matter what type of family or background I did come from! This man is actually trying to play me, but I'm smarter than him anyway. What type of old ass man has anything in common with my young ass, I thought to myself. This cornball came to the block as an adult, who does that? I bet I could run circles around him when I finished with schooling. This old fart is going to be eating out of my hands someday, just watch it. I'd be driving up and down in my brand new Benz each year, my friend! That next morning, and after the class the teacher came back to me again. I informed her on how my husband didn't think that changing my major to accounting was a good idea. This Bitch was all ready for the bullshit. She had printouts of salary structures from both majors. The information processing major that I was in currently, and the accounting major that she suggested. She showed me both the starting as well as the median salaries of both fields. She proved to me that if I could make this change in my major now, that I stood a chance of doubling my prospective income. My eyes popped out of my head as I heard all of this. Now, she knew that she had earned my attention, so she asked a question "don't you have a baby at home, I hear you talk about your kid at home?" I replied yes. She responded "and clearly you have another bun cooking in the oven" as she pointed to my belly. I was six months pregnant with my daughter. Again she asked "don't you want to be able to take care of your kids? You know, just in case this man doesn't remain in your life forever?" She looked into my eyes as if she knew that I was married to a piece of shit! She gave me the... Bitch, that man is gonna keep dragging you look. I still wasn't convinced though. She didn't know what I had to deal with every day with that monster at home. The monster that saved me from a nightmare only to tangle me up inside of his own. It's like being saved by a wolf and living in fear every day because the wolf is more dangerous than what it saved you from.

This persistent lady must have been an angel, because she walked me down to the administration office herself and practically forced my hand. There was something inside of me that got stronger with every single step that we took closer to that office. Why does she even give a shit about me anyway? I could feel the anxiety choking me, I could hardly breathe. I was having a panic attack right there in that office. The tears were rolling down my face as I signed those papers. It didn't matter because I was signing them papers!! I knew good and well that I was about to get tortured every single day of my life for making that decision which was meant to change my life. It was worth it and I wasn't afraid of the beatings anymore, I was used to it already.

I was so proud for believing in myself as much as that white lady did. It felt so good to believe in something.

By the next semester, one of my classes was accounting 101. This dude saw those new accounting books coming home and he lost his cool. "So you're going against the grain Sherrie, right? You're still that rebellious little girl that your mother couldn't control right? OK! Since you're so grown let's see how you get to school without my help. I tried to help you but you don't want my help. You think you're so grown, and that you can do it on your own... let me see you try. I won't give you any more rides for wasting my time with this kiddy little girl shit. I'm a grown-ass man Sherrie let me see you do this shit on your own." He was so mad at me and he meant every last word he said. I now had to be taking the bus with my son, that lousy son of a bitch was really serious... Guess what? I'd show him that I could do this shit with or without him. This is about my son, not this old ass insecure momma's boy. How in the world did I even end up with two kids for this miserable thing called a man? I can't cry over spilled milk now though.

My daughter's delivery date came and passed. Gosh! I'm now convinced that my baby's always get stuck inside me. They induced my labor a week later. I was so ready to get this baby out that once they started the Pitocin, I didn't even want any pain relieving meds. I remember that the epidural they gave me for my son's delivery slowed the whole labor down. I didn't want any parts of that. Now, I'm about to do this like a gangster. Three to four pushes later, and she was out. BOOM! Oh my gosh, she was a little chunky butterball plump weighing 8 pounds, 4 ounces and 20 inches of long. I named her Faith especially because I was on bed rest since my second month of pregnancy with her. I could only go to school and back home to lay down. I experienced all the things that any woman would fear during her pregnancy. I had asthmatic attacks, high blood pressure, gestational diabetes and that illness that makes your feet swell. Now my baby was here and all of those pregnancy illnesses were finally over. I have my life back! Two babies and an old ass husband who treats me like shit, and it's just 3 months from my 20th birthday. Yeah! Go me! Living my life like it's golden or whatever! No really... Whatever!

The next semester starts in two weeks. If I don't make it through this one, I'll be sure to drop out of college and I'd never be able to become independent. Tennille my cousin at this time was still living with my husband and I, and was able to watch the babies, so I could start schooling this next semester. She watched them for a few more semesters, though soon something came up which she called me up in a sudden to inform me that she'd be moving out won't be able to watch my kids anymore. I knew for sure that this bitch was hating. Why wouldn't she want to help me anymore? She doesn't have anything else to do and I pay her, so she's making money. She probably does not want to see me finish college just like she watched me finish high school. Anyway, I registered my son in the daycare which was around the corner and found a private daycare center to register my baby in.

Once Faith was about nine months old I felt so bad about missing out on her baby stages, so I decided to take a semester off in order to gain more time with her. Also I'd been having back pains for some time, so I did physical therapy for close to a year though that wasn't enough to make the pain go away. I was still having back spasms at the time. I finally decided to schedule my breast reduction during this downtime. My husband convinced me that having a breast reduction would help me out and I wouldn't have to wake him up in the middle of the night anymore in pain. My boobs were so huge that I wore a 46F bra size.

My shirts were a 26 and my pants were a size 22W. I was a big ass hot mess considering the fact that I was only a size 10 when I met this dude. My body was completely stretched out of size, and I had stretch marks everywhere, and now with boobs that are down to my kneecaps. My breast reduction surgery took seven whole hours. They removed six and a half pounds off of each breast. Thirteen pounds of total breast tissue removed from my body. The surgery was successful, though I still used a D-Cup bra size. I needed so much help after my surgery. I could not do anything on my own. Especially changing my own bandages. I had a husband at home who had agreed to do this for me. I didn't think that there would be a problem with getting the help that I needed, being a married woman. Well, of course, there was a problem. He didn't want to do it, all of a sudden. He would get all squeamish and freak out at the sight of blood and the open wounds.. He said I had to change it myself. I felt like he wanted me to beg him to help me, so I chose to try to do it on my own. That was a bad choice though. I should have asked someone else to help me, but I didn't and both of my breasts got infected. I visited the doctor for surgery and removal of the dead tissue that had started to form around my nipple and down my incision. It was a greenish-black colored skin which scared the shit out of me! I keep thinking about how tough Robert pretends to be; beating up women, but neither being able to stand the sight of blood, stitches, nor his own son's head coming through my young vagina.

I didn't have the necessary help that I needed with the two babies at home. Somehow, I busted open my stitches to the point that my breast's flesh was hanging out of its stitches. I had to be scheduled to get a skin graft to cover up the flesh that had spilled out of my boobs. Then I had a visiting nurse coming around three times a day to pack and stuff gauze strips inside the huge holes that had formed in my boobs. They put me back on the Percocet which I had stopped taking, because the pain of my original surgery wasn't as bad as this one. Plus, I didn't like the nightmares that those pills gave me. The fact that I couldn't get anything done, which I needed to get done around the house while I was on those pain pills made me desire not to take them anymore. I didn't have any help with the kids, so I couldn't be too sedated around them. Like clockwork, my nurse came every day; three times each day to pack my boobs with the saline solution and gauze. I was home helpless with a toddler and an infant. After about three weeks of nursing my breast injuries, luckily all that was left was pain when she inserted or removed the gauze. However, I still did take those pills faithfully. I'm taking them now just to escape the horrible reality that I don't have any more use of this man. Now, I have two kids to take care of while this man goes out to screw any and every one. I was really getting high with these drugs, and I was loving the feeling. The unpredicted complications after my surgery caused me to miss the following semester at school, but I was not going to stay home though. I was still getting my breast packed, with another three to four weeks to go with this nurse. However, I must be getting out of this damn house before my master starts tripping again; I thought.

Then, I discovered Robert Half AccounTemps had an opening downtown for an Accounting Clerk at Phoenix Investments. I quickly applied for the position knowing that I only had a few more credits left to finish school. Soon they contacted my school, got my transcripts, saw that I had completed all of my accounting classes and hired me! I was downtown Hartford in the same building where I always saw Gayle King come out of whenever she left the news station. This is the bus stop that I waited at heading to East Hartford to catch Robert cheating, that time. I'd waited at the bus stop in the front of this building for years, but never have I found myself inside any building this fancy. I mean the interior doors were heavy just like court doors but were much fancier. Wow! Look at this elevator! I've made it big! I get upstairs to find this huge office space with a ton of cubicles, and of course the one I was assigned to was on the other side of this room. So I get to walk past all of the desks of all of these people of high-class, living their best lives, working their high paying job in this fancy building every day. I actually couldn't believe this dream come true! This is so unreal! I'm 20 years old now and all of this hard work is paying off greatly. My desk was set up just like those ones you see on TV. It had a computer, monitor, keyboard, a mouse and even a cup with pens in it. You know the colorful little sticky notes that you walk past at Wal-Mart because they're so expensive, they even had those there too. I also had a personal filing cabinet attached to my desk, Oh My Gosh! I was the youngest worker there and obviously the only one from the hood up in this place. I was the only black person in the accounting department and the whole 8th floor. Anyway, I was only a temporary staff there to cover someone's maternity leave. I knew that this assignment would last just for two months and then this fantasy would be over. I felt so important walking in-and-out of that building every day though. I finally felt like I am a member of the elite society. And like clockwork, every day I got off to and from work, caught two different buses to get my kids, brought everyone home, fed, gave them a bath and put them in bed. I would pop a Percocet and pass out right there on the couch for hours until the old man came home in the middle of the night to put me in the bed. Some nights he would sleep right there on the other couch. Those were the nights that I knew for sure that he didn't come home till the early morning hours of the following day. I saw him one night or one morning I should say, as he snuck in the door and didn't want to make so much noise by going all the way past the couch to the room, so he just sat right there on that first couch, took his shoes off, lay down and fell asleep. He was a professional cheater. And who the fuck cares, anyway? Let them hoes have him. Hopefully, someone comes and scoops him off his feet and takes me out of my misery. But it never happens though and I'm stuck home popping these pills to escape my miserable life. Finally, my doctor cut me off when he noticed it was becoming an addiction. Doc told me I shouldn't be in any type of pain any longer, so he prescribed some Motrin 800 to me. I had a right mind to rob his ass in that private practice bro. I went home weeping knowing that I only had about 20 more pills left in my bottle. It was scary to know that I'm now addicted to these pills, and if I let it get out of control the way the dust addiction had gotten, I'd end up getting my children taken from me.

My father's only sister was having a 40th birthday party down in Atlanta. I decided to rent a minivan so that a bunch of us could drive down together. I and my father, big sister, my cousin Byron and Robert were all ready for this trip. The only person who couldn't drive among us was my sister, so the trip shouldn't be that bad with four drivers. We arrived in Atlanta having experienced no problem. The party was a whole vibe, my dad was dancing all over the place and was indeed the center of attention. The next day Robert and I drove to his daughters' house which was an hour and a half away. We were gone the entire day, and everyone else who drove with us to ATL was pissed that we had the van all day. My dad had the most to say about our trip without them because he already didn't like my husband. Later that night we all drove to a nightclub named 112. It was at the corner of a shopping plaza, and difinitely the first nightclub that I'd ever seen with multiple floors. On walking in, you'd find yourself on the main floor. However, you could either go upstairs or downstairs, similar to a split level house. We didn't stay that long because the drive back to the hotel was about an hour. The following day we all went out to do a little shopping at the mall before hitting the road to get home. The trip back home was so horrible.

Everybody got upset about us leaving for the day, and now refused to pay their share of the money for the rental. It was cool because I was never again going to include everyone in my plans. Of course nobody wanted to drive and had every excuse not to drive, but my dad took first place. He drove us from Georgia all the way to the end of Virginia into Maryland. Byron was supposed to be next but he kept on saying that he was too tired as it was 4am then. I was hoping to get back to my kids soon, so I woke up and took the wheel. I drove for five solid hours, all the way through the New Jersey turnpike into New York. However, I had a fear of heights and was terrified to drive over the George Washington Bridge. I wasn't aware if my fears were due to the double layer nature of the bridge or the fact that it took so long to get across this big ass bridge, but I'm not having it, Period! We all had a 30-minute argument about paying the last tow which was $10. Robert was telling us how all he had was a hundred-dollar bill to his name. That was him trying to get other people to come out of their pockets, because it seemed like he and I were the only ones paying all of the tows coming and going.

One heated word led to another and my dad had a knife up to my husband's neck. I was driving while Robert was in the passenger seat, and my dad right behind him. I could see my dad's arm wrapped around my husband's neck to keep him secure, and the knife almost tearing his skin. Everybody began to scream. My sister and my cousin both sat in the back seat trying to calm my father down and talk him out of releasing the knife. The whole time, I tried to avoid sudden stops or potholes since sudden movements would cause my husband's neck to open up whether my dad wanted to stab him or not. By this time I'd already got on the bridge. I couldn't turn back or change my mind about this bridge, I'm driving over it no matter what. My dad was about to kill the man that had been beating my ass but I couldn't allow him to take my children's father out of their lives. Especially not over a ten-dollar toll booth fare. I'd rather he came and saved me from one of his ass whippings than kill him right now over this bullshit. I actually denied every question my dad had asked me about Robert putting his hands on me, so at this point daddy doesn't have any reason to kill my husband other than his own selfish and personal disregard for this man. I finally came to an abrupt stop at the middle of the bridge, with hundreds of cars being packed up as a result of my stopping. All of these cars started blowing their horns and yelling out of their windows for us to move out of their way. The backseat passengers were still getting my dad to release Robert's neck, however, I finally started driving again and I made it across the bridge. Once we got back to Hartford, none of us were on speaking terms for months. That was a road trip from hell, but we made it back. The best part of the trip though was that Robert knew that my father would kill him over some petty shit. Robert now knew that daddy would certainly take his life because of me.

I was still employed by this temp agency firm, and they now had me assigned to Konica Minolta out in Windsor Locks. I was making fifteen dollars an hour in this new gig, and my salty husband was so intimidated since he was only making twelve dollars at the time. Remember that job he had while I was pregnant with my son, four years ago? Yeah that job... he'd been making just twelve dollars an hour all this time. I thought that was hilarious, especially because he told me that I couldn't even do Accounting. How hard he laughed at the idea of me working in the Accounting field, but now I am here making more money than he is on a job that I just started a couple of weeks ago. Oh yeah... I am floating over here! Maybe it's the pills that got me floating... I'm not quite sure, but I am really high on life right now knowing that I've won! I beat this hater in his own damn game! He's such a hater, I see because he got so mad that he turned around and had me paying all the bills, the monthly rent, and all of the utilities.

I bought a white minivan so he wouldn't deny me rides anymore. I chose a minivan because I loved how the one we drove to Atlanta moved. Since we were married, the salesman desired that my husband also came on to sign the forms. This way the dealer could prove that I wasn't deciding without the consent of my husband. Robert's name was on the loan as the cosigner. The car note was the only bill that he agreed to pay which was about 350 bucks monthly. He had a plan even back then, though I had no clue why he insisted on paying this bill and not the others. He actually told me that it was because he had a direct deposit and a bank account so it would be easier for the money to come directly out of his bank account.

He made me feel guilty for him having to take care of me all of these years while I went to high school and college. I owed him and I should take care of him at least that was what he suggested as being fair. I was broke every single week that I got my pay because most of my money was spent taking care of the kids and the bills. The whole time he was getting himself new outfits and sneakers on a weekly basis, while my children and I suffered and looked poor and abandoned. Most times I couldn't even afford ordinary pampers and a few other necessities, but he didn't care though. We looked just like slaves, while he stayed fresh to death for other women to see and think he was balling. He drove my minivan most times and left me with no means of transportation to leave the house. He usually left his own car in the garage; that same Honda Accord that I couldn't get a ride to school in. That Honda was actually a stick shift and I couldn't drive a stick, so he would take my van and leave me with a car that I can't drive. I hated him... My family hated him. They knew that he was a monster, but nobody could tell me. I pretended that everything was fine at home, but they knew better though. I was fucking miserable, and I wore it on my face every single day.

10

ALL WE GOT IS US

One particular weekend, Robert went out of town with his friends. Supposedly he was visiting Washington DC., for Howard University's home coming. I knew and I suspected he wasn't... When does he ever want to go out of town and what friends does he have anyway? Whatever! I'd finally get a break from his troubles for a couple of days once again, so I'm not even tripping. I'm done with him! I just need to learn how to survive on my own before I practically walk out of his life. Mentally, I was already gone! He wasn't available all weekend and not one call was answered or returned. It was cool because I was already plotting my escape. Paying all these bills and taking care of the kids on my own, I was just getting stronger and stronger. I'm trying to figure out how I was going to actually leave since I'm so afraid for my life.

Reginae was with me that weekend. Reginae; Robert's middle daughter and three years older than

Tre had lived with me for the majority of her life. Reginae's mother Andrea was the same age as my mother, I repeat "My Mother!" Andrea's birthday was on my fucking birthday too. Talk about a freak show, Andrea was trash though. She would walk around with her ass hanging out. I should have known right then that these were the types of women that he liked. I mean how in the world did you go and have unprotected sex with someone or something like that? She's so embarrassing, I wouldn't dare let anyone know that I had a baby for the same man that she did. She didn't even want her own baby, though. Andrea also had an older son whose father actually took away from her because she was unfit. She really had this baby thinking that Robert would keep her, but he never even had any real relationship with her. Both Andrea and Robert were irresponsible parents. I sympathized with the baby because I knew exactly how it felt to want your parents to love you and relate with you. So, I stepped in and taught this girl all of life's lessons including her ABC's, 123's, how to tie her shoe, how to spell her twelve letter name, how to groom herself, everything! I've been in this girl's life since she was six months old and I was the only mother that she'd known, simply because her real mother always had her dropped off somewhere at some stranger's house. Every chance I had to get her with me, I did. She wanted a mother so bad that she would call me mommy and become one of my children. I even went as far as all of her parent's conference meetings too. Anything that had to do with her, I did it because she had two real parents that didn't give a shit about her. Anyway, Reginae was home the weekend that Robert went to DC. The day before Robert came back home, I was on the phone telling one of my cousins that Robert had been away all weekend and I don't know where he is. When I got off the phone, Reginae told me that her mom and her dad were together going out of town to pick up her mom's furniture. I was devastated as this six-year-old who has been exposed to any and everything up under the sun would be telling me about some adult business that she had no business even knowing about. That nasty hoe was out of town with my husband? Oh hell no! No wonder this bitch stays and her feelings. He is still fucking this slut-bag. OMG! I can't believe how much of a fool I've been for letting this man run all over me. He can do whatever he wants, lay up with whoever he wants, get caught and I never leave him. He's been getting caught for years with countless women, and lately the beds that he chose to lay in were getting closer and closer to our home. It was like some sort of a game to him I guess. I was a young girl with two kids and he thought he trapped me. He had no clue that I'd been learning from all of these life experiences. He unconsciously taught me how to raise and support my family without him. Dummy!

I got two of my younger cousins Sara and Keosha to come over and watch the three kids for me. All they wanted was some money! I was so glad that I had a million little cousins to fall back on though. I called Byron that night and drove over to his mother's house where he had moved back in after breaking up with his baby mama. He always knew how to clear my mind and would get mad at me that I only called him when I was having problems in my relationship. This time around I'm married and I cannot cheat on my husband, though he already had this crazy idea of role-playing about the desperate wife that needs attention. He held and kissed me all night, but we didn't have sexual intercourse. Honestly, I was scared that somehow Robert would be able to tell that I was with someone else and end my life! My anxiety was making me feel like all of a sudden he would find my car like I always found his. Not realizing that once I did find his car, I had been driving across town for hours looking for it. But I was really freaking out and even began to make Byron nervous! He calmed me down with his massaging hands caressing my body.

After that night, I returned to my miserable life, but this time I was recharged and ready for whatever was to come. I didn't know what would happen next though. While with Byron for about 10 hours, I informed him about Reginae snitching on Robert and Andrea. He made mention that he knew Andrea and that his baby mama is the one who braids Reginae's hair and she lives right next door to Andrea! Now Byron's spiteful ass is gonna go back and tell his baby momma that he was with me to piss her off because she knows how much he's still in love with me. Who the hell knew that she would be so hurt and destroyed by him still having anything to do with me after all of these years. I mean, she did think she actually took him from me and afterward bore her first two kids for him, after watching how my abortion for this man ruined my self-worth. This little bald-headed hoe told Andrea; who of course couldn't wait to tell Robert about his young dream girl cheating on him.

Robert was so intimidated by the then so-called 'little boy', that every time he heard his name he would lose his damn mind. Now he knew for sure that I was still in contact with Byron after all these years. It was a nice payback even though I didn't have sex with Byron that night!

That maniac screamed at the top of his lungs, jacked me up and told me how he couldn't believe that I cheated on him. He was hurt to the point that I thought he was going to kill me. I yelled back as I rolled up in a ball trying to protect my face; "I didn't cheat on you!" We were stuck in that moment arguing for so long that I now needed to get to the bathroom. I rolled on the floor to get away and crouched into the bathroom. As my pee was streamed in the toilet bowl, he grabbed me by my neck and lifted me off the toilet seat to the point that I couldn't even breathe but still was peeing. The pee dripped down my legs and splashed everywhere. I was so high off the toilet seat that I could stand on it and he had my back pinned to the wall behind the toilet bowl. He lifted me so high with so much power that I thought I was floating. That was actually the oxygen blockage to my brain getting me lightheaded. He was strangling me and wasn't letting go. I couldn't breathe but I kept fighting back to break free. Now he's starting to squeeze even tighter around my throat. I can't pull his hands off of my neck! Oh my God he's killing me! The way I'm pinned to this wall is actually cutting off my circulation, I thought. I'm too weak to continue this fight... I give up. My eyes are actually rolling to the back of my head! BOOM!!!!

When Robert finally let me go, he just dropped me in mid-air and let me fall back to the toilet seat so hard that it nearly broke my hip bone. "This man is crazy for real. If I live past today, I would use whatever breath left in me to 'never look back.' With the pee still dripping down my legs, I attempted to run and I made it to the couch. Why the couch? I don't know, maybe he'll realize that he's about to kill me on the same tacky ass couch that all of his kids take naps on. That psycho wanted me dead rather than live with the thoughts of being with a young nice dude whom he actually knew loved me more than he ever could. His screaming and beating me up like a maniac never kept me from yelling back at him, because I wasn't scared of him at all. No matter how many times he whooped my ass, I wasn't gonna let this punk ass motherfucker keep beating me up like that without fighting him back. I knew he was gonna fight me anyway, but I was about to tell him how I feel about this whole marriage. I had blood dripping from mouth and my nose, and I had two black eyes. I was crying so loud and so hard that my four-year-old son came running out of the room, risking his own ass to save mine. He didn't have fear in his heart either, all he saw was that his father making me a punch bag. He ran and wrapped his body around my neck like a monkey holding on to their mom. He stuck himself on to me and tried to cover my body with his. Robert started yelling at my son and began to tell him to get back in the room so he could finish beating my ass. I heard my baby's desperate cry as he squeezed me tighter trying to protect me. My man child was practically pulling my hair as that was the only thing that he could grab to stay attached to me as his father pealed his little fragile body off of me. Tre was screaming hysterically, kicking and punching trying to help me fight his father off of me! He was tired of watching his mother get beat up by a man. Today he was willing to take the ass whipping for me. Once his father finally broke his tight grip off of me, I saw all of my blood on my baby's white T-shirt. It was so much blood that I thought Tre was bleeding too. How can I subject my child to so much trauma? I'm actually creating a favorable environment for him to repeat these vicious cycles in his adult life. I have to get the fuck out of this situation and as fast as possible if I ever want to give my son a normal life. I jumped up begging him not to hurt my son and that If he let Tre go, I wouldn't fight back anymore. Of course my son had already witnessed too much!

My face was purple with bloodshot freckles all over it. I also had strangled marks all over my neck for the next couple of weeks! My face was one huge blood clot. Both of my eyes were blood red as if they were bleeding too. I couldn't believe myself. I'd never seen anyone look like that, and I was pretty sure that death was so near! I had black eye lids, busted nostrils, split lips, fractured cheekbones, and unlike this time, I'd never looked in the mirror to see the death that this man almost caused me in a fight. I saw my flesh struggling to survive. It was so purple; what you would consider black-and-blue, but covering my entire face. I look like I died and came back to life. He really tried to kill me this time and Tre knew it and saved my life. My son saved my life for the second time! The first time was from me killing myself and now he has saved me from his father killing me! I can't give up now, I have to stay strong for my children.

Over the next few months, I pretended that nothing ever happened. I still hated my life, but now I had two kids to keep climbing hard for, so I had to handle it. "Handle it," is what I would say in my head when things got too rough. "Handle it" ...and I did just that. I played the game for a little while longer as I learned all the rules on how to raise my children on my own. This dumb monster was clueless. He thought I was still young and dumb, but I learned a lot in secret like a slave hiding knowledge from their master. I had to hide my inner growth and inner strength like my master would hurt me if he found out that I learned about life. He honestly thought that I was just a young chick and I let him think so. The more he thought he was playing me, the more I was learning and getting determined to grow up and become self-sufficient. I was getting stronger, wiser and more independent every single minute. I could feel freedom like field negro waiting for master to die. I was so close to my freedom that I could taste the underground railroad. I'm never coming back to this man once I break free. After the big fight, he told me every day how he was gonna leave my immature ass and how he was sick of my immature rebellious ways, and how he needed a real woman and not a little girl. Every time he said those words, a piece of me would break off and a new inner strength wall would replace it. I was a step higher and higher like stepping stones. With every word, he built bricks for me to escape. He skipped a few days of telling me how horrible I was and how much he needed a real woman, though I woke up every morning planning my escape step by step. On those days when he didn't say anything negative to me, I would ask him "honey are you still leaving me?" He thought I was a little girl incapable of surviving on my own with 2 kids. He thought it was a big old joke and he kept doing the reckless shit. Some weekend later, he didn't return home after leaving the house and I didn't call his phone, not even once. I didn't want him to come back either. I was hoping that this is what he'd been threatening me about all these months. When he finally came home that Sunday night, he saw that all of his personal property was packed up. I think he was a little insulted that this young girl was kicking him out. He walked out telling me that he would be back for all of his stuff, and not just his clothing. He did inDanad come back the next day after work, driving the car of the white lady at his job. I didn't even give a fuck whose car he was driving, I just wanted him gone. He was packing up, bringing bags downstairs as well as boxes, and several kinds of things. Then he started grabbing the things that I purchased with my own money to be spiteful. Now I called the police. The police answered me saying that he had every right to any piece of furniture and belonging, because we were legally married, and we would only have to handle that in a civil court. I asked the officer if it was okay for me to leave, so my children don't have to witness any of this, and he replied that it was fine to do so. So I packed my kids up and we left the house. When we returned home that night, we couldn't get in; neither through the front nor the back door. This man broke the key to the front door inside the lock and then placed a chair up to the back door so that no one could get in through either of the doors. The kids and I stood outside of the house that we couldn't get in, so we left for the night. The next day I had to call a locksmith and pay them to take the lock off the door and replace it. While the man was still there, I just had him replace all of the locks in the house.

We were finally in the house and I realized that there was nothing left; but walls, and my children's beds. He took all of the TVs, movies, 3 air conditioners, window fans, food, and microwave. He took everything except the fish tank, since it belonged to the kids. However, every last fish inside that tank died a boiling death in that midsummer heat without any air conditioners. It was as hot as a sauna in that house. The kids were looking around at their empty seven room house, dead fish and the tears came rolling down my face. Now, Tre was four years old and Faith was two. I couldn't believe that this sorry bastard would take away from his very little children just to spite me. That's when I knew that all we had was us!

11

THE LAST STROKE

For the past year, I had been working at The Salvation Army as the Payroll Supervisor for the entire Southern New England Region. It was a weird place to work, with the prayer calls at lunchtime. It was a real church, but this whole time I thought it was an army. Oh! Salvation! Duhhhh!

My boss's name was Major Brewer. He was in charge of finance for the district. The Army had real officer titles like captain, cadet, major, and sergeant. You had to address them as such too.

I'd only been separated from Robert for about 30 days and I really and truly missed him , although I had to stay strong for my babies. He tried to get me fired by coming up to the job place, causing a scene and distracting me from my duties. He already took my Van during the separation, and now attempting to get me fired. At the time, I was using my mother's car to get the kids to daycare and to get to work every day. Faith attended the daycare center across the street which was run by the company I worked for, and that was very convenient for us.

Once upon a time, my mom had a doctor's appointment and I took a lunch break to pick her up and have her drop me back, off at work since I worked right down the street from the hospital. I got into the passenger seat as soon as I pulled up, in order to make an easy jump out of the car, so she could roll on to her appointment smoothly. Halfway through the five-minute trip back to my office, her hands slipped off the steering wheel. I looked over at her and asked if she was okay. She brushed it off as though it wasn't anything serious, saying that she was just tired, and so continued to drop me off at work. Within thirty minutes of dropping me off at work, I received a call from the hospital telling me that mommy had a stroke. The only thing I knew about a stroke was that when grandma had one, she fell on her face in front of me and later died the next day. I began to freak out, recalling how quickly my grandmother died after having a stroke. I left work and ran straight to the hospital since it was only 6 blocks down the street. When I got to the hospital, they directed me straight to my mom's room immediately. She was excited when she saw me, but she could barely talk; she was stuttering tremendously. Now, I'm thinking to myself "what the hell did they do to her when she got here, because she was still talking fine when she dropped me off?"

Mom had to stay in the hospital for a couple of months. Terrance, Shanon and I moved her things out of her apartment, when she gets out of the hospital she'll be living with me. This was one of the first and longest times Shanon and I ever spent with each other considering that I was his primary caregiver throughout mom's recovery. I had to beat the little dude up that first month though. Mom spoiled him to rottenness. He was a total brat; plus the fact he was still dealing with my mom's and his father's violent break up and the nasty battles that occurred. Shan and I got closer by the time mom was admitted to her new home. My kids couldn't understand what was going on with grandma. Faith was only two years old and all she knew was that she loved her grandma. I brought the kids to the hospital and Faith ran up to her to climb into her laps, while she was sitting in the chair. Mom was totally paralyzed on her left side, so we tried to tell Faith that she shouldn't climb up there. We pointed out that grandma was hurt on her left side, so faith tried to climb up her other side. We all laughed to prevent us from crying, this was a very sad time and everyone was afraid of the unknown.

I was so busy with my mom, Shan and the kids that I couldn't even think about my separation. At this point, I'm like "Robert who?" I hated that my mom had to go through anything like that, but I was so glad that this was finally going to be the end of me and what's his name. I now have to be busy taking care of mom right? I called Robert's mom to tell her that my mom had a stroke and that I needed help with my kids while going back and forth to the Hospital. She simply told me that I was lying, and that I made the story up so I could go out partying to celebrate my separation. "I can't just get a fucking break with this lady! I don't know why she hates me so much... but at this point, I'm done!"

Robert was still out there assuming that we would get back together once things calmed down. He would call me every few days or so to remind me that he's a man with needs. If I plan on getting back together, we might as well do it right now before he fulfilled those needs elsewhere. LOL! I'm thinking to myself, "now you can do it without any remorse." I am finally free baby! I am free inDanad! Carry on boo!

My mom was finally discharged from the hospital and it was such a relief to have her back home. No more having to go up to the hospital every day and coming home to feed the kids, get them ready for bed and wake up to do that all over again. That was one step out of my life which I didn't have to do anymore. I didn't quite understand what was going on, but the more my mom was able to walk and function on her own, the more I would hang out in the streets getting drunk and partying. I was extremely fat though, and extremely unhappy whenever I looked into the mirror. I stayed in my bedroom for hours and danced to dancehall music every morning, afternoon and night. I was getting slimmer and didn't even realize so. My weight was just melting off of me. I went from a size 22 down to a 12 in about six months. About the same amount of time it took me to gain the weight, come to think of it.

We switched payroll systems from ADP to Paychex. The representative from Paychex was a young Jamaican dude from Hartford named Stan. He was cute and professional as hell. The whole time I had no clue that he was black until he came out to train me, though we'd spoken several times over the phone. Good Lord! "That's a lot for a man!" I hadn't been attracted to light skinned guys since Byron. He was there an entire week and trust me, I imagined countless times closing my office door and bending over for him. I could feel that he was feeling me too, but he had to keep it professional. We were damn near fogging up the room trying to train, while we both wanted to help each other get those clothes off. Once the training was over, we exchanged phone numbers and stayed in contact.

In all the drama I was going through, I got close to one of the other two black women working in the corporate office. Her name was Endia. She was only a couple years older than me and she was the damn Public Relations Director. I thought to myself, what the hell is Public Relations anyway? It didn't even matter because she was dope as fuck! Beautiful, brown-skinned, small waist, Howard University graduate, Jamaican, sophisticated kinda gangster and super friendly. I said all that because I was inspired to see a young successful black woman. I'm from the hood and this is very rare. Endia's office was downstairs in the public relations department between the prayer room and the lunchroom. We had a member of that department upstairs in accounting, who was in charge of nothing but public relations funding. Endia was responsible for all public news and events for the

Southern New England Region. I thought that was dope in itself because who the hell does that? I'm not into socializing at work, but after a few coffee runs passed her office, we hit it off. This was the first time I befriended someone with this type of status and lifestyle. I'm a hood chick trying to cross over to the other side and she looks like she can show me how to do it. She has a rough edge underneath all that corporate shit and she can relate to me more than anyone else here in the building.

After a few weeks, I got comfortable enough to often get to her office before getting my coffee. We were sharing personal issues and I knew she was solid. We always complained about the workload we had with the army. We both needed assistants and finally got them. Mine came from one of the captain's new foreign mail order wife. She learned English in school when she got here about a year ago. She had absolutely no payroll experience, but she was part of the army and I couldn't deny her position even if I wanted to. If I needed an assistant I had to teach her. Endia's assistant was her big sister Angie who just started school and was majoring in criminal justice or some kind of black power shit. She always talked about black owned businesses and black man this and black woman that.

Endia was able to choose her assistant because she had that much rank in her department as the Director. Angie was cool and definitely a classy gangster. She was light-skinned, big pretty eyed with a contagious smile. She was ten years older than I was, but we could relate with each other. Endia was more reserved and engaged with her son Jayden though. She would hang out sometimes, but not like that. I didn't expect her to, with a family and as a soon to be wife. Whenever we all did hang out, Angie would actually hang out for the longest time possible even when I just needed to get out of the house. Angie was in and out of a relationship with her baby daddy. She had two kids for him; Dahmani and Ivory Gem. Endia and Angie also had a younger sister named PJ. She was spunky, mysterious, very conscience and woke and definitely a diva. She went to college in Philly and married a super conscience Philly dude named Gabe. PJ and Gabe had a daughter named Paige. I was now part of this big loving Decordova family and began to get invitations to family celebrations, which happened very often. Once my divorce was finalized, I had to give up my visitation rights during birthdays and holidays just to make this man agree to divorce me. I gave up so many rights during my divorce. My three new sisters saved me from myself at a time when I needed them the most and they didn't even know it. Sometimes I would be too much for them to handle, but instead of judging me and teaching me what I should do in these situations, they would triple-team me as big sisters would do. I knew that I had pissed each one of them off with my unpredictable behaviors, but they always responded with unconditional love and helped me transition from a thugged out little girl into a sophisticated-ish young woman. I loved them so much!

I'm partying every single night and weekend now. I'm not even asking my mom if she is able to babysit, I'm just walking out. I was lost, I was sad, depressed, lonely, and afraid for a long time too. I think my mom stayed with me for about 6 months to a year. I didn't even notice this because I was so messed up in the head and had so much responsibility that I didn't know if I was coming or going. Somewhere in-between this time, my mom and Shan moved out. Mommy moved in with Kelis. I knew my situation had to be a bad one if she really had to move over there, knowing that it was just me and my kids at my house; but she moved in with Kelis and her three daughters with her oldest also having a kid. To go from having her own bedroom in a house with only three other people to a house with twice as many people told me that she just tried to get away from me. I can't quite tell what I was doing which pushed her away so badly, but I knew after years of facing perpetual abuse, it wasn't fun for anyone to be around me.

I spent the next few years dating all of the wrong types of men, trying to find out what I missed in all of these years since this man had stolen my youth away from me! I needed to find myself. I mean, I was only twenty-two but still I've been with Robert since fifteen, so yeah. Stolen!

I received a call from big sister telling me that my auntie Kim's son Chance had passed away. I hated that the news came from her because I knew that she didn't like me that much, but for some reason she wanted to funnel any family news. My father's only sibling lost her only son so I had to find a way to get me and my kids down south to Atlanta for the funeral. Of course my sister is riding with the twins; Sonsharay and Tray, and my dad's ex-wife Vicki. She wanted to be sure to let me know that we couldn't ride down south with them, but she secured me a spot with sister Patty who is good friends with auntie Kim. Sister Patty was Chance's god mother, and the aunt of the twins in the singing group Jagged Edge. She was traveling with just one person; a friend of the family, so this was a chance for me and my two kids to get a ride to Georgia. The funeral was beautiful, but it was sad to see my first cousin who was only one year older than I was being buried.

That was the first funeral that I'd ever seen cars being escorted by the police. The cars on the opposite side of the street were completely stopped until we made our pass. My cousin had a funeral similar to a veteran with the way people paid respect at the funeral ceremony.

We afterward went to the clubhouse in the housing complex where my aunt lived in. This was actually where the whole family went right after the funeral. There were tables set up six layers deep into the clubhouse for family and friends to sit and eat. Me and my kids were in the fourth row next to my big sister, the twins and their mom. On my way back to my seat, all the way from getting my kids some sweet tea, I accidentally spilled a tiny drop of tea on my sister as I squeezed passed her fat ass trying to get back to my seat. She screamed as loud as she could in effort to get the attention of everyone in the room. "Oh my god you spilled tea on me!" She kept yelling. I kept apologizing to get her to stop making a scene during this funeral repass. Her major focus at every event we found each other was to try to embarrass and invalidate me. I quickly stepped outside to get some fresh air because she wasn't going to stop being loud with her attempts to make a fool of me. I stayed outside almost the entire time because I was so overwhelmed with the reactions of this big sister of mine. She definitely can't be related to me, otherwise she would see how much hurt she causes me every time she does shit like this. I don't even want a sister anymore, I got dealt a bad hand by this one. I can't even imagine living with her as my mother's child. It's so exhausting to stay around her for long, with all of the destruction she causes everyone. I couldn't wait to get me and my kids home. I felt so bad for even being part of her fiasco at such a sad time in my aunt's life. She wasn't even able to try to find out what the issue was between the two sisters, she just had to focus on being strong for her family while this chick is showing off, looking for attention. The twin kids are preteens and I hardly have a relationship with them because of her. They're over there laughing at her dissing me. Now she has them where she wants them. She's always around them and I can never get a free moment with them without her. Whenever I try to see them, she would regulate what I do or say because she's the 'everybody's boss'. She's so Deep in the mix that I'd rather be all the way over there than to share any space with her. So hopefully one day Sonsharay and Tray will get to know me for who I am and not for who she tells them I am. Anyway, I hate that I did that in front of auntie... I'm outta here!

Once I got back home, I was over everyone. I tried to hide and make sure that no one would drive by and find out where I lived. I moved to the south end on a little side street where my two cousins lived with me at different times. Tak moved in first, she was wilding out on the streets addicted to the dust. I was a recovering addict for years and I couldn't risk my recovery nor my children's well-being. She came home one night after getting jumped by them girls from Nelton Court. One of them hit her in the head with a hammer or bottle because she had a whole chunk of her forehead missing. It was about 2 or 3 am and not only was she bleeding everywhere, but she also showed up drunk and high,and with 2 other people. Tak only wanted to come and lay down. I began to panic after seeing lots of blood dripping down her face. She was calm like the serial killers in the movies when they get hurt but it didn't matter.

"Yo! You're not about to lay up here and die in my house while my kids are home! You need to go to the hospital to get stitches. I don't want my kids to wake up and see all that blood. It'll be too traumatic for them." She couldn't just understand why she needed not to stay there that night, and it wasn't even necessary for me to explain that to her right then. Go get yourself checked out and I'd talk to you when you're feeling better. The next day, I had her call me from jail in New York. She drove a car out there with no license and crashed into someone's yard. Tak had to do a year and a half in jail for that. While she was away, another cousin of mine; Tennille came back to stay with me for a month or two until she got on her feet. While she was living there, she had to babysit my kids as she used to do when she lived with me and my husband once upon a time. She didn't like babysitting though, so she moved back with her mom. No one liked to babysit for me because whenever I said "stay for the night," I meant tomorrow afternoon and evening too! I usually paid my babysitters unless they were living with me rent-free. In that case, the free shelter was my fair exchange payment. I needed help with my kids while I went out to catch up on life that was taken from me. Nobody understood me or what I was going through. I was depressed and pretended that I was stronger than I really was. I would go party all night but cry in the morning while nobody was around. I really missed having a complete family, but I never missed that maniac whom I started procreation with.

12

FAMILY MATTERS

The end of the summer was here and time for the annual Jamaican parade. I knew each night of the weekend was going to be lit. I secured a babysitter early. I never let my kids leave home; I would always have a cousin or two to watch over them. This way they could sleep in their own beds and be home while mommy was out. I made sure that I was in bed when they woke up each morning. This weekend Sheila and Tina were babysitting for $40 each. For some reason, Tennille was mad that her sisters were over my house for the whole weekend to watch my kids. They would never watch her kids because she would never pay them. Nonetheless, what I got going on over here was none of her business. This particular morning, she called her sisters to tell them to come home. It was about noon on Saturday afternoon, I prepaid them for the whole weekend so I still had another day and another night. I heard Sheila who was the oldest yelling and pleading telling her big sister to mind her business. I snatched the phone and asked what was going on? She got very loud and irate on the phone. She said she didn't want her sisters over there watching my kids and they needed to come home immediately. First of all, Kelis was their mother and they're my little sisters too. I lived with Kelis for practically my entire life so this hater better chill out! I bluntly told her that they weren't coming home until the next day. She then started talking about some other shit that she had no business talking about... saying my kids needed a real mother and I'm never home taking care of them but always gone in the streets. The whole time I was in confusion wondering if I made my kids with her. I told her to chill out before things got worse and that she had no business getting personal and talking about me like that. I'm a better mother than she could ever be any day of the week. She never had her own place and her son never had his own things. This bitch is delusional and definitely must have forgotten everything I'd done for her. I'm pretty sure she's saying all this because she's on the phone and not face to face. I advised her one last time "If I have to come over there, I will smack the dog shit out of you!" She said some slick shit like "come right now" as if she was testing or urging me somehow.

I dropped the phone and put on my shoes, while her sisters began to ask if I would go over there for real? Yup! I drove 15 minutes down to talk to her in person so she could maintain that same energy. When I pulled up to Kelis's building on May street, I met her waiting outside there for me. She had problems with me for real, and she got me so confused about why she had so much frustration and animosity towards me. One word led to another, and she eventually walked up to push me. I couldn't just understand why she was so concerned with me not being at home with my kids on the weekends and why she was so mad to the point of trying to fight me. As soon as she pushed me, I jumped into a boxing set up position waiting for the next attack. This is my little cousin who's only a year younger and her hands aren't ready for this yet! She came back rushing at me with a tight fist but I blocked what she thought was a connection. Still not swinging on her though, she caught me off guard and capped me in the face. It was a baby punch, but enough to let me know she meant business. Initially I began to play around with her, attempting not to hurt her. She grabbed my hair and began to jerk my head as if she was trying to drag me to the ground. That's when it was over for her. Boom-Boom-Bow! Now I got to beat her like she's a hoe in the streets. I went in on her; bung; bung; bung like a drummer in a marching band. We had a rhythm like a belt whooping when the parent would say only one word per hit. Didn't - I - tell - you - to - clean - this - room type of rhythm. I wasn't sure if she knew that I would do her dirty like that. But I knew for sure that she would watch her fucking mouth talking to me thereafter. Kelis called my mom and asked what I had been hitting Tennille with, because her face got so deformed! Both the mother's called me and questioned me as if I had a weapon. I simply told them to ask Tennille who knew I didn't use any weapon. She made me feel like my life was in danger and I showed how I survive in a wilderness.

Early one morning I woke up on the couch. I saw a bat flying through the house and I really thought I was having a nightmare. I tried to wake up out of this horror story as this 'thing' flew from the kitchen, dining room, living room and back. It was soaring through the house without a worry in the world. OMG! The front door was right in front of me and I started crying because my kids were all the way in the back of the house. I sat there on the floor watching it glide while i built up the courage to face it. After about an hour of traumatic bat danger, the bat stopped flying. Where did it go? OMG! Where did it go? I was finally able to crawl to close one of my bedroom doors closest to the front door. I crawled to my room door and opened it. I had three doors in my bedroom besides my closet. One of the doors was just close to the front door and the other went into the dining room. The other door led to the hallway that connected to the bathroom, kitchen and the kid's bedroom. I could see that their bedroom door was wide open through my opened door. I sat there in the doorway looking around my room to make sure that the bat didn't fly in there. I couldn't find it anywhere in my room. I kept crawling through my bedroom looking around for a sign of movement. Once I got to the door on the other side of my room, I paused my movements and was able to see part of the kitchen towards the left side. I sat there frozen to listen again, but heard nothing as my heart began to beat even faster seeing that my kid's room could have been where this intruder had landed. I slowly crawled past the kitchen and realized that it wasn't flying in there. I looked in the bathroom which was on the right side of the hallway. "Where is it?" I paused again once I reached the kid's door. OMG! I saw the bat on the top of the window frame. Tre was on the top bunk sleeping while Faith was at the bottom also asleep. I started whispering;

calling their names to wake them up. They didn't hear me, because they were sleeping. I looked on the top of the window blind and saw the bat sitting there; chilling. I cried even harder now and snots came dripping out of my nostrils. I was Deeply terrified! "Tre!" I whispered in a louder tone. I put my finger over my lip to tell him to be quiet as he woke up. I whispered "come here, Tre". He sat up slowly, rubbing his sleepy eyes. I said "get down and wake your sister up, hurry!" He was looking down at me on the floor with tears in my eyes. He followed the movement of my eyes to turn his head and see the bat! "Ahhh! Maa!" He screamed as he moved back to his bed. The bat turned its head as if he could see Tre. "Get down now, baby! Don't move too fast, just be quiet!" I whispered in a desperate plea. Instead of quietly coming down though, he jumped off the side of the bunk bed and ran to me. I grabbed him, covered his mouth and froze to watch if the bat would fly. It did stay right there. I whispered in his ear, "go wake up your sister." He started whining because he was scared as well. I told him to crawl slowly to the bed. He climbed over there to wake Faith up, told her to hold his hand, and they both came running out of the room. I slammed the door and we were all saved! The bat remained in the house for two days before finding someone to chase it out for me. It was gone but I still couldn't live there with that nightmare.

I moved back to the north end on Kent street off of Albany Avenue with hope that they didn't have bats. I was so afraid of bats that I assumed they were everywhere! I didn't have furniture because I did abandon my furniture at the south end. I just couldn't go back there and I didn't have anyone to help me out. Besides, I don't ask people for help, if I don't do it myself then maybe I don't actually need it.

This was a really cute place to live in, but like the other apartments; I had clothes everywhere. Now that I'm not being beaten up anymore, I somehow gave up on household duties altogether. It's not like I didn't know how to do it, but the joy of not doing it and not getting beaten up became an obsession. I would throw clothes around because of course. I would do laundry and dump the bag of clean clothes on the floor. I would look at the pile of clothes or dishes and say, "Yup! I didn't do it now what are you going to do about it? Beat me up? Do it then!" But he wouldn't ever hit me, because he wasn't there and will never be here again.

One sunny afternoon, I was minding my business when I got a prank call on my cell phone. "I know who's fucking with your husband." At this point, I

really don't give a damn who's fucking my ex-husband."
I've been so much removed from him that I wasn't even
concerned a bit. After a few of those creepy calls, I
began to tell the person on the phone that I didn't care.
"I'm divorced now so please stop calling my phone."
The next call came from a very familiar voice. "Hey
Ree! This is Sania." Sania was my cousin Tommy's
girlfriend. Kelis's only son Tommy whom I spent most
of my childhood with. "Ree, I wanted to tell you that
your cousin is fucking your husband."

"What do you mean my cousin is fucking my
husband? I asked. First of all, he's not my husband and
what cousin are you talking about?"

"It's your cousin Tennille, Ree that trifling bitch
is fucking with Robert. I know for sure because I always
see daddy saved on her phone. She receives text
messages and calls from this daddy person, but when
your kids were over her house, she would tell them that
daddy was on his way when she hung up the phone.
When Daddy showed up at the door each time, it was
Robert." In disbelief, I said there was absolutely no way
this was even possible, not with all the time she lived
with me. "Tennille is my sister, so don't play these types
of games because you're beefing with her." "Ree, I'm
not lying to you, your cousin is a bitch but I never had a

problem with her. I'll prove it to you because that bitch is grimy and you needed to know; just hold on." She clicked over to the other line and called my female cousin. Sania came back on the line. "Bitch, tell your cousin that you're fucking her husband!" "Hell yeah, your cousin is on the phone and I want you to tell her that you're fucking with her husband." Click... Silence... She hung up! "See I told you, Ree! She can't even tell you the truth... she couldn't even say that she didn't do it because she knows that she did!" I could feel my body getting numb. Flashbacks of the recent fight that we had about my kids like she is my baby daddy, and each time that she spent with my ex-husband and I, and how they had plenty of time alone together. It's true! I'm really trying to convince myself that it's a lie but I can't. I can't shake off this anger and rage that's building in my mind. I'm now playing back all the scenes from the scripts in which those two played since my marriage.

I knew that my phone would ring soon and it would be her explaining the reason for the lies. I wanted to cancel all the murder plots that began to forge in my mind. Who was going to raise my kids after I end everybody!... but no call, no show. no HOE! She didn't call back; there was nothing to explain. She was guilty!

Later that night, I was still on that floor in the living room next to the phone. I was busy staring at the same spot on the wall for hours. By this time I'd had so many thoughts running through my mind in so little time, that i began to lose track of reality. My nights turned into days and I lost track of time. I was losing myself, and to the outside world I was losing my mind. My kids were at my mom's house in West Brook Village, only minutes away. Mom was able to get on the waiting list for section 8 after her stroke and moved to the projects. She was waiting until they pulled her number for her voucher so she could move to Atlanta. Tre was a student at Annie Fisher School right across the street from West Brook Village. I wanted him to go to the charter school that Faith would go to next school year. The very small school name was Breakthrough Charter Academy and you could only get in with the lottery system. You could only get in if someone else left, except you went in from preschool. Preschool is the only grade where an entire class opens up. This was how Faith got in. She was in preschool while Tre was in the first grade. If you had a sibling enrolled in the preschool, you automatically earned a spot in the lottery. Shanon was in the eighth grade about to graduate from high school. That was the year Faith got approved as my mom was listed as her guardian. Tre was gonna be automatically accepted in the following school year with his sister being a student in the preschool. The good thing was, Tre's school and my mom's house were just 2 blocks away from each other.

I lost my job at Masonite Doors in Manchester, the largest door manufacturer in the country. A few weeks before my lay off, I received a call from a detective telling me that he has a warrant for my arrest. He claimed that I stole furniture from 'Rent-A-Center'. This was the furniture that Robert took out of the house when we separated. I called the police, but they couldn't help me because it was now a civil matter. They let him take the shit and expected me to finish paying for it. I had a $1100 deficit at Rent-A-Center. I kept explaining to the store manager how I was going through a vicious divorce. However, every time they came to retrieve the furniture I let them come inside to see that I didn't have it. I guess a lot of people were stealing from them and they made an example out of me, all because I couldn't produce a police report of it being stolen by my abusive husband. I told the detective that I'd turn myself in this week once I've gotten paid in efforts to bond right out of jail. That response right there told him that I had a job. Of course, he pulls my labor record and finds my job. Now three officers walked into the accounting office, and I was sure they were here for me. I began to shut down my computer and pack up my belongings. They all went into the conference room with my boss. At this point, something is stuck in my throat and I can't swallow. "What are they talking about? Why are they here?" The other three payroll staff gossiped and joked. They were all older than me. Art was a white gay man in his late 50s who was sweet but didn't take any shit. Lauryn was a white woman in her early 60s, she was ready for retirement and everything made her moody. Lauryn was hyper like she was on cocaine, though I knew it was one of those pills she was always popping. Jeanne, a white lady in her mid-40s and too good to work with my black ass limited her interaction with me. Chris was a white man in his early 30s who smoked weed and listened to west coast rap. I was only 24 and a half and about to shit my pants! The conference doorknob turns and I hear every bit of the two metals that allow the doorknob to twist sliding against each other. That was fate trying to buy me enough time to run out of the front door. I saw my boss coming around the corner, walking into the big room that we were all in. "Sherrie, can you come real-quick?" That moment I had an out-of-body experience. I saw myself walking with my boss into the conference room where the three big white guys were waiting. She closed the door and the older guy said "Sherrie, I'm detective Peters, we talked the other day." My iris dilated in my eyes, goose bumps like mountains grew on my skin, and I began to tell myself "you had a chance to run. They were on there for 5 long minutes, you could have been getting on the highway by now. Why didn't you run?" My real body was standing there with a loud ringing noise in my ears, and my legs were weak. His voice was in the background muffled but echoing. I couldn't even tell if I was still standing or I was floating. He said a lot of things in that room, but I couldn't hear anymore over the ringing sound that lasted at least a minute. Once the loud noise in my head got lower, his words got closer and easier to understand. "We're going to get down to the station to talk about it," he said. "Wait! What? What's happening?" I replied. "Ms. Davis, you're under arrest!" They said. "No, wait you can't. I don't get paid until tomorrow and if I don't bond out, I'll be in jail all weekend. Please give me a chance officer, I'm at work and you're scaring these nice people!

Can you at least tell my boss what this is about so that I can keep my job? This is the accounting office;

I can't get arrested at work like a criminal over Rent-A-Center." My boss came back inside and I explained to her what was happening to me and how my ex-husband was still ruining my life. The officer confirmed my statement to my boss all except the ruined life part of it because I'm that dramatic. They put the handcuffs in front of me as they walked me out of the building into the police car parked right outside. The building had huge panoramic windows and I could see my colleagues watch me do the walk of shame! You could bet that they had never seen anything like it before. They were in shock, standing there in disbelief for as long as it took us to leave the parking lot. I was extremely embarrassed. I had come so far away from getting an arrest, and now my job is in jeopardy.

We arrived at the station in Hartford at about 10:30 am. I called my friend Brud so he could call my father on my behalf! I knew my dad wasn't gonna answer a call from Hartford Police Department so I needed a third party. Brud called my dad who still couldn't sign the bail bond, though he had the bond money. Brud was from Bloomfield but hung out in Sigourney Park also called Sig Box; my old block. He was a tall dark-skinned chocolate thing. Initially, I used him to get Robert jealous though he turned out to be a really cool guy. I wanted to openly fuck with someone that Robert knew. Brud used to be in the Army and now he's late 20's and in SigBox... Sounds familiar? Robert was a former Marine. Anyway, it started off really messy at first, but Brud was the first man I allowed to get close to me since my divorce. I kinda liked having him around, even though he had a whole family at home. Regardless, he was someone I could depend on, so I didn't care whom he belonged to. The way he touched my body was usually what I had missing at that exact time! He knew he was lucky bagging me... He would risk it all just to stay the night with me. Not just the night, this dude would stay for lunch! LOL!

In times like this, I knew that I could always depend on him if I didn't have anyone else.

I could overhear the officers telling my family about bail over the phone. The cops were nice to me after my arrest. They told me how they wished that they knew that I was an honest citizen before they came to get me. The sincere look in their eyes told me that they regretted this bullshit arrest. It's like they knew how hard I had to work to get to where I was in life and they have to live that karma. They were asking me about my profession and how long I've been doing Accounting? They went on to say that they were sorry for hurting my career with a larceny charge from Rent-A-Center. I told them all about my horrible marriage to a statutory rapist who had a baby with my sister/cousin. I let them know how I could NEVER get a break in life! They were sitting trying to think of how they could lower my arrest charges. They completed new paperwork and charged me with larceny third degree. This changed the felony charge to a misdemeanor. I thought of the white lady in school helping with my career; now these officers were helping me save my career. I bonded out by noon. I walked out of the building where Brud was waiting for me with a hug and kiss! "You knew I wasn't gonna leave my baby on there," he said as he squeezed me. I started crying because though he belonged to someone else, I had mad love for him after that. I was back at work by 1:30 pm because I couldn't afford to lose my job. The whole office was weird reactions when I returned that afternoon. It was as if they thought I was a murderer or something. I was certain that they never met a criminal before, and of course, it had to be me. Now I'm sure that they are uneasy about working beside one. I tried to play it off and bring up the office morale, but you would have thought that someone died in there. My colleagues whom I've been working along for 2 years were now struggling to even look me in the eyes. My boss went home for the day as I was told she was almost having a panic attack. I was the only black person in the company and now I proved them all right! Black people are criminals! I blew it! Within a month, my position was eliminated and I was offered a 2-month severance package and sent on my way.

After the whole incidence, my dad would visit me often. We were pretty close since got out of jail a few years. This Christmas was different from others, since my dad got out of jail and it was like he wanted to make up for lost time with my kids. He spent so much money on my kids that I started getting nervous. I would ask him where he got all of the money from? He quickly told me about his workers comp settlement for getting hurt on the job and how he filed two lawsuits which he got paid from. It didn't go so well with me but that was my dad and I believed him. Months later, I found out that my dad was picked up and arrested at work on bank robbery charges. Bank Robbery? Huh? How? Why? Next, all of his cars and bikes would get seized by the FBI. It was the talk of the town, and everybody had something to say about it. The bank robbery happened over a year ago and over $200 thousand was stolen from one of those grocery store banks. During his trial, the prosecutor read all of his 17 felony convictions and a list of countless other charges which dated all the way back to when I wasn't born. I always suspected my dad to be a career criminal, but to hear them list out every single conviction was something straight out of a movie. He looked back at me to see the look on my face and I couldn't even look him in the eye because I was so disappointed and overwhelmed with all of this news. I even found out that he got married again when he got arrested and his wife was in court running shit like she's been around from time immemorial. I'm staring at this woman wondering who the fuck she is and where the hell she came from. I don't even know my own father after all of these years! Either way, he'll be gone for another 5-7 years. Damn Daddy!

I moved to Sharon street; into a two-family house with my severance paycheck. The rent was $750 and $200 cheaper than Kent street. I should have known it was too good to be true, but I didn't pay attention to the warning signs due to the fact that I was gonna be able to pay my rent with a $325 weekly unemployment checks, plus my $200 biweekly child support check. I soon found out why the rent was so cheap and the move in process was a breeze. I had two crazy ass landlords who lived right upstairs above me.

The old Jamaican man didn't cause me issues until one day when he couldn't recognize me walking into the front yard. He called me the devil saying that I kept shape shifting and changing into a different person. The older couple instantly started making complaints about the weed smoke that somehow made its way upstairs through the vents. I only smoked in my bedroom late at night after the kids went to bed, and these old turds should be fast asleep as well, but they started banging on the back door and stomping on the floors daily and at night threatening me to leave their house. One day, they blocked me out of the driveway saying that I couldn't park in the back yard any longer. They had some serious issues with each other too. I would always hear them arguing about everything and anything! The wife was afraid for her life and always made peace with her husband. On a certain Saturday morning, she waited for her husband to leave the house. She pleasantly knocked on my back door with a desperate plea. "Please move out my dear. I won't charge you rent if you just move out in 30 days."

If all of the banging on the doors and yelling weren't enough, this plea bargain did it for me. I packed my shit up and left the following week because I began to feel unsafe at home, while my kids were afraid to sleep in their beds either. I sent my kids to my mom and their father for two weeks. I moved in with my cousin Jemih for two weeks while I found another apartment. Jemih was a year older than I was and she had seven kids. She took care of all of her kids and never got them taken away from her for neglect or abuse. That said a lot! She's one of my heroes for being able to raise seven kids.

Jemih's oldest children's granddad had an available attic apartment. I quickly moved to Earl street, and into that one-bedroom apartment in the attic. It was far too small for my kids and I, but that was the best I could do with my unemployment check at the time. I turned the den into the kid's bedroom because it had a door that separated the room from the rest of the apartment. The remainder of the place consisted of another main room, a kitchen, a bathroom and one bedroom in the back. It was small as hell, but it was our new home and we were safe.

On one particular afternoon, I was listening to the radio and I got to hear a live rap battle. Two guys called into the station to rap on the phone over a beat that the station played on air. I thought to myself, I could beat both of those dudes. I listened to the end of the show to find out who was the winner of the battle.

Once they announced his name, I grabbed the back of an envelope and began to write my first rhyme in almost 10 years. It was easy to write because I knew all that I had to do was embarrass the winner from the last contest by using his name in my rhymes. I wrote 16 bars of pure disrespect and it was dope. I had a whole week to practice and recite it perfectly before the next show. On the morning of the show, I had so much anxiety, but was trying to talk myself out of it. The show was to start by 6pm in the evening, but what if I don't call in time and miss my spot this week, or what If I can't rap anymore? I had to find some courage to finish what I'd started and I found it really quick. I called in and told the host that I wanted to battle. They began to laugh as soon as they heard that I was a female contestant. They put me on hold and announced my name on the radio as a contestant. My old rap name was Wyld Chyld but I couldn't use that anymore seeing that I'd grown up, with two children of my own. I just told them that my name was Ree. They played me a beat and I went crazy on that phone. By the time they allowed the champ from last week to rap, I had already won over the crowd and the hosts. When the listeners called in to vote, they were either saying my name or saying they're voting for the challenger. I was crying as

I heard all of the love I was getting on the radio from people who didn't even know me. I won the show and then I had to write more rhymes for the following week. After winning five weeks in a row, I finally got invited down to the station for a live interview with DJ Showtime the host of the station. At the radio Station, they began to call me Ree the Reezon which I hated, so I had to find a new rap name. I'd been retired from the show and at a point got invited to perform on stage at an open mic battle.

Calling the radio station really changed my life and brought back some of the happiness that was stolen from me. Another radio station had a singing contest to win $100 and a chance to go to the Grammy Awards. I called it and gave it a shot. I needed a big break of any kind! I sang a song by Monica at 7am in the morning and my voice was raspy, and had a Deep tone to it. My cousin Taky stayed the night and was wrapped up in a ball at the bottom far end of my bed. She woke up to my loud singing in my room and began to ask what was wrong. I told her to GET UP, and that they were about to play me singing on the radio. She didn't believe me until they aired the song that I was just singing. Taky sat all the way up on the bed wiping the sleep out of her eyes still asking what's going on.

The radio host announced that they would pick a winner the following morning; same time.

My cousin stayed up under my behind that whole day so that she can see if I won that next morning. We were both awake by 6am, waiting on the announcement. By 7am, they announced my name and gave me a seven minute window to call and claim my prize before they picked another winner by default. After screaming in shock and disbelief, I called and received directions on how to pick up my money. They also said that my name had entered into the lottery to win a trip to the Grammy's in which they were going to announce in two weeks. Taky instantly began to talk about me bringing her to the Grammy's with me. All I could see was us going to jail in LA, so it was a no for her. I don't even think that prize is real anyway because; who goes to the Grammy's in real life? The thoughts of being surrounded by that much number of celebrities had me getting dizzy already. The anticipation alone was enough to make me want to give up, because my anxiety was crippling. When I heard my name on the radio as the winner of the Grammy Trip, I felt nauseated. I couldn't believe that little ole me was going to the Grammy's, and I still don't know who I'm bringing with me. Once my mom found out that I had won the trip, she told me that she would go with me, and that's that! My mom was the boss, and if she said that she was going, then she was going, Period! We had about three weeks to plan for this free all-inclusive trip for two to Los Angeles.

We flew for so long that we watched two movies in the air. It was a six-hour flight through multiple time zones, and it was my first flight over 3 hours. Talk about Jet Lag. We had to pay for our own food and transportation but it was all good because the rest of the trip was free. The hotel was a luxury five-star hotel called the Wilshire Grand Hotel that sat right in the heart of downtown LA and only 2 blocks away from the Staples Center. My mom and I decided to take a trip to the Staples Center that night to see what's going on down there on the night before the awards. We walked two long city blocks to the entrance where we saw a group of people in a huddle. We got excited thinking it was some kind of tailgating thing with this large group of people hanging out. The closer we got to the group, we realized that this was a staff meeting about what to except the next day. Mom and I joined the meeting because we knew that at some point they were going inside the building where we could snap pictures. They knew we were suspicious but they couldn't put their finger on it because of how seriously we looked as we focused on our training. We looked like we belonged there and were eager to learn about how to do our jobs the following day.

As the crowd began to move inside the building, we started getting nervous because this was the moment that we waited 30 minutes in training for. We were maneuvering through the building with our newly found co-workers. As soon as we started passing by the brown and gold Grammy backdrop that the celebrities take pictures in front of, we slowed down so the group could go ahead of us. As soon as the last person turned the corner and got out of our sight, we started taking Grammy pictures. We were so scared, trying to take as many pics as possible before calling it a night and leaving the building.

That was so much fun, especially with us being silly and laughing so hard that we started crying uncontrollably. We laughed all the way back to the hotel as we recapped the entire Grammy invasion. As we walked back up the street, we passed by a tent, which I wasn't sure whether it was there on the walk to Staples. As we were approaching this tent on the sidewalk, there was a voice that shouted outside of the tent "Shut up you're too loud." We instantly paused to get a better understanding of what was happening there. "Did the homeless man in the tent tell us to shut up?" I asked. Mom replied "come on let's get out of his house, we are disturbing his peace." We laughed even louder the farther we got away from his living room.

Once we got to the hotel, mom was exhausted and wanted to lay down. It was only about 11pm which was really 8pm back in CT. I decided to go down to the lobby for a drink. I met a really nice guy that wanted to take me to Hollywood since I told him I've never been. I was afraid to leave the hotel with this stranger so I declined. I started thinking about all of the things that could happen to me in LA and I just couldn't do it. I went back upstairs and went to bed. it was an extra-long day and I needed to get ready for the show the following day.

The next morning mom was up full of excitement and ready to get to the show. She was now rushing me to do everything; "now! NOW!" We got dressed up in our best awards show attire that we bought from Macy's the previous week. We walked back down the street and found it difficult to believe the difference that a couple of hours made. There were people everywhere and we now had to follow a single file line all the way up to the door. Mom wanted to go to the Gospel side first because she wanted to see her folks. Once we made it to the other side of the building, we were right at the red carpet with the photographers and media. We saw a few popular celebrities, but when mom saw Shirley Caesar, she lost her cool. Mom started talking fast. "Ree hurry!" Whenever she walked past, I'd swing around and take my picture as she walked by. We were ready, however, Shirley took a detour and came straight at me with a cigarette in my hand. She grabbed my hand and said, "baby you are too pretty to be smoking cigarettes. My good friend died of lung cancer and I would hate for something like that to happen to your pretty self." I looked down at my cigarette and then looked up in her eyes which were still staring at mine and threw the cigarette down. She smiled and gave me a hug saying, "you don't need them baby!" Wow the legendary Shirley Caesar had a vested interest in whether I live or die of cancer? That was HUGE for me and I'd never forget it. Mom was now able to say a few words to her idol and get a real picture!

Once we got back to the other side of the building, we missed lots of stars but still got a chance to see Will.I.Am, Wyclef, Kanye West and a few other faces. We were tired of standing and wanted to get inside to our seats, which was another trip of its own. This building was gigantic. There were so many escalators and section letters, and colors to follow, that you had to have reached a certain level in education to be able to find your seat section. Of course we were in the nosebleed section, though fortunately it was right above the stage. So really, it was a front row seat in the sky. This year Jaime Fox and Alicia Keys did a duet and put their pianos together facing each other. I knew they were the next performers since I could see them set up for each new performance backstage.

After the show, they were talking about the after party on the other side of the building. My mom and I walked over to the other side of the building. I told mom to keep moving with the crowd which was moving pretty fast. We got past the first set of security when I told her to follow me. I got past the last security and looked back, while I saw her still on the other side. I signaled for her to come on, but she nodded a no; because she was too nervous to do another powow. So I turned around and we walked back to the hotel. I kept on saying "mom I was in there, what is wrong with you? I should've left you home and brought someone else with me." She felt bad that she couldn't make it through with me. I was mad, but I still had a good time on this free trip to the other side of the country. We left the following morning and were still in shock. We went to the Grammy's! Who knew?

13

LET IT BURN

Back to reality, I stayed in my little attic apartment for about 9 more months before I met a guy from New York whose name was Vendetta and one of the many men whom Terrance introduced me to. He knew of him, but he really didn't know him that much. All he knew was that Vendetta was a rapper with a swag and someone that I might like. So my brother gave my phone number to him and he called me right away. I should have known something was up with the way he was so ready to tie the knots before actually knowing what I looked like. What he had failed to mention was that he was in a halfway house and he had 90 days left before he finished his program. He was already my boyfriend before we even met, that was crazy but whatever. Once we finally met, it was like love at first sight. It was an instant attraction and one that I wasn't willing to let go and neither was he. He had a curfew, so he would come over and hang out with me during the day, then go back to the halfway house by 9pm. I was faithfully dropping his ass off every night too.

I don't quite know what happened or what actually went down but I knew he had to go back to jail to finish his bid which was 6 months. We've only been together for two months, and now I'm about to wait six months for him. The only time I ever did a bid with anyone was my dad so that didn't count. I know people who do longer than that, so I waited out for him. I kept his commissary full and left lots of airtime on my phone, and was available for every single call that he made. When he finally got out, he was so happy that he had somewhere to go and someone who stayed down for him, so he treated me like a Queen. He also introduced me to ecstasy pills. These are the pills that my friend Katie was fantasizing about in rehab. I'm not someone who is weak and let a nigga turn me out on drugs, but this is different. Well at least for me, because I know it's not Crack, Heroin, Percocet's or Dust, so it must be ok! Plus, I love the ground where he walked on, so I tried it and liked it too. That was my first relationship as an adult and I loved every minute of it. We would pop pills like there was no tomorrow, most especially on weekends. Then he started getting super freaky and I was down with it because he was my man.

We would go to the Jamaican after-hours rolling on these pills. Everything felt good, sexy and erotic. He would point out females and tell me "she's pretty" and we should take them home with us. I couldn't get jealous because I was so high, and soon it started to turn me on that it turned him on. One night a pretty dark skinned girl was dancing so erotically that I told him to go dance with her. He quickly ran over there. He would rub and touch on her as they danced in the dark. I watched how slowly he was caressing her back there on the wall in the corner. I began to get wet, and started to fantasize about how she made him feel. When the song was over, he returned with her name and number. He told me she invited us to her house that night. I was scared as hell, and instantly I sobered up. I was ready to go home. This nigga cheating in my face! We argued the whole way home. I couldn't believe I allowed him to treat me that way. However, the drugs were still in my system and that night we had explosive sex as he made me understand why he was thinking of those women. Every slow stroke, he would fantasize about some freaky adventure with him in another woman. Again it turned me on as he would whisper in my ear how he long dicked these other women. I don't know how this is turning me on but it is. I'm not even jealous anymore. Actually, I'm starting to visualize what he's saying and now I'm fantasizing about watching him have sex with another woman. Whoa! These are some crazy drugs!

We took a trip to New Orleans for the Essence fest and brought some pills along with us. That was my (I don't know) fifth trip there, so I was familiar with the French Quarters. One night on bourbon street we were in a bar that had a second floor where you could go on the patio and watch the crowd in the street below. As I was leaning over the balcony, he looked at me and said I want to bend your ass over this balcony. The thought alone sent me into an erotic trance and I wanted to pull my pants down right there in front of everybody. I walked back into the club and headed toward the bathroom. He followed me all the way in there and had his dick already in his hand. Three women were already in there and they began to scream, but I yelled "this is my boyfriend and I needed help!" Next they heard me moaning as he pinned me into the wall! It didn't take too long before we ran out the bathroom. By this time there were gangs of bitches inside and outside of the bathroom already, as if they were getting turned on by us. We left the club soon and moved into another club right next door. We decided to split up and look for bitches. I was ready because I was so turned up on those pills and I never remembered that I got creeped out the last time he tried. Now the thought of me seeking girls for my man to fuck was starting to get me off. I targeted pretty girls who I thought were prettier than me. We would get as far as him dancing and feeling on them but no luck getting away with them.

We flew back home in full-flight. The following weekend was going to be thee weekend. We went back to the after-hours spot on the avenue and I just got ready for the win. We split up for the while he was flirting and mingling. Now it's so dark in here, and nobody can see who's who until one gets close enough to see the other person's face, plus there are clouds of weed smoke in the air. I'm dancing in the crowd on my own right now and a dark skinned girl comes dancing next to me. The song was dope and we were getting down with it. All of a sudden we got looking at each other like; get it girl! She was tall and slim and could dance her ass off! Here comes Detta dancing on my butt, smiling and getting nasty. Then I move from his frontage and pull the girl in front of him, telling her to get some. She did just that! They were fucking with clothes on. I could tell he liked her alot and she definitely liked him too. Song after song, they danced. I bought her two drinks too. She was on him just as much as he was on her. I wonder if she knew what was up, but she was just down with it.

As she was whining to the next song, I whispered in her ear "can we come home with you." She replied yes. I didn't know what next to do though. I wasn't expecting that answer. I told Detta that the lady said yes to her home and he got ready to go on the spot! Gosh! We popped another pill while we asked if she wanted one. She replied that she was straight. We moved on to her house which wasn't too far away from the club. We took our shoes off at the door and all sat on the couch having him in the middle, we began to watch a movie and have a small talk. Soon in the movie he had his hand in my panties playing with my pussy. I never had public sex so I began to get nervous though the drugs were giving my nerves some pleasure as I got hotter and hotter. Then I saw his other hand rubbing her thighs in very slow comfortable strokes. It was as natural as though he knew her already. He started kissing her as his fingers began to go crazy inside me, there's a whole water fall in my panties now. I pulled out his dick and began to stroke it as I watched them kiss. That's when she joined me to stroke it. I was like, this bitch is really touching my man's dick for real. It creeped me out at first, but then she began to suck it. Now I knew for sure that she was down from the beginning. I don't know why watching his dick slide in and out of her mouth was so sexy, but I swear I came right there in his hand. She was on her knees in front of him going to work. The way he was looking at her though seemed he was falling in love. I can't lie, she was good at it, and she did all kind of tricks with her mouth. He put my hand on her tit. It was soft and squeezable, but I felt uncomfortable touching her, so I stopped. She moved my hands down to her clit. It was skinny or boney; a lot less fat than mine. I slid my finger further inside her, and at that moment I couldn't quite pinpoint where lesbian fun emanated from. It was just a hole and far from as much fun as a dick was. I stopped touching her again and just began to touch myself. Detta held her head, while his dick went Deeper into her throat and he slid his hand down her face in a seductive way, and told her that I was scared, and asked her if she could lick my pussy to loosen me up. She agreed to, but I was as nervous as hell and froze up. He stood me up, undressed me completely and laid me down on the carpet. He got down on the floor next to me and started kissing and rubbing my pussy. She then kneeled down in front of me right on the floor and began to rub my legs. Then it all started. He's tongue kissing me now and squeezing my tits, while she's licking my clit with one hand inside of me and the other stroking his dick. I tried to climb back on the couch but he was holding me hostage. Finally, I got fully involved as she sucked the life out of me. He then put on the condom and climbed behind her. He stared me straight in my eyes and made me look at him as he stroked his dick in and out of her. He grabbed both of my hands and used me to pull himself inside her. With every stroke he said "I love you baby, look at me, I love you baby!" We had her in a sandwich. I never had that type of pleasure before and all I had to do was stop being jealous. We both came at the same time. I wasn't entirely sure if she did or not, but once we were done, we got dressed and left. When we got home, we were jumping on each other all night. That man sure knew how to please my body. Or maybe it was the drugs... Gosh!

Soon I didn't want to do pills anymore because he was getting out of control with it. It seemed he was trying to turn me into a lesbian or some sort of bisexual; when all I wanted to do was please him. One night at the west Indian club, we had a big argument, and instead of making a big scene I simply walked away from him. He chased me through the club, but I was ducking and dodging him in the big dark ass crowd. When he finally caught me, he wasn't that close enough to grab anything other than my clip-on ponytail. I stopped and realized that he grabbed it off. All I had was a knot at the top of my head that the ponytail was attached to. I WAS SUPER EMBARRASSED... I grabbed the little knot to cover it up in front of all those people. Now I got myself outside onto the patio and this mother fucker followed me still, trying to grab me. I was like "leave me alone yo". He began yelling about how sorry he was for snatching my ponytail off. I didn't want to talk to him, "just leave me alone" as I tried to reattach my hairpiece. But no, he kept on grabbing me. I pushed him off me, but he jacked me up against the wall outside; shaking me as if to calm me the fuck down. I punched him in the eye, and that's when he released me to grab his eye. The bouncer grabbed me saying "I need to restrain you not him, you can definitely handle him." They were all laughing as he was getting sympathy and assistance with his eye. The bouncer told him to leave first, and he'd let me leave in 20 minutes' time so he'd get to wherever he intended.

When I finally got home, he was already there in bed. I climbed in the bed trying to sleep. He started playing with my clit and soon he was inside me. I assumed he was sorry for his actions and honestly, I was too. When we woke up the following morning, his eye was closed shut, puffed up, with a ball that was blood shot red. I was scared that he would retaliate on me, but he started apologizing again as we saw the damage. It felt weird with him apologizing for his closed eye, so I apologized too. "It was my reflexes baby, I kept telling you to let me go but then you jacked me up against the building. He replied, "I know baby, I was wilding out last night." In my mind, it wasn't all good seeing the damage I put on this grown ass man who could have folded me but chose to temper his anger. Wow! The humiliation alone would have had a weak man ready to end me, but nope. He knew that I was about my shit and not for games after that. We didn't have many issues after that incidence. I found out that he was sneaking around with this older lady around the corner so I dropped him. I was over with the whole relationship anyway and was looking for the escape route. I needed to find a job because my unemployment claim was about to run out. I moved to two blocks over on Westland street on the corner of main street because I still had about 6 months left on my unemployment claim. My friend 'Dawn' lived right around the corner on Main street, right in front of the Gee Thang barber salon. I could see the salon from my house and I could see Dawn's backyard. Her house was the hang out spot. She had a party every day, and all types of company came over. We would be on the porch watching the barbershop customers come and go as we partied on the front porch or in the back yard. Those parties started early in the day and went on all night. I would get so drunk off Wray & Nephew Jamaican rum. Its 150 proof alcohol and sure to get you done off. That's exactly what I needed to slow down my racing thoughts and anxiety that I'd had for a while.

My cousin Byron was a barber at the barbershop. The Gee Thang had 6 salon seats and 6 barber chairs. I was only cool with KeKe, Ciara, Moe, Gee and Byron. The owner Gee needed a bookkeeper and receptionist and I needed a job. He paid me three hundred a week to answer the phones and book appointments, and calculate the commissions to pay his staff each week. Each contractor made a certain percentage of their overall client earnings each week. It was based on their personal sales. I created a spreadsheet for each person to show them their weekly pay breakdown based on the tickets and cash that they turn in throughout each day. I also received free hairdos and colors when the stylist needed a guinea pig. Since I had prior salon training at Prince Tech and then worked in Gina's salon for a year prepping clients, I also stepped on to do small jobs. One job included doing bantu knots for the mother of Anika Nonni. I did here hair for her Dream Girls Tony award ceremony! I was nervous that she was about to wear my hair hairstyle in front of Beyonce and Jennifer Hudson? Wow! She loved her hair and gave me a thirty dollar tip that I had to hide from Gee because he was a greedy dude and would have wanted to split my damn tip! Gee was married and always bragged about graduating from Morehouse and being the best barber in the whole land. He was also a big flirt too. I helped him build his budget for the new shop that he was building down the street, so he was picking my brain on the financial execution. He started to include me in his plans for the new building, as if he thought that I would be here that long. I wasn't, I had my resume out there from day one.

One night while I was doing a customer's hair, one of the young boys from outside ran in the shop and asked me if Tray was my little brother? I replied yeah and why do you ask? He said "because I just heard that he got shot in the head at five corners." 'Five corners' was an intersection of Westland and Garden street as well as Love Lane; the intersection literally had five corners. When I heard that news, I was just shocked and in disbelief. Mainly because my little brother wasn't even a street kid so this had to be some kind of mistake or misunderstanding. I had someone step in for me and I went up there to Saint Francis Hospital where a mob was waiting outside and inside the waiting room. They had a special room in the back for family so I went back there. That's where my two sisters were and the twins mother and grandmother. They confirmed everything, and everyone was very overwhelmed at the fact that Tray was dead. He was only 16 years old at the time of his death. I couldn't believe it having to bury a younger sibling, all while my dad was in jail away from all of us.

The night before the funeral I did a roller set in my little sister's hair. She had already come out of the closet about being gay, so to have a roller set wasn't sitting well with her. She wanted to look like her old tomboy self. The next morning, I got over to the house to get ready. My sisters were in the bathroom with my dad's ex-wife while they all got ready. Not knowing that I was an outsider, I was kicked out of the bathroom. My step mom told me to go use another bathroom. That hurt my feelings so badly, though I thought that she was just grieving but not until I wasn't allowed to ride to the church in the family limo. They all told me that there was no room because three of her friends were riding with them. My kids and I rode to the services with my auntie. I can't imagine being that mean to someone. I don't even understand what had occurred to cause that horrible treatment but I knew for sure that it had something to do with my hateful ass older sister. She hated me ever since she found me on the playground at school. All of these years she had attached herself to my dad's ex-wife and the twins, and every chance she had, she wanted to push me away. Regardless of her efforts, she couldn't push me out of a family that I was born in. I mean come on, I have my dad's last name. Why would I try to fight a battle that I've already won? This girl is delusional, that's why she had to find me at school instead of at a family gathering. Come to find out that my sister told my step mom that me and my mom didn't like her and my mom was talking about her. After everything that she's done for me when my mother couldn't, me nor my mom would never speak badly about her. However, I didn't find this out until a couple of years after the damage was done. Therefore, my sister pushed me away so that I wouldn't want to come around and she told them lies to make them not want me around. But right now everything is hitting the fan at my brother's funeral.

After 2 years of being rejected from employment and discouraged about my larceny charge, I got hired at Diggs Construction on the south end. Diggs was a large program management company hired by the Hartford City School Building Committee to build and/or renovate over a dozen schools with a $900 million budget. My title was financial administration and my duties were to coordinate the projects, collect the subcontractor invoices to be paid, and compile a big ass monthly invoice with all of the subs, and sub-subs, and all corresponding documents to valid each of the expenses. Every month after I collected all of the valuable data and documents, I hand delivered the package of documents about 7 inches tall to the Mayor's office at City Hall. I was also single-handedly responsible for all of the meeting minutes at the Hartford School Board Meetings. I had to create the meeting agenda and corresponding documents based on the information provided by the team throughout the month. I made about 45 meeting packets to provide attendees and had 2 days after each meeting to complete and distribute the final minutes to each member of the board as well as all of the meeting attendees. I knew all of the players on these school construction contracts. I'm the one who had to ensure that insurances were up to date and lien waivers were provided before I issued payments to anyone. It was fun for the first year or two, but after I was denied a promotion to do more accounting work I was over it. My boss depended on me to do this job and didn't want me to move to a different role in the company. So basically I was trapped with her. Nope, not happening because I also get the list of our subs classified ads for open positions within those companies. I saw that the only flooring company on our team was looking for a full charge bookkeeper. I was making $38k at my current job and this flooring company was paying $45k. That was a no brainer. I asked my operations manager to forward my resume to the owner of that company and give me a recommendation which he did. I think he was tired of me complaining about my boss trapping me and not letting me grow and again he wasn't a big fan of her evil ass either. I received a call that same day for an interview on the following week. I went to that interview and met the owner Bailey. She was 72 and still thriving. You could tell that she was the shit back in her day. She came from old money! This was her father's company and she'd been working here since she was 16 years old. She showed me all of her ledger books which she kept manual bookkeeping with. I only did manual bookkeeping in school so I was excited to handle this skill in a real life situation. I was hired on the spot but of course in order to stay in good graces with my current job, I gave a two week notice and I was out! Peace!

I loved working for this lady. She was super sarcastic because she was old and didn't have much patience any longer. She taught me everything she knew about bookkeeping. "I have 60 plus years of hands on bookkeeping in my back pocket." I was imagining running my own business and leaving it to my kids like her dad did, but whatever; I always dream in fantasy like that when I'm really interested in something or someone. Bailey was the most interesting person that I'd ever met in life. Bailey was hard on me though, she made me prove myself to her every single day. She was grooming me to run the office so she could retire. Therefore, she wanted to make sure that I could handle anything including her dark sarcasm and condescending remarks. I didn't take offense to anything, because she gave me bonus after bonus just for being her side kick. I drove her brand new Cadillac to the bank in Bloomfield every day. She purchased the car from the lot for $37k cash. She was loaded! You hear me? Old Money! That car was the newest car that I'd ever driven, it had less than one thousand miles on it. I drove a white two-door Chevy Monte Carlo with tints which I bought from a guy named Raymond who used to flirt with me. It was a piece of shit car though, but it was reliable to get back and forth. My co-worker Greg who was Bailey's first cousin, told me about a Chevy blazer that he had which was sitting in his yard for two years. He told me that I could buy it for $1200. When I gave him the money on my next payday, he handed me back $500. He charged me $700 for this jeep with only 29k miles on it. I was coming up in life because my jeep was everything and more! These people that I found myself among were some real genuine people and had changed my way of thinking about the compassion of others. They had really shown me that there were people out there in the world who could help you.

I moved off Westland street after my kids witnessed a double homicide in the yard next door. I was in the room when my kids ran and told me that there were two dead bodies in the yard. I jumped up and went to the front window where they were watching these bodies bleed out on the concrete. I told them to get out of the window but it was too late, they kept talking about the blood and how many bullets they heard. The dead bodies became a regular conversation whenever they spoke to people. They would tell random people that we had two dead bodies next door to us. I wanted to get my kids off that hot ass corner, so we moved to Martin street behind unity plaza. I didn't stay there for too long though. All the while, I didn't know that my cousin Taky's mom lived two houses down from me. On the other side of our home was another very large family that would sit on the porch and watch me come and go every day. I didn't feel safe especially knowing that a few of the guys had a crush on me and too many people knew where I lived at.

I ran into my old friend Kat in a club. We started chilling and hanging out. She told me that she was in a gay relationship. I thought it was weird for her to live with a woman since I've known her to be straight. Anyway she popped pills too, so on some weekends, I would hang out with her and her crew and we would get high and drink and chill. All of her friends weren't gay so it wasn't any open gay talk going on or anything that would make me feel uncomfortable. It was just a group of girls that partied and did the same kind of drugs. Kat lived with her girlfriend on Garden street.

Her girlfriend's mother owned the building that they lived in and she told me that the second floor apartment was available for only seven hundred a month. It was a two-bedroom flat, but that was a deal compared to the nine hundred fifty that I was currently paying. Kat and her girlfriend lived on the third floor and there was another older lady who lived on the first floor. I quickly moved in and it was nothing but parties and drugs every day. I didn't start popping pills until the weekends, but I was certainly having a drink or two almost every day and for whatever reason, I always found people who liked to drink as much as I did.

My neighbor downstairs knew some of my family in Bellevue Square. I knew some of her company as well because they were acquaintances of my mom as I was growing up. One day, the lady downstairs got into a heated argument with Kat's girlfriend and the landlord about the rents or something that had to do with the apartment. As I was walking up the steps from the curb and on to her porch, I heard her yelling and finally saying that she would burn the house down. I said "whoa, wait a minute I and my kids live here too." She began to calm down saying that she was just upset with all of the BS that was going on. I had nothing to do with anything because I just moved in and so I went upstairs to my apartment.

A couple of weeks later I called a family meeting between my two sisters and I because we hadn't been on speaking terms. I was sad that Sonsharary was finally 18 now, but we still couldn't have our own relationship because my older sister was always interfering.

During our sister's meeting, I was just crying out to my sisters about how important it was for me to have sisters. Since my older sister already had two other sisters, she thought my tears were funny and she made fun of my pain. Both her and Sonsharay were laughing out at me in my face. I quickly wiped my tears and ended the meeting. How dare they laugh at me like that? I can't even blame Sonsharay because she's only doing what she had been taught. My older sister is the only influence that she's had, so she doesn't even understand how dysfunctional she is. But Whatever! I'm done trying to be sisters! When she grows up and gets away from misery herself, we'd certainly try to pick up from where we left off.

Shanon is graduating on Friday. He had tickets enough for me alone, so my kids had to stay home. I asked Kat if she could keep an eye on my kids while I went to the High School graduation at the University of Hartford. Of course she didn't have a problem, considering that my kids didn't need supervision; they just needed to know that they are not in the building alone. They knew what to do in case of an emergency and they definitely knew not to open up my door for anybody!

At the very last minute my brother was able to get two additional tickets for his graduation and this time, my children could attend as well. Due to the last minute change, I didn't have enough time to tell my neighbor that I was taking my kids with me.

Two hours into the graduation, I looked down on my cell phone and saw that I had missed seven phone calls. That made me so nervous because I never had such number of phone calls in such a short period of time. None of the missed call numbers were from people that I had saved as contacts on my phone, so I didn't see that as an emergency. After the graduation was over, I told my mom and my big brother that I had to return a phone call. I walked away from my family as I returned the last call. It was my mother's youngest sister telling me that she thinks that my apartment is on fire, but she doesn't know exactly where I live and there's a house close to where she thinks that I live which happened to be on fire. I hung up with her and called the other numbers that called me. From the first call that I made, I did hear my neighbors screaming hysterically in the phone telling me to get home that our house was in flames. I became frozen; I just didn't know why I was shaking uncontrollably. My mom came over and got me into the passenger seat of my car before even knowing what was wrong. All she knew was that she saw me shaking and crying and that I was in no position to be driving, especially not driving her back home. My brother was going to an after party which his class mates were having after the graduation, so he was straight. When I told my mom about the fire, she flew over to Garden street. The street was blocked off 2 blocks away so I jumped out of the car and started running around the corner to my apartment. As I approached, the fire department tried to stop me from getting any closer until I told them that it was my apartment, so they let me pass the yellow tape. That's when I saw my neighbors crying and looking at the building where all three floors were on fire. The news reporter came to interview me, and by that time my kids had found me and began to cry as they were squeezing me in the middle of the street. I asked the reporter to give my kids some privacy because they were screaming out of control as we all sat there and watched the fully inflamed three family house on fire. I couldn't believe it, everything that I owned other than my children and my vehicle was gone forever. What now? Where now? The Red Cross was there on scene and gave us a two-night voucher for the hotel and seventh five dollars each for clothing and toiletries. That's it! After that, I was on my own starting over with my own two hands. I didn't even have renters' insurance which would have helped a little with getting back on my feet, but I didn't have insurance so I had to start from the scratch.

The worst part was that my mom had been planning on moving to ATL for over a year and she's leaving for good next month. What am I going to do with my lifeline leaving the state next month? My mom told me to call my father's sister and ask her if I could move in with her. My aunt agreed to let me and my kids come to ATL and move in her house while I got on my feet. Now I had a plan; I had about 5 weeks before my mom was driving down south with her haul truck.

14

ATL SHAWTY

I landed a new job within three weeks of moving to Georgia. It's now fall of 2008 and the country is in the middle of a recession. I wanted to work downtown Atlanta because I hated the city of Lawrenceville. If I had to live in this town permanently, I was sure to move back to Connecticut. I can't live out here with these long, dark, single lane streets. I mean these streets had real farm animals, barns and whatnot. I'm a 28 year old northern city girl, what do I know about living in these under populated areas in the south? I get nervous driving at night because black folks are still going missing down here.

My aunt's house is the largest house that I've ever been inside of, and now I'm a resident. Although, this was a dream come true, I can't live in a quiet suburban setting like this for too much longer.

My first job in Atlanta was a Pearson's Wine in Buckhead. Buckhead is a wealthy area inside the city of

Atlanta. If you drive down any residential street in Buckhead, you'll see nothing but big ass mansions. The commute to and from work was an hour and a half each way. It takes thirty minutes on back roads before I would even get to the highway. I cried to and from work, the traffic jams on route 316 and interstate 85 were depressing. I had to report work each morning by 7:30 am. Therefore, I had to leave the house no later than 5:45 am. I never had to wake up this early in my life.

My title was purchasing coordinator, which was something I've never done before. That's what made the job so cool to me. I was learning new skills and increasing my job knowledge so yeah I was on it. On Mondays, the reps lined up waiting outside of my office for me. Every man represented a different beverage company. There were at least 7-10 guaranteed meetings first thing in the morning right after that dreadful commute. Before each meeting, I ran a sales statistic report which showed me which items sold the most within the past month, and year. One by one I sat with each representative and went over special deals on hot ticket items from my report. Each of the deals consisted of a buy one get one type of thing. Whether we decided on the free bottles deals or the larger free cases deals, I then had a whole weeks' worth of work to get ready for these deliveries. I had to research our two main competitors prices listed on their site. Then I had to take the free bottles or cases and spread that cost amongst the other cases to lower the cost. Now, It's time to change all of prices in the system and print new bottle tags for the shelves downstairs. Delivery days are the most stressful because the soda trucks start delivering on Wednesday but those days aren't that stressful as Thursday and Fridays.

In Georgia its the law to pay for Alcohol on the spot, you cant be invoiced to pay for it later. This meant that on delivery days, we had to manually receive the orders, verify that each bottle and or case is received, process that invoice for payment and cut the check within a 20-30 minute window. Talk about high stressful environment. The cool part about it was I bought my bottles for the same price the owner buys his bottles for. I would have big bottle of top shelf alcohol for fewer than twenty dollars. I had a bar at home the size of

My aunt wanted me to stay with her for at least a year, so that I can get my life in order after the fire. However, this was my first time living in anyone's house since I was a kid. It was also was weird having a curfew and so many other restrictions. The doors had censors on and if opened after 10 pm, they would cause the entire house to wake up from the alarm.

All of this motivated me to find a place of my own because why wouldn't it? I kept trying to tell my aunt that I need to find a place of my own. However, she would shut that idea down in every conversation. She wanted to be there for me. In my mind, she has done a lot for me and my children. I could never repay her and my uncle Donald for all of their generosity.

Still, I wanted to leave. I didnt want any confrontations, so I waited for everyone to leave the house and I packed up everything we had. I didnt have much considering I had a total loss fire a few months ago.

I quickly found a 3 bedroom house to rent with my 3rd biweekly paycheck. The house was on the West Side of Atlanta. I moved off of Simpson Road (aka Joseph E Boone) on a side street named Detroit Avenue. The rent was only $800 and the house was right down the street from my mom. My Mom lived on Simpson Terrace which was walking distance for the kids to go to grandma's house. Now my job is only 20 mins away and already my quality of life has increased..

I drove around the city everyday in a different direction until I learned my way around Atlanta.

One afternoon, I was in the gas station paying for my gas when this guy from New York started talk to me. His name was kieth, he was a dark skinned, bow-legged Guanese. His eyes were so mesmerizing that I couldn't resist his pass at me. He asked for my number and called right away. It turns out that he lives around the corner by himself in a 5 bedroom house. He was going through custody issues but he had to legitimize himself as the child's father and pay child support before he could get any visitation or custody rights. I saw him fighting for his child, which was something that I've never seen before in my life. I was able to see his character and find out what type of person he was. The idea of him being a family man was enough to make me stick around and find out what he had to offer me. The answer was absolutely nothing, but I stayed to find out anyway.

After a few months in Atlanta, I met a gang banger from Los Angeles called L.A. Go figure. He was an O.G. and in his early forties. You can tell that he was Deep in the game just by the way he spoke. One day he came to get me with a purse that he had bought for me. We went to a park called Maddox park to hang out and kick it with people from the neighborhood that he knew. This park reminded me of a park named Kenney Park in Hartford so that was right up my alley to be to kicking it in the park. LA introduced me to quite a few people at the park, he was very well known even though he wasn't from that hood. I really liked LA a lot, but just like ole boy from New York, he didn't want an exclusive relationship. That's cool, but I don't want to be someone's play toy at this stage in my life. Although the big homie's pipe game was on one hundred, I rather just be friends in efforts to protect my heart.

I started getting out more and exploring the city. This is a big ass city! It just keep going and going. I'll be driving for 30 minutes and still be in Atlanta, like WTF! One day I came home from work to find that my house had been broken into. These folks stole everything that I've built after my fire. They even stole the doors to the bedroom and bathrooms. I've never seen a thief take the time to steal doors off the hinges. That's so bazaar right? Of all things like copper, appliances, they took the damn doors.

Who does that?

The boutique liquor wholesaler wasn't making money as fast as they used to due to the recession. Not long after I left the company, the owner retired, closed the business and moved to Florida. I was out of work and collecting unemployment benefits again. My weekly benefits were about $335, which equaled out to be around $1400 each month. I had to move somewhere with cheap rent and utilities under $300.

In no time of course, I moved around the corner on Anderson Avenue on the corner of Simpson road. I was alone in a big city trying to escape a traumatic life and now I'm scared because I dont know who is watching me. I have to be strong and protect my kids at all cost, but that doesnt stop me from being afraid. If there was a time to move back to Hartford, it would be now... At least if something was to happen to me or my kids, someone would know about it or know who did it. Then again, there's a (no snitching) law in the hood so I highly doubt it.

Within 2 weeks of me moving into my new place, the pipes busted in the half bathroom on the first floor. Water was shooting through the walls like a shower. I called Kieth, my friend from New York that lives 5 minutes away to help me. I can tell that he has female company over his house because he kept making excuses why he couldn't leave to come and help me. However, I made it pretty clear that if he was too busy to help me with this urgent matter, then I had no use for him in my life. He was there within five minutes.

Kieth tried to turn the water off from the basement; however, the water had to be shut off by the city so he personally called the fire department to handle this. I tried to call my new landlord about my issue with the pipes. Their response was that I had to pay my first month's rent before they could fix the pipes. That's when I knew that something was up with them. I decided to hold my rent money when the rent was due. They called me for two additional months without sending court paperwork and that further confirmed that they did not own this duplex. I hired a plumber, fixed the pipes and lived there as a squatter for 18 months before the real owners came around.

My cousin Tak moved down south to escape criminal charges in Hartford. Terrance called me one day and told me that he just put Tak on the greyhound bus because he pulled up and found her stabbing some chic. He said he brought her home to pack some bags and she'll be here in Atlanta tomorrow. Once Tak got to Atlanta, I felt more comfortable in this big city and I wasn't alone anymore. Tak and I were balling out with no jobs, she came with $200 in food stamps, and $200 weekly a week. I didn't have to pay rent in the apartment that I was scammed three hundred thirty five with so we were good.

We started going to this hole in the wall spot on Holly street. It was somebody's house that they turned it into a Juke Joint. The kitchen was the bar, the living room had a pool table, the dining room had the Juke Box and there was a little den on the other side off the kitchen where they played spades and dominoes. This place was popping every single night, no matter what day of the week it was, somebody was going to be there regardless. Tak and I went everywhere; however, she quickly ventured off and started meeting new and weird people to hang with. She didn't like the structured life that I was living on my journey to self-healing. Therefore, she would cling to almost everyone she met just to get away from me it seemed. LOL After a few months in Atlanta, Tak knew more about the south than I did. She was a whole peach, how did that happen?

As the world turns and so does the tables, I'll soon come home to learn that I've been robbed yet again! How many Flat screen TVs and video games do I have to buy? What am I doing wrong? I want to have a man in my life to protect me from this type of stuff or at least to the point where I'm not going through it alone.

First my bitter husband takes my shit, I build it back up.

Then the fire burns my shit, I bought it all back.

They the rob me and take everything including the doors, I bought it all back,

Then I got robbed again...

IM TIRED!!

I'm trying to keep going but.... GIVE ME A BREAK!!!!

Now here comes the real landlord showing up to check out the property. I had already been there for a little over a year and somehow forgot that I was squatting. I opened up my door when I saw these strangers in my yard.

I yelled out to the group of about five professionally dressed white people in the middle of the hood. "Can I help You?" The older white guy responded "Hi, can I help, You?" That's when it dawned on me. I'm going to jail.

When the sheriff showed up with the eviction notice, the paperwork listed the tenants as John Doe/Jane Doe. I wondered if they were telling me that I was dead. I have never seen any legal document listing a john doe on it. Trust and believe that I went to court trying to buy more time and let them know that I was a victim of fraud over a year ago. Yeah, I tried it!! While I sat in the hallway waiting for the mediator, the owner of the building asked me if I wanted to make a deal. They gave me an additional 60 days to move out as opposed to the 7 day process for normal evictions. This gave me 2 additional months to go out and find a job.

I moved down Bankhead highway on Peek Road into a nice 3 bedroom house with tall wooden privacy fence. I thought that this extra-large fence would make it difficult for people to rob me. What it actually did was gave them privacy to break in and take my shit through the back fence that led to the next street over. I was so done with starting over that I stopped buying anything of value. I didn't know what I was doing wrong to keep having brake ins like that. I can't even blame it on Tak because they robbed me twice before she moved to Atlanta. Plus, I don't have company, so I just don't know who is doing this.

I found a job right away at a cool ass startup company called Southeast Gold Buyers. They were located in Sandy Springs, Ga in a small building on Roswell Road. I was hired as the Payroll Manager and shared the accounting office with two other staff members. The corporate office was located in the back of the actual store where customers come in to sell their gold. There were about 10 employees total in the entire company so this job was a piece of cake. That was until the owners opened more stores, hired more employees, and repeated this process again and again. They even opened 2 additional businesses in the process.

This is one of the coolest jobs I've ever had and by far some of the best coworkers on the planet. Because we are in a recession, this new startup company was able to get the best of the best employees as we were all laid off from other companies. They recruited some of the top sales agents, marketing gurus, and business management professionals in Atlanta. Together we all cumulatively did our parts in growing this startup company. With so much younger and fresh talent, he business exploded faster than anyone had imagined. Next thing you know, our upper management team was over 30 people.

Within a year, the company moved into a much larger building with fancy office glass walls. That's when the accounting department found out that our current manager was being replaced by the wicked witch of the south.

I wanted to like this lady but she proved on several different occasions that she was not fond of my brown skin touching the company's finances. She even suggested that she has to set up segregation of duties in efforts to keep me honest. She suggested that I had the opportunity to set up a dummy employee and pay myself. I know for a fact that there were several different audit trails and traps that she could have set up if she wanted to catch a criminal. Instead, she knew damn well that I wasn't a criminal as her only mission was to degrade my character and insult my moral compass. Let's say for example that I was paying myself with a fake identity. By her mentioning it, wouldn't that make it more difficult to catch me red handed? She just wanted to let me know what she thought of me. I was nothing but a low down dirty Negro to her. Regardless of what anyone else feels about me, she holds my livelihood in her hands as my superior. I don't know what I've done to make this lady hate me so much but the way she looks at me through these glass walls is terrifying. I've never been afraid of a woman as much as this lady frightened me. It wasn't an aggressive type of vibe that I received from her little frail self. When she looks at me, it's like she can see me hanging from a damn tree. You can see it in her eyes, the way she forces a grin when there are others around.

I knew that I had to get away from this lady before I turned up missing down here in the Jim Crow south. She would never speak to me unless she absolutely had to, but she wanted to make sure that I knew about her hunting skills. She wanted to let me know that she knows how to shoot animals. Why is that? It's like some type of intimidation or something, but I'm not going for it. This bitch better leave me alone because I'm am not my ancestors. I will beat the dog shit out of her.

She quickly learned that the HR manager and I were never on good terms, however, my former manager wouldn't let her get close enough to hurt me. As soon this new gun slangin accounting manager spots an opportunity she jumped on it. It didn't take long before I could see both of their masks. The owners of the company knew that I'm loyal and will always have their backs during these growing pains so neither one of these haters with authority can touch me boo! I was single handedly processing payroll for over five hundred employees. Who can replace that without lots of pay discrepancies and hiccups? Ha! Beat it Betty! I just make this shit look easy.

One of the multiple companies that I processed payroll for, had traveling employees. The employees would fly out to different cities and set up estate sales inside hotels to purchase items from the locals in each city.. That traveling company had pay rates that depended on the position that was worked each day. One employee can have 2-3 different pay rates within one week. Because of this rate differential,, none of the major payroll companies were able to accommodate this type of pay structure which ultimately made my job miserable. We had meetings after meetings with different companies to no avail. That's when I worked day and night to find a solution; I can't let this defeat me in front of my enemies. I have to show this hater boss what I'm made of.

Within a week, I created a spreadsheet that had all types of (IF) statement formulas. When the employee selects which role they were performing on each day, the rates pertaining to that role would populate into the cells indicating how much they made that day. Time sheets came directly from the supervisors which meant they were approved upon arrival. It took a couple of weeks to come up with the entire process but that's what I do, I solve problems. Try to fire me now, Hater!

The two owners were both young Jewish guys. I'm 29 now and they were between 33 and 35. One of them, Andy, has two kids with a dope black chick named Denise. She stops by the corporate office every now and again. Every time she visits the office, she would come around to my office and chat with me for a while. We connected like this for months, but it wasn't until after the first company Christmas party that she started inviting me to events outside of company functions. When she saw me getting extra loose on the dance floor with Antoine, my gay coworker, she knew that I was with the foolishness all the way!

Denise was cool as ever though. She's a Gemini too. I literally watched her go from a regular chick like me to a rich chick and she never switched up. One year I went to her house for a party, she lived in a regular house. Then another year I got invited to a party and now she has a movie theater, elevator, gym, 3 kitchens including one by the pool, swimming pool, zip lining, playground, Jacuzzi, bedroom sized closet and she is super nonchalant about it all.. I meet celebrities in her house too.

One day, Tre was with me at Denise's house for a fight night. He was downstairs playing pool between the theater, and the basement kitchen. There are so many rooms in this house that there were several different parties going on at the same time. Tre was downstairs with all of the fighters and ex fighters. Andy got into the ultimate fighter challenges since he closed the gold buying business. Most of the people that attended his fight parties were professional fighters. I was upstairs with Denise and her group of associates. There were other women in the house, but this was a small circle of women upstairs. If you weren't part of the crew, you would feel uncomfortable on the outside of these conversations. Therefore, the other women were either in the theater watching the fight or in the basement kitchen with the guys watching the fight.

Tre ran upstairs a lot faster than he has any other time at these parties. I thought something happened to him or someone said something to him because he came sprinting towards me.

"Ma! Pam is downstairs"

What? I replied.

"Pam is downstairs!!! Gina and Pam... From the Martin show!! Pam is downstairs right now...

I've been watching her for twenty minutes and it's her mom!!"

Tre had all of our attention at this point. Denise said "Pam is downstairs where? In my house?"

"Yes right now!!!" Tre yelled!

We all went downstairs and bum rushed her! It was her! Sitting in the barstool in Denise's basement kitchen yelling at the fight with some handsome tall glass of chocolate milk! You can tell that he was some kind of professional fighter and had some money too.

We talked with her for a good while and even took a few pics. She enjoyed herself and was comfortable as ever. I didn't know that celebrities were that chill. After that, you can never tell who was going to show up at one of Andy's mansion parties.

As soon as this school year is over, I'm taking my kids out of Atlanta Public Schools. They are out here cheating on test scores and helping the kids pass the class. If students fail, the teachers take the blame and may not get hired the following year. It was so bad that teachers and board members of the Department of Education were going to jail and or resigning. Then down in clayton county, they lost their accreditation and the high school graduated couldn't get a proper diploma from an accredited school board of education. It was a big messy scandal down here in the south and I was getting my kids far away from it. I don't know what I walked my babies into.

I moved to Smyrna in a subdivision on Cobb Parkway. I paid $700 for a 3 bedroom apartment inside of an obviously cheap apartment complex. The living conditions in this building were so bad compared to how we were used to living, but I kept telling myself that I had to do this so that I can buy a house next year. I started the process by attending a (first time home buyers) course at the Urban League Atlanta. It was a 6 hours class full of guest speakers within the real estate field, and designed to get us prepared for each step in the home buying process. You get a certificate at the end and a one-on one counseling to go over your credit report and what things to do to help your credit score. When you leave the class, you know exactly what to do. It turns out that I had a year and a half, maybe two.

I sent my cousin Tommy a Greyhound ticket to come and live with me. I thought this would be a good way to get him to see a different type of living and maybe he might want to change his life. Tommy is practically my little brother. I lived with his mom Kelis off and on since I was a kid. I hate seeing my family live a life that I got so far away from and I just want to help in any way that I can. I took him everywhere when he got here. I bought him new clothes and shoes and wanted him to get himself together down here. One day, I decided to bring my family tubing down the Chattahoochee River. It was everyone's first time tubing and we had so much fun. Until Tommy saw a group of teens jumping off of a cliff into the river. He wanted to do it and it made sense since he was with us as kids when we went swimming in the dangerous sewer as kids. I knew that my brother/cousin like to do dangerous stunts so this was right up his alley. The only problem was that Tre wanted to go with him. That's when I had to draw the line. Now I had Tommy, Tre and Faith trying to convince me that I'm being irrational by not letting Tre jump off the cliff. We are getting closer to the cliff and they are triple teaming me about being an overprotective parent. Finally the pressure was too much for me and I let him go with Tommy. What I didn't know was that they planned on removing their life vest to jump. By the time I realized that my son had removed his life vest, he was already half way down into the water. He made the jump but soon learned that the river is much different than a swimming pool. He tried to swim back to the tubes that we had connected to each other, but he wasn't strong enough to swim after that big jump. I saw him slowing down and I yelled out to him.

"Tre, are you OK?" I asked him.

"Nooo" he replied!!

"TOMMY!!! Get him!!!"

As soon as I yelled for my cousin to help my son, he quickly swam over to Tre who by this time was about to drown. Tre started to panic and was going to drown Tommy as well. There was white guy nearby who heard me screaming and saw Tommy struggling to save my son. The guy swam over and grabbed Tre away from Tommy and swam him to the shore where Tre's life vest was waiting. I pushed the tubes against the current back over to the shore where Tommy and Tre were standing on some tree roots. They got back into the tube and we finished the remaining hour ride down the river.

We talked about this tubing trip the rest of the day and for the next few weeks. I even had horrible nightmares for weeks following that traumatizing event. Every time I think about tubing, I think about the time that the river almost swept my son underwater and carried his body down the river.

Eventually Tommy started doing the same old same ole. He let a guy front him some weed with a promise to pay him back. He knew that he wasn't going to pay the dude back before he took the first pack. But he was able to convince the guy to give a second loan and a much larger loan than the first one. Before it was all said and done, Tommy owed the guy about $600 and knew for sure that he wasn't going to pay it back. I didn't feel comfortable knowing that my brother could be killed down here for trying to play the same games that he plays up north. These southern will kill you over anything and I couldn't let that happen. I planned a trip for all of us to go to Connecticut. I flew up there and bought bus tickets for the kids, Tommy and Taky. Everyone had round trip tickets except for Tommy. He had to stay there and get his life together. I promised him that if he can make some significant changes in his life within six months, I'll send him another bus ticket. Within a month he went to jail for armed robbery and carjacking.

Tre was a freshman in high school and wanted to play football. He made the team and played a few games. The football team were a bunch of jocks that got into trouble and weren't serious about their education, they just only studied enough to be able to play football. Tre's grades dropped drastically and before long he got suspended from school. I put him on punishment and told him the next time he acted up in school, I was taking him off of the team. He knew that I was serious, but the peer pressure to be one of the cool kids was getting the best of him to the point where he was willing to suffer the consequences. That's when I took him off the team and knew that I had to get him out of this school district too by the time next school year came around.

Faith was starting to get chubby and self-conscious about her weight. She would completely shut down and get depressed. I told her enrolled her into basketball when the season opened up. I knew that she would get selected because she was tall and huge. She was in the seventh grade and had 2 full years to get in shape before high school. She was selected on first drafts picks. She didn't even know how to hold a basketball let alone dribble or shoot, but she was selected. The coach saw something in her and personally developed her. The other teammates were jealous because it was clear that Faith was a favorite. There were players that played last year who never got that much favoritism so you know the jealousy was everywhere. Her first few games she only got a little play time because she was still learning the game.

Her teammates used to bully her, especially the starting five. The starters never wanted her around because she was tall enough to take one of their places.

They told the other teammates not to speak to her. When they did things as a team, they would leave her out of it. This made her focus on her game. She thought that if she got better that she would be able to be a part of the team and hang out with them. Towards the end of the year, her skills got better. Some of the teammates started coming around and speaking to her outside of the game. They still thought that she was beneath them.

By the next school year I moved the kids to East Cobb. I moved in a 3 bedroom split level house with an in-law suite in the basement. The in-law suite had a kitchen, living room, bedroom and bathroom. I turned it into the kids hang out with a pool table, darts, video games, etc.

Faith was selected on the new middles school basketball team. One of the coaches was a former college basketball team player and she said that Faith reminded her of herself growing up. She took interest into making Faith a more dominant player. She gave Faith specific drills that the other team didn't have to do. She was harder on Faith than any other player. She made Faith the star of the team and when they won the championship competition, the team gave the trophy to Faith. They knew that she worked the hardest on the entire team. All the players hated Faith but could do nothing about it, she was their star player. None of the parents like me because my daughter got favoritism and they could say nothing about it.

I'm finally qualified to buy a house!! The only problem is, every time I make an offer on a house some rich investor outbids me with cash. This has been going on for close to a year. The next school year is starting soon so I have to find something quickly or else I'll have to wait until next summer. I can't really afford these homes in this area because any decent property over here is close to three hundred thousand. So If I find a property it will most likely be in a different school district.

I found a house!! It was down the street, and I'm going to see it later. I love it!! It has an in-law suite and a wraparound porch. Granite countertops, epoxy floors and Island sink! I called Kieth to come with me when I go back with the inspector. Of course my mom and the kids were going too. This was finally happening, my dream came true!

The next step in the process after I signed the contract and paid the earnest money, was to hire a home inspector. We all met the inspector at the house. The kids saw the house for the first time and they were running around and going crazy! They were happy that we were about to own our own home. It was everything that we wanted in a home. Unfortunately, the inspection failed. The older black guy told me not to buy this house. I got angry and thought that he was trying to steal it from under me and have someone else purchase it instead. He started walking around pointing out damage that I would have never noticed, The main damage was the fully cracked foundation. Once he pointed this out, I could see the crack going up through the entire house. It was split in half as if it was struck by lightning. A tornado could rip one half of the house off because of this cracked foundation. Wow! I would have never noticed that!

The inspector goes further to show me major roof damage and the very unstable wrap around porch. The house was a complete piece of shit. That's why the investors didn't buy this one yet. I thought after a year and a half of looking for my first home, I have finally found it. I cried on that shiny commercial looking dining room floor under the chandelier. I cried so hard that they all felt bad for me.

"WHY ME?? Why can't I just get one break!! " They thanked the inspector for me and got me together as he left. I wiped my tears and got up from the floor. I did one more walk through the house and then we left.

I was quite the drive home. I didn't want to look for any more houses. I now have to start looking for places to rent before school starts again.

I moved to Kennesaw. Maybe my kids will have better luck over there with the rich kids. I know that everywhere has bad apples but when you minimize those numbers you should be able to get better results. It turns out that this was the best option for them to begin with. I wanted to bring them out here when I first left Atlanta but I was scared to be that far away from the city, I had flashbacks of Lawrenceville and that horrible commute and decided to stay closer to the perimeter. I only have one more year before Tre graduates high school, and three years before its Faith's turn. When I do decide to purchase a house, they'll be finished school and I can go back to the city.

15

RECOUNT BIZ

I've been working in my accounting career for about 16 years now. I've worked in every industry from manufacturing, health care, Beauty and Spa, construction, Audio visual, Design Build, City and Government sectors. My current job is Bookkeeper for a Multi-Million Dollar General Contractor in Tucker, GA. It was on the other side of the perimeter and about a 45 minute to an hour drive each way from Cobb County. I took that position after dealing with all of the toxic energy from my management team at the Gold Buyers.

The two young owners got rich and ended up pulling out of the gold business altogether. Those chicks tried to play with my job and found themselves looking for one in the end! You see how Karma works!

Now I'm going to work for a black man which I felt really good about after dealing with two "*Karens*" in the same space. This black guy was from New Orleans and was Creole. This is black with French descent. He looks like a white man but he's a black man. White people don't accept creole as white. He's a handsome older guy and a former certified Architect.

My 1st couple of months was basically learning how he ran his company.

Over the next few months, I was able to bring lots of my talents to the company and improve some of their processes and procedures. This allowed him to see better profits based on my contribution to his company. I did so well in lifting his company to a higher level that he started giving me perks and bringing me to banquets and introducing me to public figures out in the city. This all came after I helped him formulate his electrical company. I also got him certified as a minority contractor with the city of Atlanta which led to him receiving a large contract for the electrical work at the Atlanta Airport. He was very impressed with my business skills and kept me close under his wing. One night after the award ceremony, he asked if I would like to go out for a drink. I didn't see what the problem would be because we have had drinks in the past together at other events. We went to a bar and had several drinks that night. We stayed out pretty late as well but it was definitely a professional outing. His wife clearly didn't approve of his late return home that night and I assume it raised suspicion. He was already having problems at home that I had no clue about, nor did I need to. His wife came into the office and requested to have a meeting with me. I was confused why she wanted to meet with me when she didn't even work here; she was only his wife. We went in the back conference room and sat down. She looked across the table with this evil glare expressed how she was the big kahuna and the Queen Bee of this company and she will not let anyone take that away from her. She went on to say that she knows that I'm a young girl and trying to work my way to the top but it won't be through her husband. She said some other slick shit that I sat and allowed her to finish her rants since that's what she came to do.

Once she was finished talking, I took a Deep breath and had a confident smile on my face when I replied. In all due respect, I'm not sure why we are having this meeting since I work directly for your husband. Furthermore, I've had 15+ years in my accounting career and should be charging your husband a lot more for my services. So actually Mrs. Insecurity, I'm doing you a favor.

I went on to explain how I had no clue that they had all that drama going on up on the company and I didn't have to deal with any of that bullshit!

She started to apologize because now it seems like she realizes how much she just insulted my character and now. she's afraid that I'll quit. I stood up as I expressed how disappointed I was in her for thinking that someone of my intelligence had to use my body to advance in life. My last words to her were asking her what was her profession and if that was how she got with her husband. Her blank stare and silence told me everything that I needed to know! Bitch bye! Fuck this company! I went back to my desk and gathered my things and walked out! Some nerve of her to think that I wanted her old ass husband. He didn't even have the money that she thought he had, he was barely covering payroll each week. Please! Miss me with all of the messy ratchet workplace nonsense.

That same day, I went home and sent my resume out and instantly got 3 hits. Two of the hits were live interviews and ultimately I was offered two positions. I chose the Company in Marietta because the offer was a salary of $60k, four weeks of vacation, ten sick and personal days, just to start. I was only making $47k with that ratchet homie the clown company. Plus the new company had so many benefits and sign on perks. My title was Branch Accounting and HR Manager. My branch was responsible for all Georgia and Alabama; however, the company is a global firm with over 1700 branches across the world.

I love everything about this position and this company. I worked directly under the corporate office in Louisiana because they were still looking for a Branch Manager who would be my boss. This was one of the worst locations and they hired me to fix it. There were issues in every department. The main reason for the issues is the last manager was able to do things that no other branch was doing and therefore he ran it into the ground before he left. It was like the inmates were running the asylum. The managers were white and they were taking advantage of their minority employees out in the field. The white employees had overtime when the minority employees were struggling to stay with the company by only working part time hours. The corporate office kept receiving tips about the abuse at that branch so they needed to get someone in position but went through months of interviews looking for the right fit. They wanted to hire a minority who was strong enough to regulate this type of environment, and I was just what they were looking for. I guess!

Step by step I changed procedure after procedure, making the work flow smoother from the field to the office and vice versa. There were at least fifty technicians out in the field at any given time. They never had the proper tools that they needed to do the job correctly and in turn was costing the company money. I had to study reports and time clocks to find out who was milking the clock. Once I set up these types of traps, I was able to prove theft of hours and terminated all of the violators. Corporate office wanted to fire everyone but couldn't find proof. I had to find the physical proof of certain things and present it. Over the next year I had a new boss who couldn't handle the fact that we had to terminate over 45 employees together. He made me do all the talking because when they start begging him for their job he says he'll see what he can do instead of this is it. He wasn't strong enough for what he walked into and he resigned on me.

I still had to finish implementing new systems, processes, procedures, and software for the branch. I had to train the remaining employees who just watched me fire coworkers that they've been working with for the past 10-30 years. They know that it's coming from corporate but they know It's me that is executing those orders. My former new boss is gone so Im the only one left with blood on my hands!

The numbers are looking good on the books and the head officers know my name. They are thanking me personally during our teleconferences in front of everyone. These people have been working here for decades and they never had these big guys calling out their names. I was something like a big deal at the corporate office. I had the branch producing numbers that they haven't seen in years. Granted quite a few people had to pay the price for it. However, they were costing the company money and that also meant my job so one of us had to go. In this case, it was close to 50 employees that had to go before the company could start seeing profits. I also closed the gap on most of the processes so now it doesn't take the technician as much time to do his job, saving the company money on labor also.

They had money to hire a Branch Manager thanks to me. Guess who they hire? One of the disgruntled managers who got reprimanded after one of my report discrepancies. For over two years he and I have been butting heads about the new guidelines and restrictions they corporate had me enforce at the branch. However, he was my peer and now he's coming into the corporate office to be my boss? I've expressed in writing on multiple occasions about my concerns that he may have some resentment towards me and may use his authority against me. The corporate office has assured me that this was impossible considering his new promotion and good standing with the company for over 20 years. I believed them and that was the worst thing that I could have done.

He hated me! The crazy part is that he couldn't say that I wasn't doing my job because I was doing the best job that corporate has seen in years. By the time he got to the corporate office, I'd mastered my job. The curve balls that he threw weren't fast enough because they didn't work. One of the middle eaten guys came in my office saying that he is about to quit because his boss won't give him hours and he heard other people bragging to him about fifteen hours of overtime each week. I had him write a letter explaining everything that is happening and I sent that letter to the corporate office. That manager got fired and hours were spread between all employees properly.

It pissed the little new manager, ex coworker all the way off that I went over his head after he told me that he would handle it. I knew that he wouldn't handle it because that manager was his friend for years. The manager did so much dirt that he was able to be fired behind it, and therefore, this wasn't just one case of misconduct. This was a pile of infractions that could have the entire company paying the settlement claims behind some careless racist managers.

Anyway after he had to personally fire his friend, he had it out for me. It was similar to the way my old hog hunting boss at the Gold Buyers hated me but times ten because it was personal with this little big guy. You can tell that he had a height complex the way that he walks with those stubby little toddler legs. The way he avoids eye contact with me while I'm standing up is hilarious. When he walks into my office, I stand up like when the Judge is walking into the courtroom. He watches me grow like a beanstalk out of my seat and quickly loses his train of thought and walks away pretending that he is forgetting something in his office. He was starting to catch on after a while and before I could stand up he would say, "You don't have to stand up" Oh my gawd I don't know why that was so funny to me.

Soon there would be nothing left to laugh about. This man was willing to lose everything to get the best of me. That was some shit that you don't see white people doing too often. He didn't care what it took. He was going to end me for good. He started giving me new assignments and deadlines that would be sure to throw off my other duties and deadlines. I knew what he was doing early so I prepared to take work home and work every weekend to catch up. I succeeded for a while until he kept loading me up. He removed my HR position and this is how he justified giving me more work to the corporate office. But he removed my HR position so I couldn't tell the corporate office what was going on at the branch anymore. I told the corporate office what was happening and it seemed like they were on his side. At this point I was on my own with him. He was power hungry and he used that power over me in every way that he could. Now the corporate office that used to praise me, were not impressed anymore as my work performance had declined almost fifty percent.

He told them that even with the increased workload that I should be able to complete each task because I didn't have to do the Human Resources job anymore. But that was only a fraction of my total duties. If you remove HR you have to replace those duties with comparable duties. Instead, he had me fire two of my accounting staff members and take on both of their full time jobs. They let me promote my accounting clerk but they knew that she wasn't experienced enough to cover these vital positions permanently. She was a clerk, and handled most of the administrative functions in my department, not the technical functions.

This bastard really sat up on numerous nights plotting this because there isn't enough animosity in the world to make me think about someone this much in order to create a plan to destroy them. But I was in his way and he was destined to show me what happens when one of us Negroes crosses the lines in the south. He didn't have to kill me like they did disobedient slaves back then. He could just as easily destroy my livelihood and have a somewhat similar effect on me and/or my children. All that mattered to him was that I was crossing the lines by reporting racism to the corporate office and there's no way that someone like me was going to have that much power in this branch.

Before I knew what hit me, he had loaded me up to the chopping block. The entire office had it out for me especially since I have no more authority in the branch. One by one each employee filed a complaint against me. I'm either too rude or snappy, unprofessional or unresponsive, and aggressive and abrasive.. Within 60 days I had enough complaints to fill up my personnel file.

I was over it, I can't win with so many people against me. I've even had my tire flatten and windshield busted right in the front of the building. I started driving around in circles before going home because I was afraid someone would follow me.

This is when I moved to Kennesaw. I didn't want any record of my address anywhere in this company. I don't know who I can trust now. Most of the people in the corporate office that I knew personally has resigned so I'm all alone with an entire branch wide confederate army against me. I sent one of my bosses best friends at the branch his invoices. When he receives the invoices, his reply to my email read "I got my mind on my bitches and my bitches on my mind" I forwarded that email to the corporate office and he was fired immediately. Now I'm drowning in work. Bills are getting cut off notices, deadlines are being missed. I've never been so covered up in my life.

He would rather cause the branch to run down only to force me to quit. He is a straight weirdo and I've never witnessed hatred in this capacity in my life. I would sit in my office behind closed doors and cry. That was until he realized that I was trying to hide my pain and made it mandatory to keep my door open. Everyone would walk by and smirk at me because they knew that I was miserable. It was a running joke around the office to purposely walk past my office in order to see how the manager was treating me.

One day, an older white lady came into my office. She told me that she knows what they are doing to me isn't right. She advised me to use my (EAP) employee assistance program to get a therapist. She went on to say that a therapist would get me out of work for a month if I told them what I was going through. I leaned closer letting her know that she had my attention.

She said anyone who has to deal with these types of environments can get help from a therapist. She assured me that I wouldn't have to worry about bills because I would be able to use my short term disability insurance for mental health just as I would for a physical injury. She even added the fact that white people have been doing it for years, and how black people don't believe in mental health therapy. She was trying to give me a way out without quitting and at this point, I don't have a choice but to give it a shot.

That night I called the EAP and was connected with a therapist in two days. I called out sick for three days including the day of my appointment. I drove to East Cobb and met with an older black lady. She was cool from the beginning as she gathered initial information. Now I feel very comfortable and able to relax and open up. Our session was like a Deep conversation where I was able to get it all out, the tears, anger, disgrace, everything! I used so much tissue that she had to change trash bags.. That felt good but it was only the beginning. She took me out of work alright. What I didn't know was that I had to meet with her once a week. She got to know a lot about me and my family and even had a couple of family sessions. She knew that I wasn't a fan of medication so she introduced me to essential oils. One tiny vial of this powerful oil is enough to calm you all the way down if you take a Deep whiff of it. She charged me fifteen dollars for this little container smaller than a perfume sample bottle. I paid her because I just witnessed first-hand what this stuff can do for me.

Almost six month go by and my Short Term Disability turned into Long Term Disability. What my bully manager did was triggered my other PTSD that was lying dormant. Now Im afraid for my life, I'm down here thinking that people were watching me and following me around. It even got so bad that I was afraid to go outside. I would scream at the kids when they were late from school because I thought that someone would harm my children trying to get to me. I was in bad shape and I couldn't wait to move back into the city.

I was afraid to go back to work for someone after what those people did to me. I refuse to put my entire paycheck in the hands of someone who can harm me with it. I refuse to put all of my eggs in one basket and was determined to separate my money so that if I have a problem with one person, that one personal won't be able to stop the show. All I had to do was figure out how I can take full control over my paycheck the same was that I took full control over my life. I can't keep letting people use and abuse me. I have to draw the line. I have to set boundaries. I have to be brave and do what I got to do for my life and stop allowing one company to tell me how much I'm worth while benefiting from processes that I put in place. Am I the fool or are they?

My homie girl Denise invited me to another party at the mansion. I'm going over there very regularly now. I think this was their engagement party or something like that because I believe they were flying out to get married that next day. At the party Andy asked me what was I doing for work these days? I told him that I'm in between jobs right now. He advised me that he may be having some work coming up by its part time contractor work. This is when he went on to say that I should really get out and work for myself because I have skills that small businesses need. He said larger companies can afford to hire the proper talent, us small businesses need the skills at an affordable price. He said that he would give me a call when this gig was ready for me.

This was confirmation that it was time to jump out there. I didn't know the first thing about being in business for myself but I was eager to learn. I went home and started studying bookkeeping businesses, how to advertise and find clients, and everything I needed to get the thought process going. I thought of business names first and none of them was going to work. I researched websites because I knew that I didn't want one of those cheap ones that didn't end with a dot com. I needed a logo, an official business structure set up and so much more. It took me some time to get these things in order but I was out of work on LTD and had the time to do some research along with my therapy sessions.

Little by little my vision was coming together. I had a business name, logo, website, business cards, and federal identification number. Now I had to study my competition and see what they were doing. I had to find my target market and find out what they needed. I had lots of work to do.

I had to study so much about what to do and how to do it that once I've learned it, I can now sell this services and help others start their business. I even gave a free consultation to someone that should have sent me referrals but instead she stole my information to sell it herself. These little mignons be stealing everything and still don't know what to do with it.

Any that's why I never give away all of my jewels.. You ever see someone try to do what you do but with missing pieces? Chile please!!!

16

SHRINK ME PLEASE

It's going on a year of me receiving disability benefits and I'm getting better every day. I am getting closer to getting back to work and getting back into the swing of things. Therapy is helping clear up some things that have been holding me back for years. I've never felt better about life as I can see clearly now the rain is gone. I wish I had gotten therapy much sooner. This is truly a breath of fresh air.

I recently have been in contact with my elementary school crush. His name was Benjamin but his family called him Ben. Ben used to walk me home from school in the 3rd grade when I was going to Vine Street School. However, Ben didn't actually walk me home, he walked me to my aunt's house where I would stay for weeks at a time when I wasn't living with Kelis and her kids.

Ben moved with his father not long after third grade because I would always ask his sister Denna where he was and she kept saying that he moved away. But it's been years so where was he?

Turns out that Ben moved to Virginia when we were kids because of personal issues and he's been there ever since. Well now with my down time from work and mental clarity, I'm ready to date again. With my crippling social anxieties meeting new people is very difficult for me. It's easier for me to open up to someone that I already know than to open up to a complete stranger. Ben had an advantage on other guys because he was familiar and he was someone who I had a crush on since I was a kid. Again, since it's hard to meet new acquaintances, I hold on tight to familiarity. Once we connected on Facebook it took no time for him to win me over. He didn't really have to do much, as long as he wasn't weird. We spoke daily for about two months before he decided to come visit. He was supposed to come for a weekend but he never left. I didn't force him to leave either because he was easy to be around. He wasn't too loud or too friendly with others; he didn't bother me much. He just went to work and came home and minded his business. I helped him pay for certifications and helped him get a vehicle. It didn't matter that he came empty handed, I can help him build himself up to be the provider of the household but I'm not going to discredit him because of his financial situation unless he shows me that he's a piece of shit, and then he has to go.

Tre is a senior at and is having the best academic year since we've moved to the south. Even he can't believe how focused he is about graduation. He was on it! He was an active member of about four clubs and social groups in school. I was so proud of him. Faith was a beast in basketball because now she's in her sophomore year. She has been playing for four school seasons and two years in AAU summer leagues. She played center and guard so she knew how to take a charge like a professional. I would jump up about to run on the court when I see her get knocked to the ground.. But this big ole five foot eleven weighting at 210 pounds amazon chick jumps right back up! That's my little iron baby! I don't know how she does it but she just keeps on getting back up!!

Monday is my mom's birthday and I have no clue what we're going to do for her. However, I heard on the radio that they were hosting an aerobics event at the trampoline park. I thought it would be fun for Faith, mom and me to kick off the weekend before the barbeque event tomorrow. We had a lot of fun at this trampoline park. It was only an hour workout session so we weren't there too long either. We were all sweaty after this intense instructional workout and I was glad that it was over. Mom and I were sitting down resting before the session was over. We gave it our best and we were exhausted. Faith was still full of energy because she was an athlete. She went on to other areas of the trampoline park. There was a form pit where you can jump in like the pit full of balls at McDonald's back in the day but for big kids and adults. Faith jumped into this thing twice and once she got stuck and it was hard to get out. Then she went over to the basketball dunk hoop where you jump up high enough to touch the rim. Any basketball player would love to do this especially if you can't jump high enough to do this on your own. Faith dunked quite a few times and she had a ball doing so. But I think she overdid it somewhere in the process because before we could leave the building she was in pain. Not the same pain that my mom and I were in after all of this physical activity. She started crying as she grabbed her neck saying that her neck hurts.

At first I thought that she was being her normal dramatic self because I know for a fact that I'm in pain too after all of that jumping up and down that we all just did. But by the time we got in the car and her tears turned into real cries for help, I was heading straight to the emergency room. While trying to find a station to listen to, she dropped the phone. This is no big deal because in a moving vehicle you can drop just about anything. When the phone dropped she started screaming.

"Mommy!!" Coming from the back seat.

"I cant move my leg!! Oh My God! I can't feel my hand"

I can't really recall the next events because they all became a blur.

We arrived at the emergency room within ten minutes. By the time we pulled up to the hospital, Faith's entire left side of her body was paralyzed. I literally had to lift her up and put her into the wheelchair as she could not move one side of her body and the other side of her body was in shock. After a few hours and several tests at Well star, they couldn't figure out what was wrong with my baby. They transported her to Children's Healthcare Of Atlanta where they diagnosed her within the first hour. She had Transverse Myelitis, a very rare spinal injury. It's so rare that doctors don't have enough case studies to properly treat it. What they do know is that whatever mobility functions that she doesn't redevelop within the first ninety days will be gone forever. This meant that we had work to do. I had less than three months to help my baby get back to a meaningful life where she has the freedom to use all of her limbs as she chooses. I had to completely block out all negative thoughts and emotions and get Faith focused on the end goal only. That goal was to get up out of that wheelchair and be able to live a normal life going forward.

I was up at the hospital every single day trying to keep a smile on my baby's face and keep some type of normalcy in her life. She had to stay in the hospital for two and a half months while she went through rehabilitation. During this time the hospital enrolled my household into an emergency medical assistance coverage plan through the department family and children services. Not only did faith now have medical insurance, we all did. Ben and Tre had to figure out how to survive without me as I couldn't be in two places at the same time. They both had enough tools to survive with each other and on their own. My main priority was to make sure that my daughter can walk again within these next few weeks.

First it started off with Ben requesting some cafeteria cookies before I left the hospital, to me not spending enough time at home or making sure that the boys have meals to eat at night.. After a couple of weeks, all that Tre and Ben talked about was me not being home cooking for them like they were used to me doing before Faith got injured. I couldn't believe that of all people, Ben would be adding to the pressure that I was already currently under. It's as if he has completely disregarded the fact that my daughter is laying in the hospital paralyzed. The more pressure that he put on me, the more he was pushing me away. Our live-in relationship didn't even last a year because he made me feel like I wasn't good enough because I couldn't give him all of me at the same time that my daughter was injured. He was literally forcing me to choose between my baby and him. He did it in a way that was alluding to the idea that I may be neglecting my son in the process of not being home as much.

It didn't take long before I had to cut my losses as I couldn't afford to go backwards on my mental health journey. He already perceived me as being crazy, and as long as his mind can validate those thoughts then it must be true. He tried to invalidate me so that he can feel good about himself or his actions. As long as I'm the bad guy, he's in the clear. Not! I wasn't having it. I saw right through his immature bullshit instantly. If this is the type of pressure that he's willing to put on me at a time like this, I'm all set on him. Little did I know that I was putting too much pressure on him as well. He had his eyes set on Denna's best friend's sister with the big butt. One night I went through his phone. I know I was wrong but he's been ignoring me lately and I wanted to see what had his attention. I saw a text to Denna that read "She's keeps asking about Frieda but she'll have a fit if she saw her"

I woke him up to ask why would I have a fit if I saw Frieda in person.

"Because she got a big ass." he replied.

That's when I knew that I was done with him and all of his childish games. If that's what he wanted he should have said something. But trying to invalidate me by comparing me with a broke chick with 5 kids is something I'll never accept.

Faith is starting to walk again and hopes are getting higher. But I have to keep pushing her to her max in order to get her back up to par. I'm physically and mentally drained by this point and I just need some help! But at this point in life I've realized that nobody is coming to save me.

My therapist is located in the same area as my former employer and my chest tightens up every time that I have to drive in that direction. I knew that I needed more than regular therapy sessions before my disability benefits expired. Although I really like this lady, I need more intense therapy sessions if I want to heal properly..

My therapist made a referral to the psychiatric hospital over in Smyrna, Ga. They had all types of programs available but the intake worker selected the Woman's Intensive Trauma Program for me. Because this wasn't an emergency and I was basically volunteering to enroll, I went in through an outpatient program. This meant that I could go home at night. However, when I get there in the morning, it's locked until the end of the day. They take your keys, your belt, shoe strings, anything that can cause harm to one of the psych patients or be used to harm them. This was the real deal and reminded me of my hospital stays as a kid. There were metal detectors and physical searches upon entering. Once you get in and see what is happening on the inside you'll know why they have these rules. I know for a fact that I was in there with very unstable people. Just imagine these women in the outside world, if triggered enough they could do some serious damage. These women have been to hell and back a few times. It made me feel safe and secure with my issues in a place like this.

Inside this program there were several other separate smaller programs like food disorders and personality disorders. In the food disorders group they had women who wouldn't eat and women who ate too much. In the personality disorder group, there was everyone from transgender to gothic women. In the main group we had all types of issues from sexual abuse, domestic abuse, human trafficking victims, drug addict, etc. I really depended on how bad the drug addiction is because if the addiction is stronger than the effect that the trauma had on you, you have to go straight to the drug rehabilitation program.

Needless To Say, everyone in this group is fucked up or have been fucked over in some way. We were angry and bitter and tired of being tired. It was a sisterhood and everyone was trying to heal. Throughout the day, we broke down into smaller groups and then would all meet back up in a large group before the end of the day. These smaller groups were important for everyone can have a voice and be heard. This isn't one of those AA groups where you can pass if you don't feel like sharing. It was required for you to go through the exercises and tell the groups what you are dealing with right at that moment.

Here's an example of one of my introductions.

"Hi, Im Sherrie and I'm feeling aggravated. I woke up on the wrong side of the bed and have been feeling down all morning. I'm hoping to used my process group to help me sort some things out this afternoon"

One lady in the group asked if I wanted to share in this group to see if they can help me feel better since the process groups aren't starting for a few hours.

That was a great idea and I went on to tell them about how my love life and how hard it is for me to trust men enough to let go of my fears. I explained how this has affected all areas in my life and I now I don't feel like I'm capable of being loved.

Another lady chimed in and advised me to stop focusing on love and focus on loving yourself. I didn't realize that I didn't love myself until she said that. Then everything made sense. I thought that I loved myself because I was no longer having suicidal thoughts but loving myself was more than looking in the mirror and believing that I'm beautiful, but at the very least It meant taking accountability for my self-sabotaging behaviors and identifying what my triggers are and how to avoid them..

Therapy isn't just talking to someone about your problems and going on about your day. Therapy was being completely honest and transparent with yourself and others while trying to identify the source of your problems. Once identifying the source, being able to accept the change that is necessary to promote positive energy going forward.. This is where most of us struggle, because we don't want to let go of who we used to be because that's what's comfortable and familiar.. We don't realize that we have to actually want to receive the help of a therapist in order for it to work. If you don't release yourself in those private session, you'll miss the true benefits of Mental Health Therapy.

17
REWRITE YOUR LIFE

Get yourself a notebook. Write down at least 10 of these questions individually. Answer the question in detail before moving to the next question. This will help you start thinking about your life and its meaning.

- What's the best thing in your life right now and what's the worst. Any particular challenge that you need to face?

- If you could make any change in your life what would it be? Is there anything in life that you're not happy with?

- What is the one improvement that you can make today?

- What are the things that you love about yourself?

- What lessons have you learned in the past month?

- What is your most important focus in life right now?
- What brings in negative and positive energy to your life these days? Is there any way to decrease the former and increase the latter?

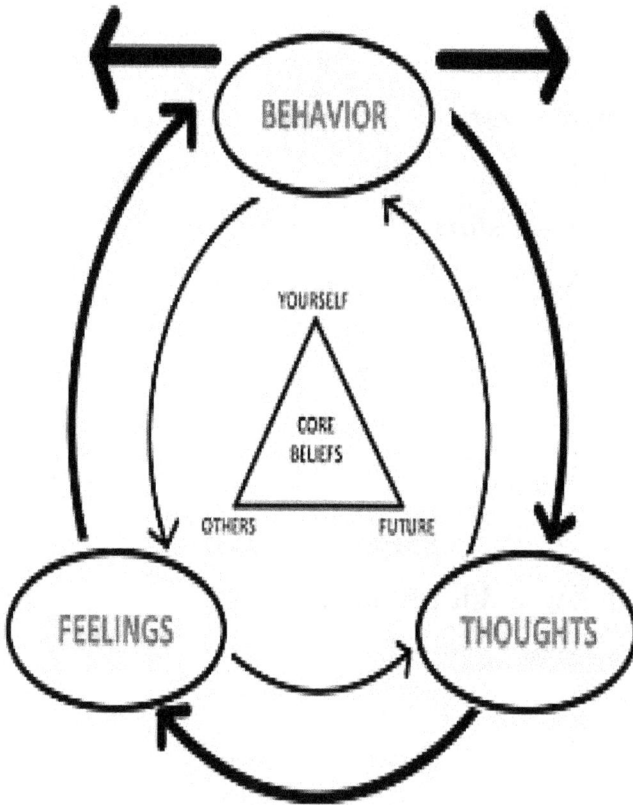

Self Discovery- Think of each of these questions and get to know yourself.

1. What matters to me most?

2. What are my most important values and how am I living in ways that are not aligned with my values?

3. What are my most important needs and desires? Does my present life fulfill them?

4. What are the operating principles of my life?

5. What is my life's purpose?

6. How do I feel about my personality type? If you don't know about your personality type, go to www.humanmetrics.com

7. What are my personal gifts?

8. Which three words describe me best?

9. What's one thing I would like to do more of and why? How can I make that happen?

10. What's one thing I would like to do less of and why? How can I make that happen?

11. What would I like to stop worrying about? What steps can I take to let go of the worry?

12. How do I move past unpleasant thoughts or experiences?

13. When I'm in physical or emotional pain, what are some of the best things I can do for myself?

14. What's keeping me awake at night?

15. What drains my energy? How can I remove it from my life or protect myself from its negative effect?

16. How do I feel about the pace of my life? Is it too fast, too slow, or just about right?

17. Do I wait for others to solve my problems? Why is that?

18. What makes me feel motivated, inspired, excited?

19. Am I holding onto something that would be better to let go of? Do I have unfinished business? With whom? What inner work needs to be done to heal this? What steps can I take to bring resolution?

20. In what areas of my life am I trading authenticity for safety, or what appears to be safety?

21. How am I censoring what I really think or feel?

22. What holds me back from being more authentic?

23. What limiting beliefs impact my life in undesirable ways? What is the origin of each belief? Is each belief still true for me today? What positive beliefs would counterbalance each one?

24. How do I feel when I enforce my personal boundaries?

25. What's behind my hesitancy to set personal boundaries, both in general and in particular situations?

26. How do I sabotage myself?

27. How much do I trust myself? Do I listen to others more than myself?

Self Confidence Assessment-

Pick at least 15 questions. Write them down and answer them in detail.

1. How do I feel about getting quiet, listening Deeply and patiently to my inner wisdom?

2. Do I hold back from asking the big questions? The hard questions? If so, what scares me?

3. How do I hesitate or refuse to take action on what my heart tells me

4. In what ways is my self-acceptance conditional, dependent upon the validation of others or specific accomplishments?

5. If I could change one thing in my life, what would I change and why?

6. Do I feel supported by my family or friends? Who supports me or who doesn't?

7. Do I surround myself with mostly positive or mostly negative people? How does that work for me?

8. What are my favorite ways to take care of myself physically, emotionally, mentally, and spiritually?

9. How do I feel about my relationship with my body?

10. Do I feel comfortable expressing myself?

11. Do I feel seen, heard, and valued?

12. Do I have any regrets about my life so far? What changes can I make so I don't continue to live with regrets?

13. How do I feel about accepting my "negative" qualities? Am I able to accept my whole self?

14. What does my inner critic tell me? How does it stop me from moving forward?

15. What important needs do I have that aren't getting met?

16. How do "shoulds" influence my choices rather than my own wishes and dreams? If you're overcome by shoulds,

17. What makes you feel most like yourself. Why?

18. Am I getting too caught up in other people's problems?

19. What's my biggest dream?

Who am I? Who do I want to be?
Where am I going? Where do I belong?

1. Make a list of 30 things that make you smile.

2. "Write about a moment experienced through your body. Making love, making breakfast, going to a party, having a fight, an experience you've had or you imagine for your character. Leave out thought and emotion, and let all information be conveyed through the body and senses."

3. If I could talk to my teenage self, the one thing I would say is . . .

4. The two moments I'll never forget in my life are . . . (Describe them in great detail, and what makes them so unforgettable.)

5. The words I'd like to live by are . . .

6. I couldn't imagine living without . . .

7. When I'm in pain—physical or emotional—the kindest thing I can do for myself is . . .

8. Make a list of the people in your life who genuinely support you, and whom you can genuinely trust. Then, make time to hang out with them.

9. What does unconditional love look like for you?

10. What things would you do if you loved yourself unconditionally? How can you act on these things,

even if you're not yet able to love yourself unconditionally?

11. I really wish others knew this about me . . .

12. Name what is enough for you.

13. If my body could talk, it would say . . .

14. Name a compassionate way you've supported a friend recently. Then, write down how you can do the same for yourself.

15. What do you love about life?

16. What always brings tears to your eyes? (As Paulo Coelho has said, "Tears are words that need to be written.")

17. Write about a time when your work felt real, necessary and satisfying to you, whether the work was paid or unpaid, professional or domestic, physical or mental.

18. Write about your first love—whether it's a person, place or thing.

19. Using 10 words, describe yourself.

20. What's surprised you the most about your life or life in general?

21. What can you learn from your biggest mistakes?

22. I feel most energized when . . .

23. "Write a list of questions to which you urgently need answers."

24. Make a list of everything that inspires you—whether books, websites, quotes, people, paintings, stores, or stars in the sky.

25. What's one topic you need to learn more about to help you live a more fulfilling life? (Then, follow through and learn more about that topic.)

26. I feel happiest in my skin when . . .

27. Make a list of everything you'd like to say no to.

28. Make a list of everything you'd like to say yes to.

29. Write the words you need to hear.

30. Who can you go to for support, advise or to vent?

Self-Awareness

This is a list of exercises and ideas to help you think about yourself, including your talents, qualities, values, and perceptions.

The point of this worksheet is to help you know and understand:

- Your beliefs and principles;
- What you value and what is important to you;
- What motivates you;
- Your own emotions
- Your thinking patterns;
- Your tendencies to react to certain situations;
- What you want out of life.

Talents

- What are your greatest talents or skills?
- Which of your talents or skills gives you the greatest sense of pride or satisfaction?

Traits/Qualities

- What are your five greatest strengths?
- What do you feel are your two biggest weaknesses?
- What qualities or traits do you most admire in others?

Values

- What are ten things that are really important to you?
- What are the three most important things to you?
- What are the values that you hold nearest to your heart?

Perception

- How is the "public you" different from the "private you"?
- What do you want people to think and say about you?

- Is it more important to be liked by others or to be yourself? Why?

Accomplishments

- What three things are you most proud of in your life to date?
- What do you hope to achieve in life?
- If you could accomplish only one thing before you died, what would it be?

Reflection

- What is something that represents you (e.g., song, animal, flower, poem, symbol, jewelry, etc.)? Why?
- What three things would you like to change most about yourself?
- List three things that you are.

Finish the Sentence

In the final section, you will be shown several prompts to complete:

- I do my best when . . .
- I struggle when . . .
- I am comfortable when . . .
- I feel stress when . . .

- I am courageous when . . .
- One of the most important things I learned was . . .
- I missed a great opportunity when . . .
- One of my favorite memories is . . .
- My toughest decisions involve . . .
- Being myself is hard because . . .
- I can be myself when . . .
- I wish I were more . . .
- I wish I could . . .
- I wish I would regularly . . .
- I wish I had . . .
- I wish I knew . . .
- I wish I felt . . .
- I wish I saw . . .
- I wish I thought . . .
- Life should be about . . .
- I am going to make my life about . . .

Once you finish this chapter, you should have plenty of insight into who you really are and what is most important to you. Use your answers to inform your decisions about what goals you choose to strive toward, what you would like to do in the future, and what moves to make next.

Empathy Map

An empathy map can help you engage in a valuable and informative process of self-reflection, using all of your senses to help you identify your needs and the disconnections between what you say and what you do. Don't worry—we all have a disconnect between what we say and what we do.

This exercise can help you figure out where you have these disconnects and how you can best address them to become the person you want to be.

To create your empathy map, simply draw four quadrants on a piece of paper. Each quadrant represents a different aspect of yourself:

- Seeing;
- Doing;
- Thinking;
- Feeling.

Next, consider a situation that evokes a specific strong emotion in you, like having a fight with your spouse or significant other. In each quadrant, write down the relevant aspects of each perspective.

For example, for the fight scenario, you could write down something like the following:

- Seeing: What are some of the things you saw during the situation?

- Doing: What actions did you do and which behaviors did you notice in yourself? What is the behavioral pattern you can identify?

- Thinking: What were you thinking in that situation? What does this tell you about your beliefs?

- Feeling: What emotions were you feeling? Why? Which past situation do they most remind you of?

On the backside of your piece of paper, on another piece of paper, or next to your four quadrants, create a fifth section. Here, you will write down your insights and ideas based on your empathy map.

The following questions can help you with the self-reflection process while you're working on your map:

- How is the situation connected to your fears and hopes? What are your fears? What are your hopes? Which of your needs are met or not met in that situation?

- What was the environment in which you encountered the situation? What do you remember from the environment? How did you find yourself in that environment and why? What was your sight focused on?

- What hurts you most in the situation or makes you feel good about the situation?
- What was the feedback you gathered from your environment or other people?
- What are all the positives about the situation? What can you learn about yourself, others, and the world by experiencing that kind of a situation?

Do your best to avoid falling prey to cognitive distortions or reinforcing negative feelings while answering these questions. Go Deep, and identify why you feel like you do. Observe, but don't judge.

Life Satisfaction Chart

A life satisfaction chart is a great way to assess how well you are meeting your goals and furthering your hopes for the future. You can complete this chart periodically to track your progress toward your goals and see what needs to be revised, improved, reduced, or eliminated to help you strive toward them.

Draw a scale from 1 (not at all satisfied) to 10 (extremely satisfied) horizontally, and list the following ten areas of life vertically:

- You;
- Health;
- Relationships;
- Money;
- Career;
- Emotions;
- Competencies;
- Fun;
- Spirituality;
- Technology.

Assess your satisfaction in each of the 10 areas using the scale you created.

Next, take a second look at all the areas where you are only somewhat satisfied (where you used a rating between 4 and 7). It can be hard to effectively reflect when you don't have a clear idea of whether you are satisfied with a specific area or not.

Go back through these "somewhat satisfied" areas and rate your satisfaction again, but use only ratings between 1 and 3 or 8 and 10. Limiting your options to either "very satisfied" or "not very satisfied" will help you to make a more decisive judgment about your satisfaction in each area.

Highlight every section rated with a 1, 2, or 3 with red, and highlight every section rated with an 8, 9, or 10 with green. Finally, for all ten areas of life, ask yourself, Why did you rate each area how you did? What would make you change your rating?

Repeat this exercise as often as you'd like to help you keep track of your satisfaction with the way your life is going.

How to Create Healthy Boundaries

"An intimate relationship is one in which neither party silences, sacrifices, or betrays the self and each party expresses strength and vulnerability, weakness and competence in a balanced way." ~Harriet Lerner

Setting boundaries is essential if we want to be both physically and emotionally healthy. Creating healthy boundaries is empowering. By recognizing the need to set and enforce limits, you protect your selfesteem, maintain self-respect, and enjoy healthy relationships.

Unhealthy boundaries cause emotional pain that can lead to dependency, depression, anxiety, and even stress-induced physical illness. A lack of boundaries is like leaving the door to your home unlocked: anyone, including unwelcome guests, can enter at will. On the other hand, having too rigid boundaries can lead to isolation, like living in a locked-up castle surrounded by a mote. No one can get in, and you can't get out.

What Are Boundaries?

Boundaries are guidelines, rules or limits that a person creates to identify for themselves what are reasonable, safe and permissible ways for other people to behave around them and how they will respond when someone steps outside those limits.

The easiest way to think about a boundary is a property line. We have all seen "No Trespassing" signs, which send a clear message that if you violate that boundary, there will be a consequence. This type of boundary is easy to picture and understand because you can see the sign and the border it protects.

Personal boundaries can be harder to define because the lines are invisible, can change, and are unique to each individual. Personal boundaries, just like the "No Trespassing" sign, define where you end and others begin and are determined by the amount of physical and emotional space you allow between yourself and others.

Personal boundaries help you decide what types of communication, behavior, and interaction are acceptable.

Why is it important to set boundaries?

• To practice self-care and self-respect

• To communicate your needs in a relationship

• To make time and space for positive interactions

• To set limits in a relationship in a way that is healthy

Physical Boundaries

Physical boundaries provide a barrier between you and an intruding force, like a Band-Aid protects a wound from bacteria. Physical boundaries include your body, sense of personal space, sexual orientation, and privacy. These boundaries are expressed through clothing, shelter, noise tolerance, verbal instruction, and body language.

An example of physical boundary violation: a close talker.

Your immediate and automatic reaction is to step back in order to reset your personal space. By doing this, you send a non-verbal message that when this person stands so close you feel an invasion of your personal space. If the person continues to move closer, you might verbally protect your boundary by telling him/her to stop crowding you.

Other examples of physical boundary invasions are:

• Inappropriate touching, such as unwanted sexual advances.

• Looking through others' personal files and emails.

• Not allowing others their personal space. (e.g., barging into your boss's office without knocking)

Emotional and Intellectual Boundaries

These boundaries protect your sense of self-esteem and ability to separate your feelings from others'. When you have weak emotional boundaries, it's like getting caught in the midst of a hurricane with no protection. You expose yourself to being greatly affected by others' words, thoughts, and actions and end up feeling bruised, wounded, and battered. These include beliefs, behaviors, choices, sense of responsibility, and your ability to be intimate with others.

Examples of emotional and intellectual boundary invasions are:

- Not knowing how to separate your feelings from your partner's and allowing his/her mood to dictate your level of happiness or sadness (a.k.a. codependency).

- Sacrificing your plans, dreams, and goals in order to please others.

- Not taking responsibility for yourself and blaming others for your problems.

Barriers to Boundary Setting It seems obvious that no one would want his/her boundaries violated. So why do we allow it? Why do we NOT enforce or uphold our boundaries?

- FEAR of rejection and, ultimately, abandonment.
  o FEAR of confrontation.
  o GUILT.
  o We were not taught healthy boundaries.
  o Safety Concerns
- Assess the current state of your boundaries
- HEALTHY BOUNDARIES allow you to:
  o Have high self-esteem and self-respect.
  o Share personal information gradually, in a mutually sharing and trusting relationship.

- o Protect physical and emotional space from intrusion.
- o Have an equal partnership where responsibility and power are shared. • Be assertive. Confidently and truthfully say "yes" or "no" and be okay when others say "no" to you.
- o Separate your needs, thoughts, feelings, and desires from others. Recognize that your boundaries and needs are different from others.
- o Empower yourself to make healthy choices and take responsibility for yourself.

If you are dealing with someone who is physically dangerous or threatening to you, it may not be safe to attempt to set explicit boundaries with them. If you are in this situation, it can be helpful to work with a counselor, therapist or advocate to create a safety plan and boundary setting may be a part of this.

UNHEALTHY BOUNDARIES are characterized by:

- • Sharing too much too soon or, at the other end of the spectrum, closing yourself off and not expressing your need and wants.

- Feeling responsible for others' happiness.
- Inability to say "no" for fear of rejection or abandonment.
- Weak sense of your own identity. You base how you feel about yourself on how others treat you.
- Disempowerment. You allow others to make decisions for you; consequently, you feel powerless and do not take responsibility for your own life.

When you identify the need to set a boundary, do it clearly, calmly, firmly, respectfully, and in as few words as possible. Do not justify, get angry, or apologize for the boundary you are setting. You are not responsible for the other person's reaction to the boundary you are setting for your personal life. You are only responsible for communicating your boundary in a respectful manner. If it upset them, know it is their problem.

Some people, especially those accustomed to controlling, abusing, or manipulating you, might test you. Plan on it, expect it, but remain firm. Remember, your behavior must match the boundaries you are setting. You cannot successfully establish a clear boundary if you send mixed messages by apologizing.

At first, you will probably feel selfish, guilty, or embarrassed when you set a boundary. _Do it anyway and remind yourself you have a right to self-care._

Setting boundaries takes practice and determination. Don't let anxiety, fear or guilt prevent you from taking care of yourself. When you feel anger or resentment or find yourself whining or complaining, you probably need to set a boundary. Listen to yourself, determine what you need to do or say, then communicate assertively.

Learning to set healthy boundaries takes time. It is a process. Set them in your own time frame, not when someone else tells you. Develop a support system of people who respect your right to set boundaries. Eliminate toxic persons from your life— those who want to manipulate, abuse, and control you. Adapted by the Violence Intervention and Prevention Center from PositivelyPositive.com, outofthefog.net and Boundaries: Where You End and I Begin by Anne Katherine.

HEALTHY COPING SKILLS

Mental	Physical
o Reach out for support	o Hot bath or shower
o Practice non-judgement (watch thoughts and behaviors objectively)	o Deep breathing
o Positive daily readings	o Walk in nature
o Visualize a stop sign	o Abstain from caffeine and alcohol
o Get lost in a good book	o Meditative yoga
o Talk to a friend	o Listen to body signals
o Go surfing	o Go for a walk
o Watch a movie	o Go swimming
o Watch TV. shows that elicit laughter	o Get a massage
o Google colouring sheets (Disney)	o Rest
o Journaling	o Scream
o Do a puzzle or crossword	o Breathe
o Complete a thought record	o Garden
o Do a craft	o Gentle stretching
Emotional	**Spiritual**
o Listen to music	o Guided meditation
o Cry	o Journaling
o Group therapy	o Praying
o See a counsellor	o Practice mindfulness throughout the day
o Cook *(if this is safe)*	
o Knit	o Be in nature
o Get a manicure / pedicure	o Volunteer
o Go shopping *(if this is safe)*	o Do yoga
o Meditate	o Hold a baby
o Sing	o Go to church
o Play with your child or pet	o Be in nature
o Have sex *(be physically + emotionally safe)*	o Listen to music
o See a therapist	o Finish a task or chore
o Carry affirmation cards	o Carry a picture of self as a child

Cognitive Distortions

Cognitive distortions are irrational thoughts that can influence our emotions. Everyone experiences cognitive distortions to some degree, but in their more extreme forms they can be maladaptive

Magnification and Minimization: Exaggerating or minimizing the importance of events. One might believe their own achievements are unimportant, or that their mistakes are excessively important.

Catastrophizing: Seeing only the worst possible outcomes of a situation.

Overgeneralization: Making broad interpretations from a single or few events. "I felt awkward during my first job interview. I am always so awkward."

Magical thinking: The belief that acts will influence unrelated situations. "I am a good person—Bad things shouldn't happen to me."

Personalization: The belief that one is responsible for events outside of their own control. "My mother is always upset. It must be because I have not done enough to help her."

Jumping to conclusions: Interpreting the meaning of a situation with little or no evidence.

Mind reading: Interpreting the thoughts and beliefs of others without adequate evidence. "She would not go on a date with me. She must think I am ugly."

Fortune telling: The expectation that a situation will turn out badly without adequate evidence.

Emotional reasoning: The assumption that emotions reflect the way things really are. "I feel like a bad friend, therefore I must be a bad friend."

Disqualifying the positive: Recognizing only negative aspects of a situation while ignoring the positive. One might receive many compliments on an evaluation but focus on the single piece of negative feedback.

Should statements: The belief that things should be a certain way. "I should always be friendly."

All-or-nothing thinking: Thinking in absolutes such as "always", "never", or "every". "I never do a good job on my work."

Are you Codependent?

1. Do you take better care of other people than yourself?

2. Do you obsess about other people by thinking about them, feeling anxious about them, and checking up on them?

3. Do you know what other people feel, think, like and dislike, but are unsure what your own feelings, thoughts, likes, and dislikes are?

4. Do you feel responsible for other people's choices?

5. Do you change yourself hoping that other people will also change?

6. Do you feel stuck and victimized?

7. Do you try to fix and control people, places, and things?

8. Do you deny reality to cope?

9. Do you have difficulty knowing what your boundaries should be?

10. Do you have difficulty saying no without feeling guilty?

11. Do you allow yourself to be manipulated and controlled by others?

12. Do you lie and cover-up for others' mistakes?

13. Do you distrust your decisions and feelings?

14. Do you people please, because you fear rejection and desperately need approval?

15. Do you know what is right for everyone else but have difficulty making decisions about your own life?

If you answered YES to two or more questions, you are Codependent.

Mildly Codependent 2-5
Moderately Codependent 5-10
Extremely Codependent 10-15

10 Types of Emotional Manipulator

1. The Constant Victim - This kind of individual will always finds a way to end up as a victim in their relationships.

2. One-Upmanship Expert – This person uses put downs, snide remarks and criticisms, to show that they're superior, and know much more than you.

3. Powerful Dependents – They hide behind the mask of being weak and powerless – then use their helplessness to dominate relationships. That is, they send the subtle message "you must not let me down."

4. Triangulators – This person tries to get other people on their side. They're quick to put you down, and to say some nasty things. They separate good friends or drive a wedge in families.

5. The Blasters – They blast you with their anger or they blow up suddenly. That stops you asking questions - in case there's a showdown.

6. The Projector – This person thinks they're perfect and others have the flaws. They take no ownership – because they're never, ever wrong.

7. The Deliberate Mis-Interpreter – They seem like a nice person – but they twist and use your words. They spread misinformation and misinterpret you. Thus, they deliberately present you in a false, negative way.

8. The Flirt – This person uses flirting to get their way in life. They want to be admired and to have an audience. However, your feelings and your needs are of no concern to them.

9. The Iron Fist – They use intimidation and throw their weight around, to use you for their ends, and to get their way in life.

10. The Multiple Offender – This person uses several of the techniques we've described – and they'll often switch between them if it suits their purposes.

Impact of Childhood Trauma

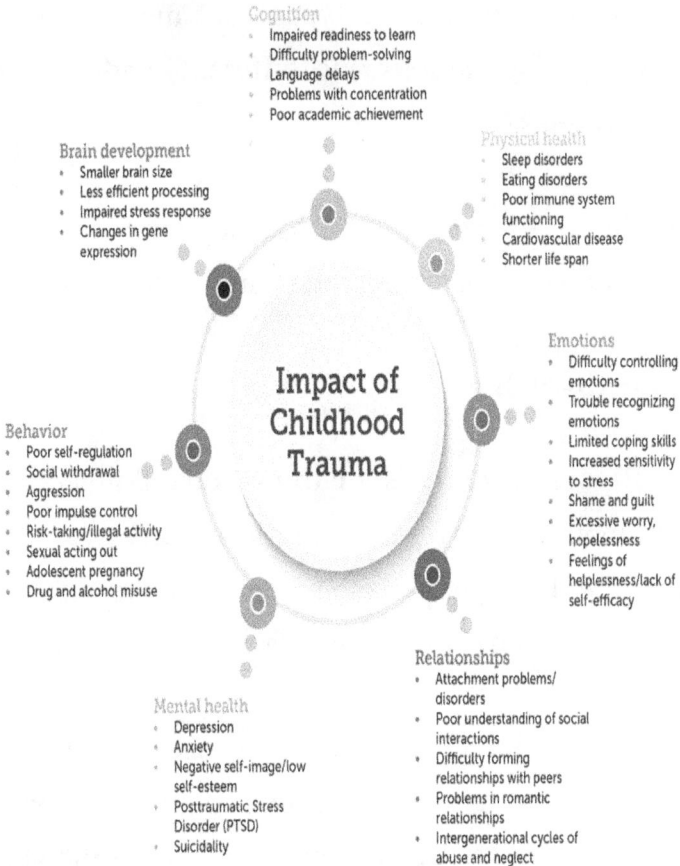

Cognition
- Impaired readiness to learn
- Difficulty problem-solving
- Language delays
- Problems with concentration
- Poor academic achievement

Brain development
- Smaller brain size
- Less efficient processing
- Impaired stress response
- Changes in gene expression

Physical health
- Sleep disorders
- Eating disorders
- Poor immune system functioning
- Cardiovascular disease
- Shorter life span

Impact of Childhood Trauma

Emotions
- Difficulty controlling emotions
- Trouble recognizing emotions
- Limited coping skills
- Increased sensitivity to stress
- Shame and guilt
- Excessive worry, hopelessness
- Feelings of helplessness/lack of self-efficacy

Behavior
- Poor self-regulation
- Social withdrawal
- Aggression
- Poor impulse control
- Risk-taking/illegal activity
- Sexual acting out
- Adolescent pregnancy
- Drug and alcohol misuse

Relationships
- Attachment problems/ disorders
- Poor understanding of social interactions
- Difficulty forming relationships with peers
- Problems in romantic relationships
- Intergenerational cycles of abuse and neglect

Mental health
- Depression
- Anxiety
- Negative self-image/low self-esteem
- Posttraumatic Stress Disorder (PTSD)
- Suicidality

Mental Health Disorders

There are many types of mental health disorders. In fact, almost 300 different conditions are listed in DSM-5.

These are some of the most common mental illnesses affecting people in the United States:

Bipolar disorder

Bipolar disorder is a chronic mental illness that affects about 2.6 percent of Americans each year. It is characterized by episodes of energetic, manic highs and extreme, sometimes depressive lows.

These can affect a person's energy level and ability to think reasonably. Mood swings caused by bipolar disorder are much more severe than the small ups and downs most people experience on a daily basis.

Persistent depressive disorder

Persistent depressive disorder is a chronic type of depression. It is also known as dysthymia. While dysthymic depression isn't intense, it can interfere with daily life. People with this condition experience symptoms for at least two years.

About 1.5 percent of American adults experience dysthymia each year.

Generalized anxiety disorder

Generalized anxiety disorder (GAD) goes beyond regular everyday anxiety, like being nervous before a presentation. It causes a person to become extremely worried about many things, even when there's little or no reason to worry.

Those with GAD may feel very nervous about getting through the day. They may think things won't ever work in their favor. Sometimes worrying can keep people with GAD from accomplishing everyday tasks and chores. GAD affects about 3 percent of Americans every year.

Major depressive disorder

Major depressive disorder (MDD) causes feelings of extreme sadness or hopelessness that lasts for at least two weeks. This condition is also called also called clinical depression.

People with MDD may become so upset about their lives that they think about or try to commit suicide. About 7 percent of Americans experience at least one major depressive episode each year.

Obsessive-compulsive disorder

Obsessive-compulsive disorder (OCD) causes constant and repetitive thoughts, or obsessions. These thoughts happen with unnecessary and unreasonable desires to carry out certain behaviors, or compulsions.

Many people with OCD realize that their thoughts and actions are unreasonable, yet they cannot stop them. More than 2 percent of Americans are diagnosed with OCD at some point in their lifetime.

Post-traumatic stress disorder (PTSD)

Post-traumatic stress disorder (PTSD) is a mental illness that's triggered after experiencing or witnessing a traumatic event. Experiences that can cause PTSD can range from extreme events, like war and national disasters, to verbal or physical abuse.

Symptoms of PTSD may include flashbacks or being easily startled. It's estimated that 3.5 percent of American adults experience PTSD.

Schizophrenia

Schizophrenia impairs a person's perception of reality and the world around them. It interferes with their connection to other people. It's a serious condition that needs treatment.

They might experience hallucinations, have delusions, and hear voices. These can potentially put them in a dangerous situation if left untreated. It's estimated that 1 percent of the American population experiences schizophrenia.

Social anxiety disorder

Social anxiety disorder, sometimes called social phobia, causes an extreme fear of social situations. People with social anxiety may become very nervous about being around other people. They may feel like they're being judged.

This can make it hard to meet new people and attend social gatherings. Approximately 15 million adults in the United States experience social anxiety each year.

Coping with mental illnesses

The symptoms of many mental illnesses may get worse if they're left untreated. Reach out for psychological help if you or someone you know may have a mental illness.

If you're unsure where to start, visit your primary care doctor. They can help with the initial diagnosis and provide a referral to a psychiatrist.

It's important to know that you can still have a full and happy life with a mental illness. Working with a therapist and other members of your mental health team will help you learn healthy ways to manage your condition.

Mental health symptoms

Each type of mental illness causes its own symptoms. But many share some common characteristics.

Common signs of several mental illnesses may include:

- not eating enough or overeating

- having insomnia or sleeping too much

- distancing yourself from other people and favorite activities

- feeling fatigue even with enough sleep

- feeling numbness or lacking empathy

- experiencing unexplainable body pains or achiness

- feeling hopeless, helpless or lost

- smoking, drinking, or using illicit drugs more than ever before

- feeling confusion, forgetfulness, irritability, anger, anxiety, sadness, or fright

- constantly fighting or arguing with friends and family

- having extreme mood swings that cause relationship problems

- having constant flashbacks or thoughts that you can't get out of your head

- hearing voices in your head that you can't stop

- having thoughts of hurting yourself or other people

- being unable to carry out day-to-day activities and chores

Stress and periods of emotional distress can lead to an episode of symptoms. That may make it difficult for you to maintain normal behavior and activities. This period is sometimes called a nervous or mental breakdown. Read more about these episodes and the symptoms they cause.

Mental health diagnosis

Diagnosing a mental health disorder is a multi-step process. During a first appointment, your doctor may perform a physical exam to look for signs of physical issues that could be contributing to your symptoms.

Some doctors may order a series of laboratory tests to screen for underlying or less obvious possible causes.

Your doctor may ask you to fill out a mental health questionnaire. You may also undergo a psychological evaluation. You might not have a diagnosis after your first appointment.

Your doctor may refer you to a mental health expert. Because mental health can be complex and symptoms may vary from person to person, it may take a few appointments for you to get a full diagnosis.

Mental health treatment

Treatment for mental health disorders is not one size fits all, and it does not offer a cure. Instead, treatment aims to reduce symptoms, address underlying causes, and make the condition manageable.

You and your doctor will work together to find a plan. It may be a combination of treatments because some people have better results with a multi-angle approach. Here are the most common mental health treatments:

Medications

The four main categories of medications used to treat mental health disorders are antidepressants, anti-anxiety medications, antipsychotic medications, and mood-stabilizing medications.

Which type is best for you will depend on the symptoms you experience and other health issues you may face. People may try a few medications at different doses before finding something that's right for them.

Psychotherapy

Talk therapy is an opportunity for you to talk with a mental health provider about your experiences, feelings, thoughts, and ideas. Therapists primarily act as a sounding board and neutral mediator, helping you learn coping techniques and strategies to manage symptoms.

Hospital and residential treatment

Some people may need brief periods of intensive treatment at hospitals or residential treatment facilities. These programs allow an overnight stay for in-depth treatment. There are also daytime programs, where people can participate in shorter periods of treatment.

Lifestyle treatments and home remedies

Alternative treatments can be used in addition to mainstream treatments as a supplement. These steps won't eliminate mental health issues alone, but they can be helpful.

They include sticking to your treatment plan as closely as possible, avoiding alcohol and drugs, and adopting a healthy lifestyle that incorporates foods that may be a benefit to your brain. This includes omega-3 fatty acids, a type of fish oil that occurs naturally in some high-fat fish.

Mental health therapy

The term therapy refers to several styles of talk therapy. Therapy can be used to treat a variety of disorders, including panic disorders, anxiety, depression, anger issues, bipolar disorder, and post-traumatic stress disorder.

Therapy helps people identify mental health issues and unhealthy behaviors or thought patterns. During sessions you and your therapist can work to change these thoughts and behaviors.

In most cases, therapists focus on current issues, things that are affecting your daily life, and help you find solutions to what you're experiencing in real time, but each doctor's approach is different. Read more about the different types and what results you might expect from therapy.

ACKNOWLEDGEMENTS

I am filled with enormous gratitude to so many people who have helped me with this project. This book would not have been written without the support from my tribe. This is the most vulnerable I've ever been my life. I've suffered from Mental Illness for three decades before I found out that I needed help. Thank you for allowing me to live in my truth and heal those deeply buried wounds that I've been carrying around with me for so long. I've sacrificed my secrets to help you with yours.

To my magical mommy and my super hero, thank you for pushing me so hard to finish this. I know that this was hard for you as well. That's why the first chapter is yours. I wanted to make sure that my readers understood the conditions that you were raised in as well. I love you to the moon and back girl! Thank you for being my biggest fan.

To my dad.... No matter how old we get, little girls will ALWAYS need their dad!

To my dear cousin Crystal, I have no clue where I would be if you weren't there for my mom and me. I love you forever and a day.

To my advisory board of big sisters, Valerie Ward, Anjeanette McKenzie, Endia Decordova, PJ Decordova, Terese Walker, Donna Gray, Christina Hawkins, Dawn Googe, Karen Baxter, Carol Perry and Leslie Gomez. You all have played a significant part in my life and I want to thank you all for the wisdom, support, advice and for simply being there exactly when I needed you. It's truly a blessing to have such a well-rounded group of dope women right in my back pocket! #BLOOP

To the man who took me off the streets and gave me my two beautiful children, Thank You for everything!!!

SHOUT OUT TO MY SPONSORS who preordered this book because you were tired of me sitting on it..... You guys paid for EVERYTHING!! Thank you!!

April Brooks, Carleen Evans, Crystal Copeland, Darryl Biggs, Darryl Copeland, Destiny Little, Donna Gray, Iris Copeland, Jamal Pennick, Kareem Copeland, Katara Thorton, Kiesha Sirobe, Kim Brown, Kristina White, Latoya White, Marge Gary, Monica Burgess, Monique Butler, Monroe Scott, Octavia Lockhart, Shandese Williams, Shanon Copeland, Shari Barnes, Sheila White, Sherry Turner, Shumia Brown, Stacey Copeland,

Takneesha Copeland, Terese Walker, Terrina Copeland, Tiffany Edison, Tonia Acosta, Val Ward, Whitney Evans.

Special Thank you to Sheilah White, Ella White, Carleen Jernigan and Corey Camby for giving me permission to use this cover as it was the last picture that I have with my grandma before she passed. She always had a snack and only gave me a bite. LOL

Last but not least I want to thank my children for saving my life. The day that I became a mother is the day that I started living with a purpose. I couldn't imagine my life without my team. I can't wait to come and live in your houses and eat your food.

ABOUT THE AUTHOR

Sherrie Davis is mother of two young adults, but don't let her brag too much about being an empty nester at the tender age of forty. She's also spent over twenty years in her Accounting career so cut her some slack and get her to the nearest beach! She has twenty plus years of self-healing experience under her belt. In the process of healing and promoting self-love and self-care, she helps others to find their inner strength to keep fighting the fight.

Sherrie has started six business ventures and has been self-employed since opening her bookkeeping company in 2015. One of her ventures happens to be a natural skin and hair care business that promotes self-love and self-healing. She started this business for her daughter.

She does her best writing near beaches, lakes and rivers. I said beach again! She also loves quarantining at home in her little apartment in Atlanta. Okay, one more time BEACH PLEASE!

- facebook.com/thereezonwhy
- twitter: @thereezonwhy
- Instagram.com/thereezonwhy
- www.sherriemicheledavis.com

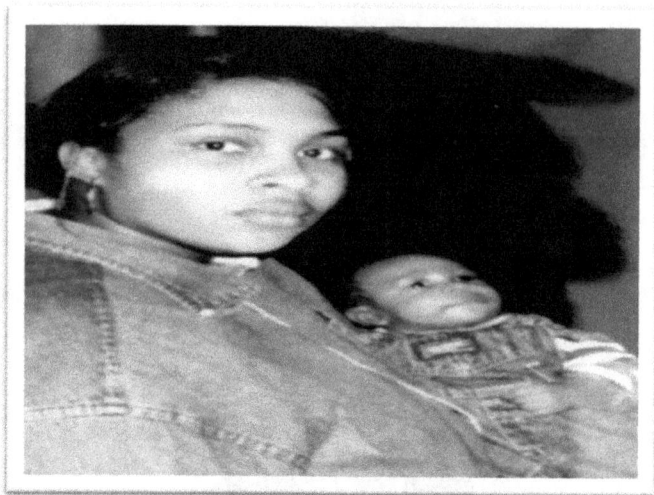

My son Tre and I...

My whole world!! Faith, Tre and I....

www.ingramcontent.com/pod-product-compliance
Lightning Source LLC
Chambersburg PA
CBHW062107040426
42336CB00042B/2259

9781735198880